Shades of Difference

Shades of Difference

Why Skin Color Matters

Edited by Evelyn Nakano Glenn

Stanford University Press
Stanford, California

Stanford University Press

Stanford, California

Printed in the United States of America on acid-free, archival-quality paper

Library of Congress Cataloging-in-Publication Data

Shades of difference : why skin color matters / edited by Evelyn Nakano Glenn.
    p. cm.
  Includes bibliographical references and index.
  ISBN 978-0-8047-5998-4 (cloth : alk. paper)—ISBN 978-0-8047-5999-1 (pbk. : alk paper)
  1. Human skin color—Social aspects. 2. Human skin color—Economic aspects. 3. Racism.
4. Race relations. I. Glenn, Evelyn Nakano.
  GN197.S524 2009
  305.8—dc22   2008043086

Typeset by Publishers' Design and Production Services, Inc. in 10/14 Minion

Contents

Contributors

TAUNYA LOVELL BANKS is the Jacob A. France Professor of Equality Jurisprudence at the University of Maryland School of Law. She has worked as a civil rights lawyer and as a senior trial attorney. She is a contributing co-editor of *Screening Justice—The Cinema of Law: Films of Law, Order, and Social Justice* (William S. Hein & Company, 2006).

EDUARDO BONILLA-SILVA is Professor of Sociology at Duke University. His interests are in race relations and racial stratifications. He is the author of *Racism without Racists: Color-Blind Racism and the Persistence of Racial Inequality in the United States, 2nd Edition* (Rowman & Littlefield, 2006) and *White Supremacy and Racism in the Post-Civil Rights Era* (Lynne Rienner Publishers, 2001), and co-editor with Ashley W. Doane of *White Out: The Continuing Significance of Racism* (Routledge, 2003).

MAXINE LEEDS CRAIG is Associate Professor in the Sociology and Social Services Department at California State University, East Bay. She is the author of *Ain't I a Beauty Queen? Black Women, Beauty and the Politics of Race* (Oxford University Press, 2002), which was awarded the Best Book on the Political History of Ethnic and Racial Minorities in the United States by the Section on Race, Ethnicity, and Politics of the American Political Science Association.

DAVID R. DIETRICH is a Ph.D. student in sociology at Duke University. His primary interests are race and ethnic relations, and social movements. His research includes recent conservative movements, such as the anti-Affirmative Action movements on college campuses, the Black Power Movement, and the current immigration debate.

EVELYN NAKANO GLENN is a Professor with the Departments of Gender & Women's Studies and Ethnic Studies, and Director of the Center for Race and Gender at the University of California, Berkeley. She is the author of *Issei, Nisei, War Bride: Three Generations of Japanese American Women in Domestic Service* (Temple University

Press, 1986), *Mothering: Ideology, Experience and Agency* (Routledge, 1994), and *Unequal Freedom: How Race and Gender Shaped American Citizenship and Labor* (Harvard University Press, 2002).

ANGELA P. HARRIS is Professor at Boalt Hall School of Law at the University of California, Berkeley. Her recent books include *Economic Justice: Race, Gender, Identity, and Economics* (with Emma Coleman Jordan, Foundation Press, 2005) and *Race and Races: Cases and Materials for a Diverse America* (with Richard Delgado, Juan Perea, Jean Stefancic, and Stephanie Wildman, Foundation Press, 2007).

TANYA KATERÍ HERNÁNDEZ is Professor of Law at George Washington University Law School. She is the co-author of the forthcoming book *The Long Lingering Shadow: Law, Liberalism and Cultures of Racial Hierarchy and Identity in the Americas* (University of North Carolina Press, 2009).

TRINA JONES is Professor of Law at Duke University Law School where she directs the Jean E. and Christine P. Mills Conversation Series on Race. Her recent work includes *Law and Class in America: Trends Since the Cold War* (co-edited with Professor Paul Carrington, New York University Press, 2006).

VERNA M. KEITH is Professor of Sociology and Faculty Associate in the Center for Demography and Population Health at Florida State University. She is editor of *In and Out of Our Right Minds: The Mental Health of African American Women* (with Diane Brown, Columbia University Press, 2003) and *Skin Deep: How Race and Complexion Matter in the "Color-Blind" Era* (with Cedric Herring and Hayward Horton, Institute for Research on Race and Public Policy, 2003).

AISHA KHAN is Associate Professor of Anthropology at New York University. She is the author of *Callaloo Nation: Metaphors of Race and Religious Identity among South Asians in Trinidad* (Duke University Press, 2004); co-editor of *Ethnographies, Histories, and Power: Critical Engagements with the Work of Sidney W. Mintz* (University of North Carolina Press, forthcoming); and co-editor of *Women Anthropologists: Biographical Sketches* (University of Illinois Press, 1989).

JOANNE L. RONDILLA is a doctoral candidate in the Department of Ethnic Studies at the University of California, Berkeley, where she is currently working on her dissertation, which examines Filipinas and skin lightening both in the Philippines and the United States. She is the co-author of *Is Lighter Better? Skin-Tone Discrimination among Asian Americans* (with Paul Spickard) and co-editor of *Pacific Diaspora: Island Peoples in the United States and across the Pacific* (with Paul Spickard and Debbie Hippolite-Wright, Rowman & Littlefield, 2007).

CHRISTINA A. SUE is a doctoral candidate at the University of California, Los Angeles. She is currently completing her dissertation on the everyday meaning of race, color, and national ideology in Mexico.

EDWARD TELLES is Professor of Sociology at the University of California, Los Angeles. He was the 2006 recipient of the Distinguished Scholarly Publication Award from the American Sociological Association for his book *Race in Another America: The Significance of Skin Color in Brazil* (Princeton University Press, 2006).

LYNN M. THOMAS is Associate Professor of History and Adjunct Associate Professor of Women's Studies at the University of Washington. She is the author of *Politics of the Womb: Women, Reproduction, and the State in Kenya* (University of California Press, 2003).

CHARIS THOMPSON is Associate Professor in the Departments of Gender and Women's Studies and Rhetoric, at the University of California, Berkeley, and is also Co-director of the Science, Technology, and Society Center, and the author of *Making Parents: The Ontological Choreography of Reproductive Technologies* (The MIT Press, 2005).

JYOTSNA VAID is Professor of Psycholinguistics at Texas A&M University. She founded the Committee on South Asian Women, and has authored publications on South Asian women's groups in North America in *Making Waves* (Beacon Press, 1989) and the *Amerasia Journal*.

Shades of Difference

Introduction

Economies of Color

Angela P. Harris

MOST POPULAR AND SCHOLARLY discussions of racism take one of two approaches to the topic. The "prejudice" approach treats racism as interpersonal, and explores how processes of cognition, reasoning, and emotion function to make racial difference real and to make demeaning treatment of the racial "other" seem natural, normal, and necessary. The "white supremacy" approach treats racism as institutional and explores how groups successfully defining themselves as "white" have been able to marshal political, economic, and social power for themselves at the expense of those they define as "nonwhite." The essays in this collection, however, illuminate a third approach to analyzing racism: the constitution of racism through economies of difference—in this case, *economies of color*.

As a threshold matter, the essays in this volume demonstrate that *colorism* and *racism* are not exactly the same. Jyotsna Vaid and Joanne L. Rondilla argue, for example, that the valuing of light skin has evolved in many regions—such as East and South Asia and the Philippines—independently (at least in part) of the black–white, European–African dynamics of race that have so characterized the Americas and Europe. Edward Telles and Christina A. Sue show that in some countries, such as Brazil and Mexico, popular discussions about "race" are difficult or impossible to conduct, yet everyone is able to talk in great detail about "color." Colorism and racism are not only not identical; hierarchies of color can destabilize hierarchies based on race. In the United States, as Trina Jones, Taunya Lovell Banks, and Tanya Katerí Hernández show, colorism often confounds lawyers and judges, who are used to conceptualizing antidiscrimination laws solely in terms of white versus nonwhite.

Despite the fact that colorism and racism can move independently, the essays in this volume show how the two nevertheless remain linked. Some of the authors suggest that colorism gives us a way to understand how racism's "color line" is changing in the twenty-first century. The team of Eduardo Bonilla-Silva and David R. Dietrich, for instance, argue that the United States is moving away from a binary hierarchy of privilege and subordination (whether white–black or white–nonwhite) and toward a social and political "pigmentocracy" that will comprise three panethnic categories: white (including "honorary white"), brown, and black. This shift, they argue, will bring the United States into the Latin American fold.

So colorism operates sometimes to confound and sometimes to restructure racial hierarchy. Meanwhile, the circulating meanings attached to color shape the meaning of race. The description of symbolic relations as "economies" has become a cliché in cultural studies. In the case of colorism, though, the term works at multiple levels. First, the language of color "circulates" at a number of levels of scale—local, regional, ethnic, national—picking up inflections, nuances, and connotations along the way. As Charis Thompson remarks in her chapter, ordinary people do not perceive skin color objectively, as an artist might; skin color is always read in the context of hair, dress, gender, age, and season, among other factors. Moreover, there are not one but many discourses of color, shaped variously by labor and migration patterns, by histories of conquest and subjugation, by class, by gender, and by national identity. The economic metaphor highlights the mobile and dynamic quality of color, as well as its complexity.

Second, colorism as a series of symbolic economies is embedded in material economies of production, exchange, and consumption. The chapters by Evelyn Nakano Glenn and Lynn M. Thomas, for example, reveal a close and harmonious relationship between status hierarchies and consumer capitalism. The medium of advertising shows us how we can overcome personal barriers to success through the consumption of products for sale, and the burgeoning market in products designed to lighten, brighten, and whiten speaks to corporate capital's desire to sell us the dream that we can individually transcend oppressive systems. Creams, lotions, and surgical procedures promise us the ability to defy racism, in the same way that they promise us the ability to defy aging.

The beauty industry's close relationship to the aesthetics of racism also illustrates the central role of gender in relations of consumption. As historians have shown, consumer capitalism was born with the recognition and embrace of women as consumers, and so it is not surprising that women should be so prominent among the shoppers for skin-lightening products. At the same time, the beauty industry's focus on women reflects the long history of women viewed as products themselves, intended for men's consumption. These chapters reiterate the truth of Simone de Beauvoir's comment that "one is not born, but rather becomes, a woman." Beauty projects relating to color are just some of the many projects urged upon gendered-female subjects to improve and perfect themselves. (Contemporary capitalism has not only colonized these projects with enthusiasm, but has helped extend the realm of the pursuit of beauty and desirability to men as well, as the U.S. television show *Queer Eye for the Straight Guy* illustrates. It will be interesting in this context to see whether men as well as women begin to feel the pressure to lighten their skin!)

Third, thinking about color as a series of economies tips us off to colorism's relationship to class as social mobility. Most discussions of white supremacy implicitly or explicitly adopt what might be called a "Marxian" paradigm, examining how groups marked *white* struggle to exploit groups marked *nonwhite*. These chapters suggest that racism also works through a "Weberian" or status paradigm. Within this paradigm, individuals and groups are ordered and compete with one another in terms of their access to and ability to utilize what Evelyn Nakano Glenn describes as *symbolic capital,* which means, in part, skin color (as well as the other aspects of physiognomy associated with race, such as eye shape and hair texture). The pursuit of higher status along the color line may occur on the individual level, such as when a woman purchases a skin-lightening cream or straightens her hair to get a job; it may occur on the family level, such as when a potential marriage partner, or egg donor, is rejected because the resulting children might come out "too dark"; or it may occur on the national level, such as in the projects taken up in Peru, Mexico, Puerto Rico, and elsewhere to "improve" the nation by lightening its people.

For example, Aisha Khan argues that Indo-Trinidadians strategically negotiate ambiguous color and race identifications in Trinidad society, in part to avoid the stigma of blackness, in part to claim an "Indianness" that is "light" or "clear." Maxine Leeds Craig, looking at a 1960s African American beauty pageant, finds the contestants and spectators engaged in an argument about the relationship of color to racial identity and pride, with an eye to the standing of African Americans in U.S. society. Verna M. Keith, using data about African American women collected from 1979 to 1980, identifies a positive relationship between lighter skin color and educational attainment, occupational standing, and family income. And Christina A. Sue and Jyotsna Vaid show how marriage is an important institution for amassing and mobilizing the symbolic capital of light skin, as partners evaluate the lightness or darkness of their own skin, their potential partner's, and that of their actual or hypothetical children. The examination of color through a Weberian language of status/class and symbolic capital thus highlights the efforts of individuals, families, nations, and other social groups to achieve a variety of goals—beauty, desirability, wealth, political power, ethnic pride, social respectability—through the discursive categories of race.

Last, the economic metaphor is useful to the examination of colorism because of the different modes of social regulation to which color and race are linked. For example, in the United States, and in some countries in Latin America, the state plays an active role in managing race relations, but a passive one in managing color relations. In the United States, U.S. Supreme Court opinions have declared a "public" colorblind liberalism in which racial classification itself is prohibited, whereas social inequalities in what is deemed the "private" sphere are considered beyond the power of the state to address. The formal dismantling of the racial state (by declaring racial classifications illegal) thus does not dismantle the racial hierarchies that continue to perpetuate inequality in the workplace, in schools, in popular culture and the media, in neighborhoods, and in families. To the contrary, racial liberalism makes it possible to characterize behavior that maintains racial hierarchy as the product of individual "choice," free of racist taint.

Looking at colorism through the lens of this racial liberalism, it is clear that the dismantling of the racial state may have little or no effect on the racial market. Indeed, the actual erosion of traditional categorical racism, state driven or not, may intensify rather than ameliorate colorism. As several of the chapters in this volume indicate, the erasure of a strict color line between white and nonwhite may enable, rather than dampen, conflict. Rather than being equally shut out of prestigious jobs, for example, persons of African descent may now compete with one another, including along lines of color. Several chapters also suggest that in the coming era, the highest status will not be whiteness itself, but a color status that is light without being white. In this economy, perhaps *café con crema* skin becomes a signifier of the postracial society that celebrates multiculturalism and rejects white supremacy. Yet, ironically, this economy continues to rely, covertly, on the racial hierarchy it claims to abandon.

One of the most seductive aspects of color has been central to its value to the hierarchies of race: its seemingly natural, unmediated quality. Skin color seems to just be there—a natural fact. And the danger of racial liberalism is that it leaves people without a language in which to talk about inequality. One of the challenges for scholars and activists concerned with colorism is thus to disrupt—and if possible prevent—"Latin Americanization," in which color hierarchy is pervasive yet its relationship to racism denied. Recent events in Brazil indicate that the effect can, in fact, be turned around. This is good news, because it would be unfortunate if the debate about color worldwide took on the characteristics of debate about class in the United States, in which relational understandings of class as a system of exploitation, not just stratification, are unavailable to most ordinary people.

Last, race and color both circulate in an economy of cultural fantasy. Color is haunted by race both in the substitutability of color for race in the naturalization process, and also in what it communicates about the human. The idea of race, as many people have argued, is connected profoundly to modernity, and lies at the convergence of the grand narratives of History and Science. Color, like race, situates peoples along the path of History: More white is more European, and more European is more refined; less European is more primitive, and more primitive is more dark. Color, like race, also situates us within the discourse of Science as a practice that can tell us who we really are and ultimately how to change who we are into something else. We no longer have a science of race, but, as Charis Thompson's chapter argues, we have new sciences of better living through reproductive technologies that will allow us to manipulate ourselves and our children to fit our fantasies of perfection. Skin color here carries fantasies about personal identity and family unity as well as the confirmation, or disruption, of racial orders.

If the study of racism alerts us to the "big picture" of class struggle, the study of colorism shows us the fine-grained details of how everyday body practices, abetted by everyday technologies of knowledge and exchange, help to make and remake racial difference. These chapters illustrate how economies of color constitute, and are constituted by, economies of race.

The Significance of Skin Color
Transnational Divergences and Convergences

THROUGH COMPARISON OF LATIN AMERICA and the United States, the chapters in this section address two crucial issues: First, what is the relationship between colorism and racism? Second, in what ways are racism and colorism changing in response to forces such as migration, globalization, and economic restructuring?

The question of whether the concepts of race and color are analytically distinct is a matter of serious contention. On the one hand, in the United States context one can argue that "race" is premised on the existence of distinct, bounded categories, to which individuals can be assigned based on ancestry, while skin color is premised on the existence of a continuum from light to dark. That is, skin color varies among individuals within as well as between racial categories. Thus, while racism in the United States is usually thought of as discrimination toward members of one category by members of another, colorism often takes the form of intra-category discrimination. On the other hand, in Brazil and in other Latin American contexts, one can argue that race and color are not analytically distinct. In his chapter on Brazil, Edward Telles shows that the idea of "color" in Brazil is similar to the idea of "race" in the United States in that it is inspired by ideas of white supremacy and a hierarchy of colors ranked from white at the top to black at the bottom; the main difference is that the Brazilian system of hierarchy takes the form of a continuum in which colors shade into one another.

Certainly, at the symbolic level, the meanings of skin color and race are inextricably linked, even when explicit reference to race is absent. Skin color as well as other phenotypic characteristics, such as hair texture and facial features, matter because they signify race. Both in the United States and Brazil dark skin signifies "blackness" and light skin signifies "whiteness." However, as the chapters in this section reveal, societies with biracial systems (notably the United States) and societies with multiracial systems (notably Brazil and other Latin American and Caribbean countries) differ in their approaches to race and color. Societies with biracial systems emphasize race and racial difference, valorize racial purity, and emphasize lineage over actual skin color, whereas societies with multiracial systems deny the salience of race and racism, valorize racial mixing (*mestizaje*), and emphasize skin color differences.

Still, discrimination based on skin tone is prevalent in both types of societies. Telles (on Brazil) and Verna Keith (on the United States) marshal evidence documenting the social and economic disadvantage of being darker skinned in both Brazil and the United States despite their divergent histories of race relations. Regarding changes and convergences over time, Edward Telles, Eduardo Bonilla-Silva, and David R. Dietrich provide unique perspectives on the issue of recent transformation in race and color formation, and a seeming convergence between the United States and Western Europe on the one hand, and Brazil and other Latin American countries on the other. Bonilla-Silva and Dietrich argue that the United States and Europe are moving toward a Latin American triracial system as a consequence of increased immigration and intermixing, and a decline of white numerical dominance. They predict that skin color will become a more significant factor in racial assignment than in the past. In the other direction, Telles argues that the U.S. Civil Rights Movement has had influence in Brazil. The growth of a viable Black Movement has created new racial politics in which more "brown" African Brazilians are identifying as "black," and the university system has responded by adopting race-based U.S.–style affirmative action policies. These convergences point to the growing complexity in the politics of race and color in both regions and the need for comparative studies to understand the complexity.

E.N.G.

1 The Social Consequences of Skin Color in Brazil

Edward Telles

IN 1968, THE U.S. STATE DEPARTMENT SPONSORED A GROUP of about eighty young Brazilian college students to visit various American institutions. As part of their agenda, the Brazilian contingent met with two African American student leaders at Harvard University who spoke to them about recent U.S. Civil Rights gains for blacks. In the ensuing discussion, some of the Brazilian students opined that the U.S. reforms on race did not affect capitalism, the central problem plaguing most modern societies. Radically distinct conceptions of fundamental social problems emerged but, at one point, realizing their ideological impasse, the two North Americans noted that among the roughly eighty Brazilians, only seven or eight were black. Where was their racial democracy if blacks were so underrepresented in their group? After the meeting, the Brazilians began to self-reflect but, rather than raising concerns about black underrepresentation, they were mostly bewildered about how more than one or two persons in their delegation could be considered black. Given Brazilian connotations of blackness, the individuals they referred to must have felt insulted and embarrassed.

Above all, the incident demonstrated how blackness is distinctly understood in Brazil and the United States.[1] A person who is black in the United States is often not so in Brazil. Indeed, some U.S. blacks may be considered white in Brazil. After all, only very dark skin color defines blackness in Brazil. Although the value given to blackness is similarly low everywhere, who gets classified as black is not. Also, the notion of who is black, mixed, or white in Brazil may change greatly within Brazil depending on the classifier, the situation, or the region. The black category is much more elusive in Brazil. Brazilians generally seek to escape from it if they can, but occasionally, for reasons of political expediency, as in the case of the new affirmative action policies, they may seek to be included in it. Stuart Hall's idea of race as the "floating signifier" is thus particularly appropriate, where meanings about race are not fixed, but are relational and subject to redefinition in different cultures.[2]

Another difference between the two countries is in the use of the term *race*. In Brazil, the term *côr*, or literally *color*, is more commonly used than *race*. *Color* is often preferred because it captures the continuous aspects of Brazilian racial concepts in which groups shade into one another whereas *race* in Brazilian Portuguese (*raça*) is mostly understood, until recently, to mean *willpower* or *desire* or even *nationality*. Relatedly, the idea that each individual belongs to a racial group is less common in Brazil than in the United States. However, color/*cor* captures the Brazilian equivalent of the English language term *race* and is based on a combination of physical characteristics, including skin color, hair type, nose shape, and lip shape.[3]

Comparatively, Brazilians often refer to color differences within the entire Brazilian population whereas in the United States, color differences generally refer to skin tone differences only within the black or Latino populations. Whites in the United States are considered uniformly pale, or at least any color differences among them have no significant meaning. More important, like race, one's color in Brazil commonly carries connotations about one's value in accordance with general Western racial ideology that valorizes lightness and denigrates darkness.

Whether one uses *color* or *race,* persons are typically categorized racially and their perceived status depends on their racial or color categorization. Racial distinctions greatly affect Brazilians' life chances, regardless of their own self-identity or the fuzziness of the categories themselves. External definitions of race and color are especially important because they often impart power and privilege in social interactions to lighter skinned persons. According to the general Brazilian societal norm, bodily appearance, influenced somewhat by gender, status, and the social situation, determines who is black, mulatto, or white. Indeed, the Brazilian system allows many persons with African ancestry to self-identify in intermediate categories, including mulatto, as well as white. On the other hand, although some persons may be able to escape being black or nonwhite, others cannot. Some remain black (*negro*) no matter how wealthy or educated they become.

In Brazil, the existence of a mulatto category is both the cause and consequence of an ideology of miscegenation and not an automatic result of the actual biological process of race mixture. Miscegenation does not create "mixed-race persons" as the U.S. case shows. Here, mixed-race persons are simply black. In the Brazilian ideology, mulattos are valued as the quintessential Brazilians in national beliefs, although they are often marginalized in reality and are much more similar to blacks than to whites in the Brazilian class structure. Racialization occurs on a color gradient, where the meanings attached to different skin colors account for different levels of discrimination. Blacks (*pretos* or *negros*) in popular conceptions of the term are those at the darkest end of the color continuum, but in an increasingly used sense of the term (*negro*), it includes mulattos or browns as well. Thus, *black* may refer to a small proportion of the national population or to half of the population, depending on whose definition is used.

These differences in racial classification between Brazil and the United States derive from distinct histories, particularly their decisions about how to classify mixed-race persons and whether to institute legal segregation. Although the so-called races could be easily delimited when Europeans, Africans, and Indians first met, the strategies for classifying the progeny of race mixture varied widely. In the United States, both before and after slavery, mulattos were often recognized as a distinct category, and the U.S. Bureau of the Census used a mulatto category from 1850 to 1910. However, with the legalization of segregation, the more common one-drop or hypodescent rule became law, thus largely overriding local traditions of recognizing *mulattos*.[4] Depending on the state, blacks were legally defined as those who had at least 1/8, 1/16, or 1/32 of African ancestry. Not surprisingly, Brazilians have trouble understanding the mathematics of this—that 1/32 determines your race despite the other 31/32. Although those laws were abolished in the 1960s, such racial ancestry rules continue to influence the classification of U.S. blacks.

South Africans adopted yet other racial classification rules for apartheid, which combined descent and appearance criteria, although their laws also created a separate classification for the intermediate *colored* category.[5] Nonetheless, race-based laws in both the United States and South Africa required highly specified classification systems to eliminate or reduce uncertainty about who belonged in which category. Despite the end of legal segregation and apartheid, a tradition of following these rules keeps racial classification fairly rigid in both countries. These traditions have been so internalized that many Americans and South Africans often still believe that those classification systems represent an essential or natural division of the human species, even though their definitions were constructed according to particular social, political, and cultural contexts.

Unlike the United States and South Africa, Brazil has never had laws that define racial group membership, at least during the postabolition period. The decision by Brazil's elites to promote whitening through miscegenation, rather than to establish segregation by category, precluded the need for formal rules of classification. Thus, classification was based on appearance and was left to individual perception. As a result, racial classification in Brazil became more complex, ambiguous, and fluid than in those countries with segregatory legal traditions.[6] Now that forty years having passed since the end of segregation in the United States, there are signs of growing ambiguity here, too, as in the biracial movement.

The ambiguity of Brazilian racial classification is apparent both in how particular persons are classified and in the racial categories themselves. There are at least three major systems of classification. These systems use different conceptions of race, each implying different levels of ambiguity and, when they use the same terms, their conceptions vary depending on the system. Currently, three major systems of racial classification are used to characterize the vast majority of Brazilians along the white-to-black color continuum; each system consists of a distinct set of categories that vary in number and degree of ambiguity.[7] The first two systems have been around for many decades. These are (1) the census system with its three major categories along the continuum; (2) the popular system, which uses an indeterminate number of categories, including the popular but especially ambiguous term *Moreno;* and (3) the newer classification system that is most like that of the United States and uses only two terms, *negro* and *branco,* or black and white, and which I call the Black Movement system, because that is where it originated. Each of these are described in the following sections.

Race in the Brazilian Census

The Brazilian Institute of Geography and Statistics (IBGE) is the governmental agency responsible for designing and collecting the decennial population census. Since 1950, the IBGE has used the categories white (*branco*), brown (*pardo*), black (*preto*), and Asian/yellow (*amarelo*), and it added Indigenous (*Indígena*) in 1991. Because Asians and indigenous peoples comprise less than 1 percent of the national population, the three categories along the black-to-white continuum account for more than 99 percent of Brazilians. Although *white* and *black* refer to the ends of the continuum, the census *brown* category (*pardo*) serves as an umbrella category for the various mixed-race terms used in popular discourse. *Pardo*, usually translated as *brown*, actually refers to an arid grayish brown color (the pardo envelope). Although often used as a proxy for *mulattos* or persons with white and black admixture, it may also include other categories, including *caboclos* (i.e., civilized Indians or persons of mostly indigenous ancestry).

These terms, although not as ambiguous as the popular classification system, are nonetheless ambiguously used. Presumably, the census is based on self-classification; but, in reality, others, including household members and the interviewers themselves, usually do the classifying. In one sense, who does the classifying does not really matter because one can name advantages to using either other or self-classification. However, racial identification, even in the census, is not exact because of the inconsistency between how people classify themselves and how they are classified by others. In a survey in which I analyzed both self and other classification, 89 percent of respondents who self-identified as white were similarly classified by the interviewer, compared with only 71 percent of self-identified browns and 59 percent of self-identified blacks being similarly classified by interviewers. Thus, interviewers and respondents are more able to agree more on who is white than who is brown or black, demonstrating that the white–nonwhite distinction is the conceptually clearest racial divide in the minds of Brazilians.

Race in Popular Discourse

The second classification system refers to racial classification in popular Brazilian discourse. It is characterized by a plethora of race or color terms, although there is evidence that the number of popular terms and the ambiguity of their use may be declining. A commonly cited finding is that a national survey in 1976 revealed the use of more than 100 terms in an open-ended question about color. These included such terms as *purple, dark chocolate,* or *Pelé colored.* However, the fact that fully 95 percent of those respondents used only six terms is often ignored.[8] In my reanalysis of the 1976 data, I found that 135 terms were used in the sample of 82,577 Brazilians. Most (or, specifically, 86) of those terms were used by only 279 of the respondents (0.3% of the population). Thus, it is true that Brazilians can be found to use a large number of racial terms, but the vast majority of them use only a few terms.

Analysis of a 1995 national survey yielded similar results. In that survey, the interviewers asked respondents their color, using an open-ended format as

Table 1.1 Frequency of Respondent's Preferred Color Label in Open-Ended Format, Adult Population in Urban Brazil, 1995

Color Label	Percentage	Cumulative Percentage
Branco	42	42
Moreno	32	74
Pardo	7	81
Moreno claro	6	87
Preto	5	92
Negro	3	95
Claro	2	97
All others*	3	100
Total	100	—

*All others less than 1 percent each including mulatto (0.8). escuro (0.7, and moreno-escuro (0.5).

they did in the 1976 survey. Results are shown in Table 1.1. The top row shows that *branco* (or white) was the most common category chosen, at 42 percent. However, the second most popular category was the unofficial *moreno* category, chosen by 32 percent of all Brazilians. *Moreno* also translates as brown, like the census term *pardo,* but is much more commonly used in everyday discourse. The term *pardo* was used by only 7 percent of the population. *Moreno claro* (light *moreno*) was used by another 6 percent of the population. Five percent of the population classified themselves as *preto,* the census term for *black,* whereas only 3 percent of the sample classified themselves as *negro,* which also translates as black. Last, the remaining 5 percent used many terms, including 2 percent who classified themselves as *claro* (light); no other term was used by a full 1 percent of the population.[9] Thus, fully 97 percent of the non-Asian and non-Indian population used only seven color terms in 1995, but only 54 percent chose the three official census terms.

The term *moreno* is particularly noteworthy for the high frequency of its use and for its extreme ambiguity. *Moreno* and its variant *moreno claro* were used by fully 38 percent of the population. Ethnographers have found the term ambiguous enough to substitute for almost any other color category.[10] Its connotations include (1) light-skinned persons with dark hair, (2) a person of mixed "race" or parentage who generally has brunette hair, and (3) a black person.[11] The widespread use of *moreno* is remarkable when one considers that it has never once been officially used in the more than 100-year existence of Brazilian censuses. Its centrality in the popular Brazilian classification may be the result of its ambiguity and its propensity to downplay racial differences and emphasize a common "Brazilianness."[12] Gilberto Freyre, the master architect of Brazilian national identity, proclaimed that *moreno* represented the fusion of blacks, Indians, and Europeans into a single Brazilian *metarace*. *Moreno,* some have suggested, is *the* Brazilian race category par excellence, because it permits discussion of race through inclusion by subverting clear distinctions and thus masking racial hierarchy.

The Black Movement System of Racial Classification

The Black Movement has long used a third classification system, which has only recently become widely accepted by the government, media, and academia. This system of classification uses only two terms: *black (negro)* and *white (branco)*. This newly emergent system most approximates the U.S. system in that it eliminates the intermediate categories. Some claim that it reveals a convergence in classification by the two countries and a growing acceptance of hypodescent in Brazil. This system is distinguished from the other two systems because of the importance of the term *negro,* just as *moreno* is important in the popular system. The term *negro,* like *moreno,* has never been used in the census. Although the term was considered highly offensive in the past, and in some situations may continue to be so, *negro* has now largely become a term of ethnic pride and affirmation, because Black Movement activists have made the term *negro* into a political category since at least the 1930s.[13] In contrast to *moreno,* which represents a Brazilian tradition of universalism through racial ambiguity, the term *negro,* by making race explicit, represents the complete opposite. *Negro,* in the modern sense, is used by those who seek to diminish ambiguity and destigmatize blackness. Black Movement activists maintain that, unlike the United States, the official and popular Brazilian use of multiple "color" categories and the unofficial hierarchy in which brown is superior to black has inhibited the formation of a collective black identity around which African Brazilians can mobilize in response to shared discrimination and exclusion.[14]

The use of the Black Movement system was consolidated among government officials when the president and the ministry of justice broke with Brazilian government tradition by beginning to use *negro* in 1996 and recommending that the IBGE do so as well. The IBGE has yet to adopt the Black Movement system, although they considered proposals to do so in 1991 and 2000. This

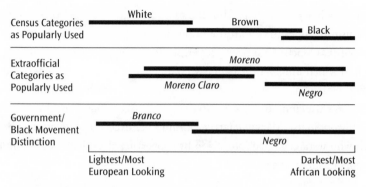

Figure 1.1 Use of Brazilian Racial Categories Along the Color Continuum

institutionalization of the *negro* category in government affirmative action programs has infuriated some scholars in Brazil because, for the first time, the government set criteria for membership in a racial category and violated popular (*emic*) notions of *negro* by including many persons (especially *pardos* as defined by the census) who would never consider themselves as *negro*.[15] The Brazilian government had sought to dichotomize, or worse (North) "Americanize," racial classification in a society that up to now had used and even celebrated intermediate terms.

To summarize, Figure 1.1 schematically illustrates how the racial categories used in the three classification systems are distributed along a color continuum that runs from the lightest and most European-looking persons on the left to the darkest and most African-looking persons on the right. The census system is illustrated at the top of Figure 1.1 and shows the three terms and the extent to which they overlap along the color continuum. The extent of overlap between browns and blacks in the census is significantly greater than between whites and browns. The middle of Figure 1.1 shows the categories most often used by ordinary Brazilians in everyday discourse. Most notably, the commonly used term *moreno* refers to a range of persons occupying nearly the entire color continuum. The bottom of Figure 1.1 shows that the Black Movement system combines combine browns and blacks as defined by the census into a single *negro* group.

Genetic Roulette?

Although mixed-race persons with a generous amount of European appearance can sometimes deny being black, this is considered deception or "passing" in the United States, whereas the same person may be legitimately classified as white in the Brazilian system. Thus, in terms of racial classification, miscegenation tends to whiten the population in Brazil whereas in the United States the same process blackens the population. I often hear disagreements about the extent to which Brazilians who call themselves white, have nonwhite ancestry. Many Brazilians understand this possibility, but Americans often assume that white is a "racially pure" category.

Anthropologist Marvin Harris[16] found cases of full-blooded siblings in Brazil who were classified into different racial categories, including white. Although his study demonstrated that ancestry did not exclusively determine race, current data allow us to probe much deeper. When comparing race or color between Brazil and the United States, the distinction between appearance and race often comes up. But to what extent is racial classification by appearance and ancestry correlated?

A random survey of the state of Rio de Janeiro in 2000 asked respondents if they had any ancestors who were European, African, or indigenous. The results are summarized in Table 1.2. Fully 38 percent of persons who self-classified as white claimed to have some African ancestry, whereas another 14 percent claimed mixed indigenous and European ancestry. Only 48 percent of self-identified whites claimed to have strictly European ancestry.[17] This reveals that for the many Brazilians who identify as white, admitting to having nonwhite ancestors is not problematic. Although the whitening ideology may lead them to downplay these ancestors, claiming African ancestry and identifying as white is thus not inconsistent in the Brazilian system.[18] At the same time, the stigma

Table 1.2 Ancestry of Self-Classified Whites, Browns, and Blacks, State of Rio de Janeiro, 2000

	Self-Classified Color		
Breakdown by Ancestry	*White*	*Brown*	*Black*
European only	48	6	—
African only	—	12	25
Indigenous only	—	2	—
African and European	23	34	31
Indigenous and European	14	6	—
African and indigenous	—	4	9
African, indigenous, and European	15	36	35
Total	100	100	100
Any African	38	86	100

SOURCE: Edward Telles, *Race in Another America: The Significance of Skin Color in Brazil* (Princeton: Princeton University Press, 2004), 92–93.

associated with being Indian and especially African may have prevented others from making similar declarations. Among those self-identifying as black, only 25 percent claim that they have only black ancestry and another 9 percent report black and indigenous ancestry only. Therefore, fully 66 percent of blacks claim to have some European ancestry.

Genetics research supports these findings. Researchers at the Federal University of Minas Gerais, in a study of Y chromosomes among a regionally representative sample of 200 unrelated Brazilian males that self-identified as white, found that only 2.5 percent of the sample had lineage in the male line from sub-Saharan Africa, and no one in the sample revealed Amerindian lineage in that line.[19] However, examination of their matrilineage using mitochondrial DNA, revealed that Amerindians contributed 33 percent and Africans another 28 percent of the total mitochondrial DNA pool of white Brazilians, revealing that many Brazilians that identify as white have a significant degree of non-European ancestry. This finding of substantial race mixture along the maternal line is consistent with Brazil's history of miscegenation between Portuguese males and African or indigenous females. The fact that such high levels of mixture were found among whites demonstrates the irrelevance of the racial purity concept to racial classification in Brazil; in contrast, the very definition of whites as it was coded in U.S. law until recent years would exclude anyone with a drop of African blood.

Black–Brown Differences

Given these definitions of race or color in Brazil, I now want to examine differences in income. Figure 1.2 shows the overall income status of Brazilians according to the 3 color categories used in the census. The figure reveals that the average income of black and brown families is about 40 and 45 percent, respectively, of those of white families. Black and brown Brazilians have much lower incomes than whites, but black family income is close to (90% of) brown family income. Thus, there is a huge white–nonwhite gap, and a relatively small gap between blacks and browns. In terms of actual income, then, the primary racial boundary in Brazil is clearly between whites and nonwhites.

Similar findings might be expected in the United States. Data from the National Survey of Black Americans (NSBA), which is also presented in Figure 1.2, demonstrate that family incomes of African Americans range from 53 percent of mean white income for the darkest subgroup to 80 percent of white income for the lightest. These results demonstrate greater differences between dark-

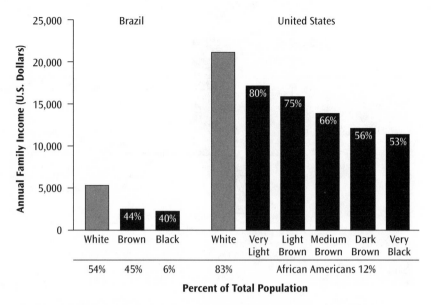

Figure 1.2 Mean Annual Family Income in Brazil and the United States for Whites and by Skin Color Among African-Origin Population, 1980

and light-skinned Africans in the United States than in Brazil,[20] and the gap between white and brown is much greater in Brazil than in the United States. Ironically, a color continuum thus better characterizes racial income differences in the United States than in Brazil, even though subjective and classificatory notions of race are based on a dichotomy in the United States but a color continuum in Brazil.

Human capital studies of race in Brazil, particularly Nelson do Valle Silva's (1978, 1985) pioneering work,[21] did much to demystify racial democracy and the belief that income differences had nothing to do with discrimination. Based on national census and household survey data, these studies showed that as much as one third of the differences in income between whites and nonwhites cannot be explained by racial differences in variables like education, work experience, social origins, and region. This unexplained portion of the difference has traditionally been believed to be a proxy for the extent of labor market discrimination. Given strong evidence from human capital models showing the persistence of unexplained white–nonwhite income differences, the scholarly discussion has turned mostly to the extent of black–brown differences.

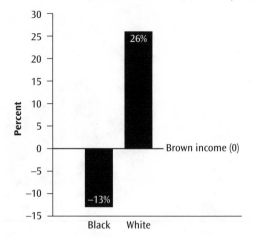

Figure 1.3 Income Gap Between Whites and Browns and Blacks and Browns in Brazil, Net of Controls

In a research article that I published with Nelson Lim in *Demography*, I used data from the 1995 Data Folha Survey to investigate the claim that browns earn incomes that are more similar to white income than black income when race is assessed by others. I treat the complex methodological issues in that article but present a summary of the results in Figure 1.3.[22] After controlling for a range of human capital (gender, education, age) and labor market characteristics (region, size of urban area), Figure 1.3 shows that whites earn fully 26 percent more than browns when race is based on interviewer classification, whereas income for persons classified as black is 12 percent lower than that for browns. Using similar methodologies, several researchers have found that U.S. black men suffered a 12 to 15 percent loss in earnings resulting from labor market discrimination.[23] The loss for brown, and especially black, men is thus greater in Brazil than it is in the United States.

The income disadvantage of browns relative to whites, based on interviewer classification, is roughly two-thirds as large as that for blacks. Thus, the primary racial cleavage is between white and nonwhite, even though blacks tend to be more discriminated against than browns. Given the especially high-income concentration among the top 10 percent of the population, and the highly skewed returns on education found in Brazil, especially large white–nonwhite differences in *actual* income are not surprising. Also, the greater residential disadvantages of browns compared with blacks offsets what would otherwise be larger black–brown differences in actual income.

The finding of greater inequality when color is classified by the interviewer is mainly a result of persons who self-classified as brown but were classified as white by interviewers. Such persons had fully 26 percent more income than persons classified as brown by both interviewer and respondents. Persons who self-classified as white but were classified as brown by interviewers had only 4 percent more income than consistently classified browns. These findings therefore indicate that official statistics, to the extent they are based on self-classification, tend to inflate brown income and, conversely, deflate white income.

Similar tests by Keith, Herring,[24] and others have shown the existence of greater racial discrimination in the labor market and in education for darker skinned African Americans and U.S. Latinos. I have also used the National Chicano Survey in 1979 and the 1979 Survey of Black Americans[25] and found skin color differences. Darker blacks and darker Latinos experience greater earnings or educational loss than their lighter skinned counterparts, even after controlling for all other effects. This strongly suggests that they experience greater discrimination. At least that is what the results showed overall.

However, more recent evidence suggests that this effect is not as strong as it used to be. Using the NSBA from 1979 and the 1982 General Social Survey, sociologist Aaron Gullickson[26] has recently shown that dark-skinned African Americans born in the 1950s and later do not suffer from significantly more discrimination than light-skinned blacks, like earlier birth cohorts did. He speculates, although he cannot prove it, that the gatekeepers during segregation were other blacks who paid much attention to skin color differences whereas today's gatekeepers are likely to be white, who presumably pay less attention to within-group color differences. I analyzed a 1998–2000 survey of Mexican Americans in Los Angeles and San Antonio aged 35 to 55 and found very few color differences. These findings are based on limited data. The need for more recent national data on color is great.

The Debate on Classification in Affirmative Action

Sociologists are good at discovering and explaining social problems. However, designing effective policy is another matter. Nevertheless, I next describe the complicated policy issues that have arisen on the ambiguous issue of color or racial classification in Brazil.

Brazil's first modern race-conscious policy was adopted in 2001. The institution of affirmative action in several Brazilian universities since 2001 has been the greatest challenge to the Brazilian color system in recent memory. Race is important because of how others are treated in social interactions. Therefore, it is perfectly reasonable that the Brazilian state has developed [begun developing developed] affirmative action policies to counteract the problems created by this social notion of race or color. However, this issue faces especially great problems in Brazil, because adverse treatment on the basis of race depends on the situation, the classifier, and other variables. Unlike gender, the lack of discrete racial categories with precise boundaries in a system in which colors shade into one another and multiple categories are recognized, makes it difficult to define racial boundaries for policymakers to decide who should benefit from affirmative action and, especially, from quotas. In Brazil, the racial *other*, although often clear, is sometimes ambiguous. Therefore, race-conscious policies need some cutoff or threshold at which one is deemed white or not, but in Brazil, the racial other, although often clear, is sometimes ambiguous. In the United States, because segregation required clear classification rules, the old rules of classification became functional to the new measures designed to achieve racial equality.

Figure 1.4 compares racial classification and the *branco–negro* divide as is used for race-conscious policies in Brazil compared with the black–white divide in the United States. It plots the division between beneficiaries of these policies and whites on a scale showing the extent of African admixture or appearance among the population. The line separating black from white is at the limit of anyone having African admixture in the United States generally being

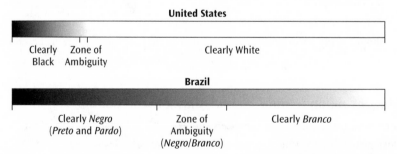

Figure 1.4 Primary Racial Boundaries in Classification Along the Black–White Continuum in Brazil and the United States, Both Using Black–White System

considered black, whereas many persons having African admixture are [with small amounts of black blood or appearance are generally] considered white in Brazil. The reality is even more complicated because many persons have indigenous admixtures as well. Most important, though, Figure 1.4 shows that although there is a zone of ambiguity in both countries, a considerably larger proportion of the Brazilian population falls into that zone. Despite the rhetoric of activists claiming that everyone knows who is black, the reality is far different.

Browns (*pardos*) are now generally included as *negros* in race-conscious policies, like the new affirmative action quotas in several Brazilian universities, even though they do not generally perceive themselves as *negros*. However, given strong data that they suffer socioeconomically because of racial discrimination, this inclusion seems justified. But besides browns, do we include or exclude the large proportion of Brazilians who call themselves *morenos,* or whites who claim to have black ancestors? Certainly, in the legal cases against the State University of Rio de Janeiro, such persons claim they should be included. Where do we draw the line between potential beneficiaries and dominant group members in the absence of clear rules for making racial distinctions?

The criterion of self-identification, more so than any other criteria, seems to have become well accepted in Brazil and around the world.[27] However, this criterion is problematic, especially because it may not reflect one's classification by typical members of Brazilian society. Its ambiguity is highlighted by President Cardoso's speech reserving slots for blacks in the Foreign Diplomacy School. He announced that

> the criteria of Brazil is a criteria of self-identification. There is no discriminatory criteria: This one is white, this one is *moreno,* this one is mulatto, this one is yellow, this one is *negro*. Because that is too difficult. The rainbow is too large. But each one knows their own identity or one they would like to have and they should apply according to their cultural preference, and naturally, based on their life trajectory and some physical characteristic, though not necessarily.[28]

As mentioned earlier, about 40 percent of self-identified whites in the state of Rio de Janeiro similarly have no problem admitting that they have black ancestors. Darkening one's identification to benefit from affirmative action is a clear possibility for many Brazilians. Because the Brazilian system is based on appearance rather than ancestry, the potential opportunity of having a quality university education for free may lead some former "white persons" to declare themselves black or brown. For the first time, having black blood may thus offer a strategic advantage. Even Fernando Henrique Cardoso claimed to have "a foot in the kitchen," by which he meant that he has black ancestors, when he sought black votes for his reelection in 1998. If the president would seek to benefit from such a racial opportunity, why wouldn't many Brazilians who normally consider themselves white?

Although I do not think anywhere near the 40 percent of whites in Rio de Janeiro with African ancestors will seek to identify as *negro,* I do believe that Brazil's ambiguity could present major challenges to the implementation of racial quotas. In a conversation I had in 1999 with Januário Garcia, the photographer of a program called (Centro Brasileiro de Informação e Documentação do Artista Negro) [CIDAN]) that promoted hundreds of black models and actors by putting their photos and resumes on a website, related at least one incident of such ambiguity. Garcia told me that a young man, whom he described as clearly white and "surfer-looking," came in asking to be photographed for the website. Garcia carefully asked the young man if he knew the purpose of the program and the model responded, "Yeah, I know. My grandmother was a *negra,* so I guess that makes me a *negro.*" Garcia thought, "Who was I to decide whether he was a *negro?*" so he photographed the model and posted his picture, and resumé, on the CIDAN website. However, a perusal of the CIDAN website reveals that the vast majority of persons who availed themselves of this free service to promote *negros* could easily be classified as brown or black.

For the strict quotas to work, when persons need to qualify as *negro,* there needs to be a fairly strict classification system, and the third or Black Movement system is often adopted. The National University of Brasilia has recently come under fire for using a commission to judge whether quota students are authentically black. This flies in the face of the Brazilian system of ambiguity. Although a recent *New York Times* article,[29] shows that the new DNA tests have shown that some whites have discovered they have African blood, allowing them to check off the "black" box on their college applications, no such genetics test is really needed in Brazil. Many white Brazilians have long known that they have black blood, but their appearances have enabled them to benefit from white skin privilege. Now there seems to be one case in which privilege is reversed, and this has created a new problem. Notions of racial purity imported from the United States are now used to confound policies that seek to redress Brazil's very real color discrimination. To date, these policies have had trouble dealing with the ambiguity inherent in a color rather than a racial system.

2 A Colorstruck World

Skin Tone, Achievement, and Self-Esteem Among African American Women

Verna M. Keith

Don't play in the sun. You're going to have to get a light-skinned husband for the sake of your children as it is.[1]

MANY AFRICAN AMERICAN WOMEN are intimately familiar with the warning and advice conveyed to author Marita Golden by her mother in the opening quote to this chapter. Black girls are cautioned about playing in the sun because the sun will make their skin darker, perhaps black, if they are already a very dark brown. Black girls and women are often encouraged to "marry light," with the implied message that if you can't save yourself from the hurt that comes with having a dark complexion (spoken aloud) and being less attractive (often not spoken aloud), at least you can "save your children."[2] Such admonitions may seem cruel, and perhaps they are, but they are given out of love and a deep, historical understanding that we live in a colorstruck world, where distinctions based on skin tone have historically intersected with racism, sexism, and class to influence how African American and other women of color evaluate themselves, who they will date and marry, how much education they will attain, what kinds of jobs they will have, and what overall standard of living they will achieve.

Colorism, the privileging of light skin tone over dark skin tone, has historically been important to our understanding of racialized social processes and experiences in the United States, especially as they affect African Americans.[3] Complexion, along with other Eurocentric physical features—blue, gray, or green eyes; straight hair texture; thin lips; and a narrow nose—has been accorded higher status both within and outside the African American community. Conversely, dark complexion and Afrocentric features—broad nose, kinky hair, full lips, and brown eyes—has been devalued. The hierarchical ranking of these phenotypic characteristics has meant that African Americans with more European features are viewed as being more attractive and intelligent than

25

those with fewer or none of these features.[4] As Rockquemore and Brunsma note, skin tone and other physical features are not value-neutral bodily differences, but instead carry symbolic, racialized meanings.[5] These racialized meanings, in turn, are central to the lived experiences of African Americans on many different levels.

For nearly three-quarters of a century, researchers have documented the many ways that colorism affects the African American community. Two major areas of interest have been the advantages of light skin complexion for status achievement and for aspects of personal psychology such as self-worth, perceived attractiveness, and overall quality of life.[6] Other research finds more discrimination reported by darker African Americans and an association between negative stereotypic traits (e.g., drug use, laziness) and Afrocentric features.[7]

Colorism affects African Americans of both genders, but the complexion hierarchy is more central in the lives of women than men. The gendered nature of colorism stems from the close link between skin tone and perceptions of physical attractiveness, and from a double standard that applies expectations of attractiveness more rigidly to women.[8] In a society where whiteness of skin is a highly esteemed dimension of idealized beauty, women with darker skin and Afrocentric features are at a disadvantage. In addition, for all women, attractiveness is linked to a host of positive personality characteristics—kind, interesting, sexy, and poised.[9] Issues of complexion, identity, attractiveness, and self-concept are often a major focus of African American women in clinical encounters—a testament to the importance of complexion in women's emotional experiences.[10] As a marker of beauty, skin tone is also a form of social capital that grants access to resources of many different types, including marriage to higher status men, higher self-esteem, and access to "visible" occupations.[11]

This chapter explores the linkages between skin tone, socioeconomic achievement, and self-esteem among African American women. After briefly exploring the historical underpinnings of colorism, I address skin tone variations in women's schooling, occupational status, income, and self-esteem. In addition, I present empirical findings that shed light on the triangulation of complexion, achievement, and self-esteem. At the outset, it is important to state a caveat. Maintaining that a more European appearance is associated with privilege is not synonymous with maintaining that light-skinned African Americans do not experience racism or discrimination. As Hunter notes, race and skin tone represent two different systems of oppression, although they overlap.[12]

Complexion and Slavery: The Historical Legacy

Racial formation theory argues that racial projects construct the meaning of race via images and explanations about racial categories that are manipulated to maintain white dominance.[13] White supremacy, one such racial project, and miscegenation are the two primary forces that gave rise to the color hierarchy in the African American community.[14] As part of the ideological rationale for slavery, blackness was defined as barbaric, savage, ugly, and evil whereas whiteness was defined as civilized, virtuous, and beautiful. As a result of miscegenation, which produced an African American population characterized by a continuum of color and physical types, phenotypic traits came to represent these abstract concepts physically that were attached to blackness and whiteness.

A prevailing view that is often disputed is that visible white ancestry became the basis of differential access to privilege among both slaves and free persons of color. Myrdal wrote that slaves more European in appearance commanded higher prices in the slave markets and were preferred as personal servants to white masters because they were considered to be more aesthetically appealing and intellectually superior to slaves with pure African ancestry.[15] Some evidence also suggests that slaves of mixed ancestry were more likely to be granted desirable skilled and domestic positions, better food and clothing, and manumission and educational opportunities; and were treated less harshly by owners and overseers.[16] The aesthetic appeal and kinship bonds between slave owners and their slave children may have accounted for some of these advantages and for the overrepresentation of mixed-raced blacks in the free population.[17] Within the free black population, there is evidence that mulattos were privileged. Bodenhorn, for example, uncovered evidence that light-skinned blacks in Virginia enjoyed a height advantage over dark-skinned blacks that may have signaled access to better nutrition and general living conditions.[18] Both Frazier and Myrdal argued that the superiority of mixed-raced blacks was widely accepted in the slave population as a whole as a result of the status advantages and similarities between whites and mulattos in physical appearance, speech, dress, and behavior. Through this structure of privilege, buttressed by ideological underpinnings of the superiority of white blood, colorism took hold in the African American community.

Mixed-raced African Americans became the social and economic elite of black communities after the Civil War because of the advantages they had received as slaves and free persons of color. Although their jobs as small businessmen and service workers with white patrons were not prestigious in the modern sense, these were privileged positions compared with the opportunities available to their darker contemporaries. Membership in the mulatto elite was based on a combination of light skin, family background, a heritage of freedom before emancipation, and a lifestyle modeled after affluent whites.[19] Socially, mulattos distanced themselves from the larger African American community by excluding darker blacks from their social organizations. By avoiding intermarriage with darker blacks, continuing their associations with whites, and passing their advantages on to their children, the original mulatto elite maintained their position at the top of the social hierarchy until the beginning of the 20th century.[20]

By World War I, the influence of skin color on social status appears to have been on the decline. Prestige in the African American community was increasingly dependent on education, occupation, and economic success resulting from the gradual extension of education opportunities to the black masses and growing competition from white immigrants for service jobs previously held by the old mulatto elite.[21] The mass migration of blacks from the South in the 1920s also produced an increasing demand for African American professionals that could not be met by the old elite. As darker skinned blacks became more successful, they married into the old mulatto elite, although this was more likely for males than for females.[22] By the 1950s, the complexion of the African American middle and upper classes had darkened considerably. Although the significance of complexion may have diminished since the mid century, research conducted during the past 5 decades argues strongly that complexion has continued to matter not just for status attainment but also for such diverse areas as mate selection and health status.[23] In the remainder of this chapter, I explore how color matters for African American women.

Complexion and Achievement

Status achievement is most generally evaluated by measuring education, occupation, and income. Much of our most recent information on skin tone and socioeconomic status (SES) among African American women in the post-Civil Rights era comes from the NSBA. The NSBA, fielded in 1979–1980, was until recently the only large, nationally representative study of adults widely available to scholars that includes an assessment of African Americans' complexion.[24] In the NSBA, African American interviewers rated respondents' skin color on a 5-point scale: 1, very dark brown; 2, dark brown, 3, medium brown, 4, light brown, and 5, very light brown. Previous analyses of data from the NSBA indicate that lighter skin tone is associated with higher SES.[25] Thus, complexion operates as a form of social capital that can be converted to human capital assets, although at differing rates depending on skin shade.

Understanding just how this process works is largely limited to speculation. One possible explanation is that the advantages of light skin have been passed down through family networks that were established by the old mulatto elite. This seems unlikely given that the advantage of light skin persists when family SES is controlled. A second set of hypotheses focuses on the educational system. Davis and Dollard suggested an indirect link between skin tone and educational attainment via parental SES.[26] They found that, in the 1930s, when complexion was still closely linked to class standing, higher status black children received preferential treatment from teachers. They argued that praise from teachers reduced student anxiety and encouraged learning, which then prompted "circular reinforcement" on the part of teachers. Making a more direct argument, Hunter theorizes that teachers make attributions regarding who is and who is not smart based on attractiveness and that, given the association between skin tone and perceived attractiveness, teachers may lower their expectations of darker students, challenge them less, and may indeed rate them lower on assignments.[27] A third explanation focuses on discrimination on the part of employers. Several studies have found that darker African Americans report more job discrimination and are up to eleven times more likely to report experiencing racial discrimination in general than light-skinned African Americans.[28]

Recently, Gullickson questioned the persistence of a light skin advantage in achievement.[29] Using data from the original NSBA, three NSBA follow-up waves (1987–1988, 1989–1990, and 1992), and the 1982 General Social Survey, he concluded that the strength of the skin tone effect on education declined significantly for cohorts born after 1945 and had no effect for cohorts born after 1953. Indeed, upward occupational mobility was greater for dark and medium-brown blacks than for lighter skinned blacks from 1980 to 1992, creating a convergence among cohorts still in the labor force. He suggested that the changes engendered by the Civil Rights Movement increasingly brought African Americans into contact with white gatekeepers for whom skin tone variations were less salient.[30] Gullickson did not present data separately by gender, perhaps because of sample size limitations in the NSBA follow-up waves and the 1982 General Social Survey data. Nor did he examine interaction effects between cohort and gender. Furthermore, he found that the significance of lighter complexion remained for mate selection, and marriage has been an important avenue for women's economic security. Thus, it is unclear whether the salience of skin tone declined for both men and women or, if it did, if there were gender differences in the steepness of the decline.

Although I did not attempt to replicate Gullickson's findings using birth cohorts, I did revisit the original 1979–1980 NSBA data to assess whether the effects of skin tone on women's achievement and self-esteem were conditioned by age (i.e., interaction effects). I did this measuring age as both a continuous variable and as a categorical variable that contrasted women who became adults and eligible to work before and after the Civil Rights Movement: roughly women ages 21 to 35 and 36 to 80. In these analyses, light- and very light-brown women were combined into one category as a result of the small number of very light women.

1. *Education:* The bivariate relationship between skin tone and education is presented in Figure 2.1. The figures show that there is a monotonic relationship between complexion and education ($F = 10.35$; $p = .000$). As complexion lightens, education increases, and there is more than a year's difference in schooling between very dark-brown women and light-/very light-brown women. I compared the dark, very dark, and medium groups with the light/very light group in multivariate analyses (data not shown).[31] These findings confirm the initial observations

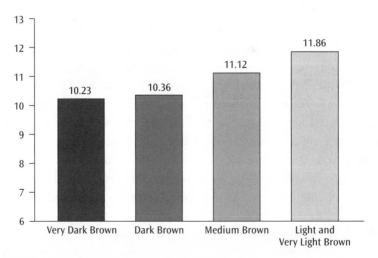

Figure 2.1 Mean Years of Education by Skin Tone
SOURCE: National Survey of Black Americans, 1979–1980.

in Figure 2.1, and I found that the relationship between complexion and education did not vary by age, measured either continuously or categorically.

2. *Occupational Status:* Occupational status also increases as skin tone becomes lighter for women in the NSBA, although the relationship is not monotonic (χ^2 = 42.31; p = .000). Figure 2.2 shows that although employment in professional and managerial occupations was highest for women of light (19.6%) and medium (14.9%) complexion, a higher percentage of very dark-brown women (10.7%) than dark-brown women (6.4%) were so employed. When other characteristics were controlled in the multivariate analysis (data not presented), the general trend indicates occupational advantages for lighter women.[32] As with education, there were no significant interaction effects.

3. *Income:* Figure 2.3 shows that lighter skin tone is associated with greater personal (F = 7.70; $p \leq$ .000) and family (F = 13.37; $p \leq$ .000) income. However, multivariate analyses indicated that the relationship between complexion and personal income is no longer significant when controls for other factors are introduced. On the other hand, findings for family income indicate an advantage for lighter women net of controls for other characteristics.[33] Tests for interaction effects revealed that the relationship between skin tone and income was not conditioned by age.

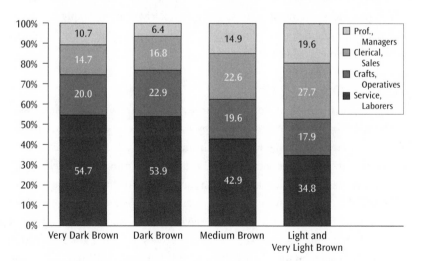

Figure 2.2 Occupation by Skin Tone

SOURCE: National Survey of Black Americans, 1979–1980.

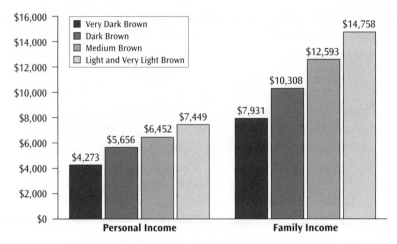

Figure 2.3 Personal and Family Income by Skin Tone
SOURCE: National Survey of Black Americans, 1979–1980.

In summary, based on these analyses from the NSBA, as late as 1980, complexion continued to matter for African American women's educational attainment, occupational standing, and family income net of family background and other characteristics. I also did not find interaction effects by age that would argue for waning effects of skin tone over time.[34] These analyses did not replicate the cohort approach used by Gullickson, but both media images that appear to place more value on light skin and scholarly research imply that more evidence is needed before we conclude that skin complexion no longer plays a role in achievement.[35]

Skin Tone and Self-Concept

Building upon the work of Goffman, Harvey and colleagues conceptualize skin tone as a form of social stigma whereby dark skin tone deviates from attributes considered acceptable within a particular context.[36] For African American women, skin tone has been a central trait for determining one's self-image. Historically, dark-skinned black women have been positioned at the bottom of the social ladder, and were viewed as least attractive and marriageable. For generations, African American women have been pressured to live up to the white ideal of beauty. As a consequence, they have sought to lighten their skin with bleach, straighten their hair with heat and chemicals, and change their eye color with contact lenses. Increasingly, African American women are undergoing such cosmetic procedures as lip reduction and nose jobs to Anglicize their features.[37] Although African American women do not want to be white, such exercises point to high levels of dissatisfaction with physical appearance among a significant number of them. But what does it tell us about the inner self?

Self-esteem, the evaluative dimension of the self, is defined by Porter and Washington as "feelings of intrinsic worth, competence, and self approval rather than self-rejection and self-contempt" (61).[38] It consists of feeling good, liking yourself, and perceiving that you are liked and treated well. Self-esteem is influenced by the social comparisons we make of ourselves with others and by the reactions that others have toward us—reflected appraisal.[39] Self-concept is derived from interactions with others, but it is also intertwined with structural features such as SES.[40] Individuals with a higher SES tend to have higher levels of self-esteem and, as we have seen, complexion is one determinant of achievement among black women.

African Americans, despite their status as a racialized minority, have higher or equivalent levels of global self-esteem when compared with whites, except during preschool years and extreme old age. In addressing this seeming paradox, Rosenberg[41] argued that one reason that African Americans do not have lower self-esteem than whites is because their self-self worth is based on evaluations and comparisons with their coethnics rather than the larger society. This argument has not been tested empirically, but it is plausible when antiblack racism is considered in historical context. Others suggest a strong ethnic group identity accounts for this counterintuitive finding. For example, ruling out methodological artifacts such as response formats and sample composition, Gray-Little and Hafdal argued that the out-group status of blacks promotes a stronger and more salient racial identity, which in turn, has been linked empirically to higher self-evaluations.[42]

Among adolescents, self-esteem is generally lower for females than males, most notably because appearance matters more for women; but, interestingly, the gender difference is less pronounced or nonexistent among blacks.[43] One factor accounting for the attenuation of gender differences among blacks is that African American females are more satisfied with their body image than white females.[44] Yet, because stigmatized physical features weigh more heavily in the lives of black women than black men, skin tone gradations may be more relevant for women's self-esteem, suggesting an even greater advantage for black females compared with black males when complexion is taken into consideration. At the same time, light-skinned black women also face challenges to self-definition by having their parentage and ethnic identity questioned, and also express feelings of guilt and shame about their unfair advantages.[45]

Using data from the original 1979–1980 NSBA, Maxine Thompson and I examined the effects of skin tone on self-esteem among African American men and women.[46] Using a 6-item self-esteem scale that tapped items from various instruments, and with a possible range in scores of 6 to 24 points, we found that skin tone was a more important predictor for women than for men. Although self-esteem was, on average, very high among all women, the average was lowest for very dark-brown women and increased as women's skin tone lightened. These differences persisted when we controlled for SES and other social characteristics. Figure 2.4 presents mean levels of self-esteem for each color group for women ages 21 to 80. As was the case for status achievement, no significant interactions by age were detected when I reanalyzed the NSBA data.

Two additional findings of the Thompson and Keith studies stand out. The first demonstrates the triangulation of skin tone, achievement, and self-esteem. Using interviewer ratings of attractiveness that ranged from 1 (unattractive) to 7 (attractive), we found that skin tone interacted with both personal income and attractiveness to influence self-esteem.[47] In one test, we found that having lighter skin boosted self-esteem for women with low to average incomes and, in a second test we discovered that having lighter skin increased self-esteem for women who were judged to be low or average in attractiveness. We did not have

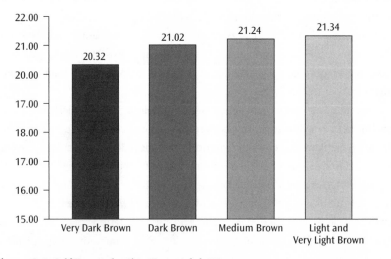

Figure 2.4 Self-Esteem by Skin Tone, Adult Women
SOURCE: National Survey of Black Americans, 1979–1980.

the statistical power to test the simultaneous effects—three-way interactions—of complexion, attractiveness, and income. However, our results do indicate that for higher income women, skin tone did not matter for self-evaluation, showing that achieved status can compensate somewhat for ascribed status based on complexion. However, for lower income women who have less access to the material *accoutrements* of status, complexion remains a source of status that figures prominently in self-evaluations. As St. Jean and Feagin observed, African American women who have learned that their (stigmatized) looks will not carry them very far, turn to other avenues.[48] Similarly, our analyses indicate that physical attractiveness can compensate somewhat for the general disparaging of dark skin color. Women deemed unattractive, however, do not escape the biases associated with colorism.

A second finding that refines our understanding of how skin tone operates for African American women's self-concept comes from our analyses regarding the racial composition of their social environments. Rosenberg demonstrated that self-esteem is higher in racially consonant (i.e., predominantly black) environments and lower in racially dissonant (i.e., predominantly white) environments, attributing these findings to fewer encounters with prejudice and discrimination in consonant environments.[49] We extended this concept to investigate the effects of skin tone on self-esteem in grade school and residential neighborhoods during childhood. Rating these social contexts on a scale ranging from 1 (all black) to 5 (almost all white), we found that racially consonant grade schools were associated with higher levels of self esteem. Although this was no surprise, our findings did reveal unexpectedly that lighter skin tone was advantaged in black school settings, but lighter skin tone was not privileged in predominantly white school settings. Thus, racially dissonant schools were more detrimental for self-esteem, but equally so for black women of all skin shades.

A recent study by Harvey and his associates points to a reversal in the relationship between skin tone, self-concept, and racial consonance.[50] Evaluating African American students in a predominantly black university, they found that "both higher perceived peer acceptance and self-esteem were correlated with darker skin tone at the black university but not at the white university" (273). The Harvey study was small and correlational, did not evaluate gender differences, and was based on self-evaluated skin color. However, evidence from the National Longitudinal Study of Adolescent Health (Add Health) provides some support that shifts have occurred. In the third wave of Add Health collected in 2001–2002, complexion was assessed by interviewers—black, dark

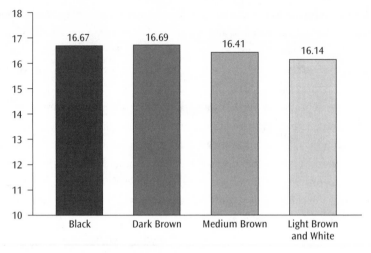

Figure 2.5 Self-Esteem by Skin Tone, Adolescents
SOURCE: National Longitudinal Survey of Adolescent Health, 2001–2002.

brown, medium brown, light brown, and white. I linked these assessments to respondents who were in grades 7 through 12 in 1994 during wave 1 data collection. The light-brown and white groups were collapsed for analyses. I found that black adolescent females rated as light brown and white had slightly lower self-esteem than medium and darker girls (Figure 2.5). These differences remained after controlling for parental education and other factors. Although these findings are preliminary and did not control for racial composition of the school or race of the interviewer, they hint at a shift in the direction of the skin tone effect.

How do we reconcile findings from the NSBA that dark skin is associated with lower self-esteem in predominantly black grammar schools, and the findings of Harvey and colleagues that dark skin is associated with higher self-esteem in a predominantly black college, supplemented by Add Health data that also show higher self-esteem among darker teens? One possible answer is that the racial activism in the 1960s and 1970s instilled pride in African American culture and history, but that the full force of these changes as they pertain to complexion are only just now being reflected in young cohorts. This explanation is plausible given the time gap between these studies. A large proportion of respondents in the NSBA would have attended grade school when *de jure* segregation was operative, and would have been in young adulthood or middle age during the "black is beautiful" era. Colorism may have already affected their self-views by that time. Craig documents resistance among older women to some of the aesthetic styles of that time, such as the Afro hairstyle.[51] Respondents in the Harvey and Add Health studies, on the other hand, would have been born and spent their childhood in a world where considerable change in the opportunity structure of African Americans had occurred and would have been exposed to a different ideology regarding blackness during their formative years. As Harvey and colleagues note, in a predominantly black setting, where dark skin tone is more favored, higher self-esteem may be a consequence of being in the favored (dark) group. Perhaps this is more generally applicable, and results from Add Health reflect black and dark brown as the favored skin shades. An alternative explanation is that rather than a linear, lagged change, the "black is beautiful" ideology reemerged in the 1990s, this time not fueled by a mass social movement but by key events such as the Reverend Jesse Jackson's bid for the presidential nomination in 1988.

A second question is why is skin tone unrelated to self-worth in predominantly white social environments? Harvey and colleagues suggested that in predominantly white environments, skin tone variations are ignored, because in such contexts greater emphasis is placed on black–white comparisons. White gatekeepers in these environments may be less likely to make distinctions based on skin tone, treating all African Americans similarly. This interpretation is consistent with Hill's finding that white interviewers see less variation in African American skin tones than black interviewers.[52] Equally likely is that given the generally small proportional representation of African Americans on white college campuses and even in grade schools among older birth cohorts in the NSBA, the need for racial solidarity reduces emphasis on intraracial differences.

Conclusions

Blacks of all phenotypes have faced obstacles to advancement, but those with darker skin have generally experienced more difficulties than their lighter counterparts. The ranking of phenotypic characteristics in a racialized hierarchy has been especially critical for women. Like men, darker women receive less schooling and have poorer jobs and a lower income than lighter skinned women. Unlike men, dark complexion also works in conjunction with achievement and attractiveness to undermine women's self-esteem, at least among older cohorts.

There are some indications that the salience of colorism is changing, although perhaps not uniformly. On the one hand, Gullickson finds that complexion is no longer relevant for status achievement. On the other hand, Harvey and colleagues, and my own preliminary research find that it still matters for self-esteem, with darker African Americans reporting the highest self-worth. An ideal shift, however, would be one in which differences in self-worth are unrelated to complexion. The historical importance of complexion to African American social, economic, and personal well-being argues strongly for continued research that clarifies why and under what circumstances such transitions are occurring. Limitations such as not disaggregating analyses by gender, lack of panel data, small sample sizes, as well as continued research linking phenotype and stereotyping indicate that we should proceed with caution before declaring that color gradations no longer matter or, if they do matter, that they now privilege darker African Americans.[53]

Despite years of research, we know very little about how complexion differences actually come to matter. As noted previously, it is conceivable that teacher expectations of African American children differ by complexion given stereotypes that associate attractiveness, competence, SES, and skin tone. Studies have shown that, in schools, unattractive youth are punished more often than less attractive youth,[54] and such evaluations may play out in how school is experienced by darker children. If such colorized expectations are operative, we need to investigate how and in what circumstances children achieve despite them.

When trying to understand less optimal opportunities for achievement among darker blacks, it would also be helpful to know to what degree hiring decisions are influenced by complexion. Qualitative studies such as the one by Kirschenman and Neckerman, in which they explored how Chicago-area employers evaluated prospective workers, should be replicated to determine whether and how colorism operates in hiring and promotion.[55] In other words, we need more research on whether, as Gullickson argued, skin color is less salient for white gatekeepers.

Many issues pertaining to skin tone and self-concept need to be investigated. If Rosenberg is indeed correct, and self-worth comes from coethnics, then studies are needed that address how ideas and values regarding skin shades are communicated in primary groups. Are issues of colorism addressed by African American parents as part of their racial socialization messages? Do these messages vary by gender? Are little dark-skinned girls still told to "marry light," and do parents impress upon them the need to achieve in other areas to compensate for devalued, stigmatized features? How do such socialization processes vary by SES? Do such messages continue to be reinforced in adulthood, and from what sources are these messages derived? To understand fully the impact of colorism on the lives of African American women, we need both survey and ethnographic studies that integrate questions concerning achievement and personal psychology.

3 The Latin Americanization of U.S. Race Relations

A New Pigmentocracy

Eduardo Bonilla-Silva and David R. Dietrich

We need to speak about the impossible because we know too much about the possible.[1]

"WE ARE ALL AMERICANS!" This, we contend, will be the racial mantra of the United States in years to come, although for many analysts (because of this country's deep history of racial divisions), this prospect seems implausible. Nationalist statements denying the salience of race are the norm all over the world. Countries such as Malaysia or Indonesia, Trinidad or Belize, or, more significant to our discussion, Iberian countries such as Puerto Rico, Cuba, Brazil, or Mexico, all exhibit this ostrich approach to racial matters. That is, they all stick their heads deep into the social ground and say, "We don't have races here. We don't have racism here. Races and racism exist in America and South Africa. We are all Mexican, Cuban, Brazilian, or Puerto Rican!"

Nevertheless, despite these claims, racial minorities in these self-styled racial democracies, tend to be worse off, comparatively speaking, than racial minorities in Western nations. In Brazil, for example, blacks and *pardos* (tan or brown) earn about 40 to 45 percent as much as whites compared with 55 to 60 percent for blacks in the United States, are twice less likely than blacks in the United States to be employed in professional jobs, are about three times less likely than blacks in the United States to attend college, and have a life expectancy, controlling for education and income, between five and six years shorter than white Brazilians—a difference similar to that between blacks and whites in the United States.[2]

In this chapter we contend that racial stratification and the rules of racial (re)cognition in the United States are becoming Latin America-like. We suggest that the biracial system typical of the United States, which was the exception in the world racial system, is becoming the norm—that is, it is evolving into a complex racial stratification system. Specifically, we argue the United States is developing a triracial system with whites at the top; an intermediary group of honorary whites, similar to the coloreds in South Africa during formal apartheid; and a nonwhite group or the collective black[3] at the bottom. As we suggest in Figure 3.1, the white group will include traditional whites, new white immigrants, and, in the near future, assimilated Latinos, some multiracials (light-skinned peoples), and other subgroups. We predict the intermediate racial group, or honorary whites, will comprise most light-skinned Latinos (e.g., most Cubans and segments of the Mexican and Puerto Rican communities),[4] Japanese Americans, Korean Americans, Asian Indians, Chinese Americans, the bulk of multiracials,[5] and most Middle Eastern Americans. Last, the collective black will include blacks, dark-skinned Latinos, Vietnamese, Cambodians, Laotians, and maybe Filipinos.

This map, however, is heuristic rather than definitive and thus is included as a guide of how we think the various ethnic groups will line up in the new

Whites

- Whites
- New whites (Russians, Albanians, etc.)
- Assimilated white Latinos
- Some multiracials (white-looking people)
- Assimilated (urban) Native Americans
- A few Asian-origin peoples

Honorary whites

- Light-skinned Latinos
- Japanese Americans
- Korean Americans
- Asian Indians
- Chinese Americans
- Middle Eastern Americans
- Most multiracials

Collective black

- Filipinos
- Vietnamese
- Hmong
- Laotians
- Dark-skinned Latinos
- Blacks
- New West Indian and African immigrants
- Reservation-bound Native Americans

Figure 3.1 Preliminary Map of a Tri-Racial System in the United States

emerging racial order. We acknowledge, however, that the position of some groups may change (e.g., Chinese Americans, Asian Indians, and Arab Americans), that the map is not inclusive of all the groups in the United States (for instance, Samoans, Micronesians, and so forth, are not in the map), and that, at this early stage of this project and given some serious data limitations, some groups may end up in a different racial stratum altogether (e.g., Filipinos may become honorary whites rather than another group in the collective black stratum).

More significant, if our Latin Americanization thesis is accurate, there will be categorical porosity as well as "pigmentocracy," making the map useful for group-level, rather than individual-level, predictions. Porosity refers to individual members of a racial stratum moving up (or down) the stratification system (e.g., a light-skinned middle-class black person marrying a white woman and moving to the honorary white stratum). *Pigmentocracy* refers to the rank ordering of groups and members of groups according to phenotype and cultural characteristics (e.g., Filipinos being at the top of the collective black stratum given their high level of education and income as well as high rate of interracial marriage with whites). This strategy for determining racial and ethnic stratification views groups is soft bounded, not hard bounded or having the definitive closure of traditional ethnic groups. Instead, these groups occupy spaces in the field of race that are not cleanly delineated; thus, they have an element of pluralism. Research suggests that there is a world tradition of preference for lightness[6] and that phenotype may be a better predictor of stratification outcomes in the United States than the three major racial–ethnic categorizations of white, Hispanic, and African American.[7] We predict that phenotype will become an even greater element of stratification in America's racially mixed future. However, we cannot make a stronger empirical case for the importance of pigmentocracy, because there are neither census data on phenotype nor a single data set that includes systematic data on the skin tone of all Americans.

We recognize that our thesis is broad (attempting to classify where everyone will fit in the racial order) and hard to verify empirically with the available data (as just mentioned, there is not a single data set that includes systematic data on the skin tone of all Americans). Nevertheless, we believe it is paramount to begin pushing for a paradigm shift in the field of race relations and consider our efforts here as a preliminary effort in that direction. In the remainder of the chapter, we do four things. First, we draw on research on race in Latin America and Caribbean societies and extract what we think are their central racial stratification features. Second, we outline five reasons why Latin Americanization is occurring at this historical juncture. Third, we examine various objective (e.g., income, education), subjective (e.g., racial views, racial self-classification), and social interaction (e.g., residential preferences, interracial marriage) indicators to assess whether the data point in the direction predicted by the Latin Americanization thesis. Last, we conclude by discussing the likely implications of Latin Americanization for the future of race relations in the United States.

How Race Works in the Americas

> *To advocate transculturation without attempting to change the systems*
> *and institutions that breed the power differential would simply help to*
> *perpetuate the utopian vision that constructs Latin America . . . as the*
> *continent of hope. (p. 32)*[8]

Eduardo Bonilla-Silva has argued elsewhere that racial stratification systems operate in most societies without races being officially acknowledged.[9] For example, although racial inequality is more pronounced in Latin America than in the United States, racial data in the former are gathered inconsistently or not gathered at all. Yet, most Latin Americans, including those most affected by racial stratification, do not view inequality between whites and nonwhites in their countries as racial. *Prejudice*—Latin Americans do not talk about *racism*—is viewed as a legacy from slavery and colonialism, and *inequality* is regarded as the product of class dynamics. Therein lies the secret of race in Latin America and why racial protest there is so sporadic. Because examining the long history that produced this state of affairs is beyond the scope of this chapter, we only sketch the six central features of Latin American (and Caribbean) racial stratification.

Miscegenation or Mestizaje

Latin American nation-states, with the exception of Argentina, Chile, Uruguay, and Costa Rica, are thoroughly racially mixed. This mixture has led many observers to align with Brazilian historian Gilberto Freyre, who described Brazil as having "almost perfect equality of opportunity for all men regardless of race and color"[10] and thus label it a *racial democracy*. However, all "racial contacts" between Europeans and the various peoples of the world involved racial mixing. The important difference is that the mixing in Latin America led to the development of a socially and, sometimes, legally recognized intermediate racial strata of *mestizos*, browns, or *trigueños*.

Racial mixing, however, in no way challenged white supremacy in colonial or postcolonial Latin America because (1) the mixing was between white men and Indian or black women, maintaining the race/gender order in place; (2) the men were fundamentally poor and/or of the working class, which helped maintain the race/class order in place; (3) the mixing followed a racially hierarchical pattern with whitening as a goal; and (4) marriages among people in the three main racial groups were (and still are) mostly homogamous.[11] The latter point requires a caveat. Although most marriages have been within-strata, they still have produced phenotypic variation. How can this be? Because members of all racial strata have variations in phenotype, members of any strata can try to "marry up" by choosing light-skinned partners *within* strata.

Triracial Stratification System

Although Portuguese and Spanish colonial states wanted to create "two societies," the demographic realities of colonial life superseded their wishes. Because most colonial outposts were scarcely populated by Europeans, all these societies developed an intermediate group of browns, *pardos,* or *mestizos* that buffered sociopolitical conflicts. Even though this group did not achieve the status of white anywhere, it nonetheless had a better status than the Indian or black masses and, therefore, developed its own distinct interest. As many commentators have observed, without this intermediate group, Latin American countries would have followed the path of Haiti (Us vs. Them). The parallels with complex class stratification orders should be obvious. Although class polarization leads to rebellion, multiplicity of classes and strata leads to diffused social conflict.

Colorism or Pigmentocracy

There is yet another layer of complexity in Latin American racial stratification systems. The three racial strata are also internally stratified by "color" (in quotation marks here because, in addition to skin tone, phenotype, hair texture, eye color, culture, education, and class matter in the racial classification of individuals in Latin America), a phenomenon known in the literature as *pigmentocracy* or *colorism.*[12] Pigmentocracy has been central to the maintenance of white power in Latin America because it has fostered (1) divisions among all those in secondary racial strata, (2) divisions *within* racial strata limiting the likelihood of *within*-stratum unity, (3) mobility viewed as individual and conditional upon whitening, and (4) white elites being regarded as legitimate representatives of the "nation," even though they do not look like the average member of the nation.

Blanqueamiento: *Whitening as Ideology and Practice*

Blanqueamiento (whitening) has been treated in the Latin American literature as an ideology. However, *blanqueamiento* is a real economic, political, and personal process; it is a "dynamic that involves culture, identity and values."[13] At the personal level, families can be color or even racially divided, and may exhibit differential treatment toward dark-skinned members. The material origin of whitening practices was noted by the 1783 *Cédulas de Gracias al Sacar,* which allowed mulattos to buy certificates declaring them officially white. Having this certificate allowed them to work in the military and in colonial administrative posts, and was a direct ticket of mobility for their offspring.[14]

As a social practice, whitening "is just not neutral mixture but hierarchical movement . . . and the most valuable movement is upward."[15] Thus, rather than showing Latin American racial flexibility, racial mixing oriented by the goal of whitening shows the effectiveness of the logic of white supremacy. This practice also works in apparently homogeneous societies such as Haiti[16] and even in Japan.[17] In both cases, slight variations in skin tone (lighter shade) and cultural affectations (being more French in Haiti or Western oriented in Japan) are regarded as valuable assets in the marriage market.

National Ideology of Mestizaje

National independence in Latin America meant, among other things, silencing any discussion about race and forging a myth of national unity. After years of attempting to unite Latin American nations under the banner of "Hispanidad,"[18] a more formidable ideology crystallized: the ideology of *mestizaje* (racial mixing) and *mulataje* or, in the words of the late Mexican philosopher José Vasconcelos, "*la raza cósmica.*" Fathers of the homeland such as Hostos and Betances in Puerto Rico, Martí in Cuba, Bolivar in Venezuela, and San Martín and Artigas in southern South America preached national unity and *mestizaje,* although none of them had clean records on racial matters.[19]

This ideology hides the salience of race and the existence of a *racial structure,*[20] unites the nation, and better safeguards white power than *Hispanidad* (regarding oneself or one's country as Spanish), an ideology that still exists among white elites in Latin American and that causes problems for the maintenance of nonracialism.[21]

"We Are All Latinoamericanos":
Race as Nationality/Culture

Most Latin Americans, even those obviously black or Indian, refuse to identify themselves in racial terms. Instead, they prefer to use national (or cultural) descriptors such as, "I am Puerto Rican" or "I am Brazilian." This behavior has been the subject of much confusion and is described as an example of the fluidity of race and racism in Latin America. However, defining the nation and the people as the *fusion of cultures* (even though the fusion is viewed in a Eurocentric manner) is the logical outcome of all the factors mentioned earlier. Nationalist statements such as "We are all Puerto Ricans" are the direct manifestation of the racial stratification peculiar to Latin America, rather than evidence of nonracialism. Although these statements also represent nonwhites' agency to carve a space in the nation, these statements, which are taught to Latinomericanos in schools and at home as historical truths, also help maintain the traditional racial hierarchy by hiding the fact of racial division and racial rule.[22]

Why Latin Americanization Now?

Why are race relations in the United States becoming Latin America-like at this point in our history? The reasons are multiple. First, the demography of the nation is changing. Racial minorities have increased to 30 percent of the population today and, as population projections suggest, may become a numerical majority in the year 2050.[23] And the projection may be an underestimation because data from the 2000 U.S. Bureau of the Census suggest that the Latino population was about 12.5 percent of the population, almost 1 percentage point higher than the highest projection, and the proportion of the white population (77.1% white or in combination) was slightly lower than originally expected.[24]

The rapid darkening of America is creating a situation similar to that of Puerto Rico, Cuba, or Venezuela in the 16th and 17th centuries, or Argentina, Chile, and Uruguay in the late 18th and early 19th centuries. During both of these historical periods, the elites realized their countries were becoming black (or nonwhite) and devised a number of strategies (unsuccessful in the former and successful in the latter) to whiten their population.[25] Although whitening the population through immigration or by classifying many newcomers as white[26] is a possible solution to the new American demography, for reasons discussed later, we do not think this is likely. Hence, a more plausible accommodation to the new racial reality is (1) to create an intermediate racial group to buffer racial conflict, (2) to allow some newcomers into the white racial stratum, and (3) to incorporate most immigrants into the collective black stratum.

Second, as part of the tremendous reorganization that has transpired in America during the post-Civil Rights era, a new kinder and gentler white supremacy has emerged that Bonilla-Silva has labeled elsewhere as the *new racism*.[27] In post-Civil Rights America, the maintenance of systemic white privilege is accomplished socially, economically, and politically through institutional, covert, and apparently nonracial practices. Whether in banks or universities, in stores or housing markets, "smiling discrimination"[28] tends to be the order of the day. This new white supremacy has produced an accompanying ideology that rings Latin America all over: the ideology of color blind racism. This ideology, as is the norm all over Latin America, denies the salience of race, scorns those who talk about race, and increasingly proclaims that "We are all Americans."[29]

Third, race relations have become globalized.[30] The once almost all-white Western nations have now "interiorized the other."[31] The new world systemic need for capital accumulation has led to the incorporation of dark foreigners as "guest workers" and even as permanent workers. Thus today, European nations have racial minorities in their midst who are progressively becoming an underclass,[32] have developed an internal "racial structure"[33] to maintain white power, and have a curious racial ideology that combines ethnonationalism with a race-blind ideology similar to the color-blind racism of the United States today.[34]

This new global racial reality, we believe, will reinforce the Latin Americanization trend in the United States as versions of color-blind racism become prevalent in most Western nations. Furthermore, as many formerly almost-all white Western countries (e.g., Germany, France, England) become more and more diverse, the Latin American model of racial stratification may surface in these societies too.

Fourth, the convergence of the political and ideological actions of the Republican Party, conservative commentators and activists, and the so-called "multiracial" movement[35] has created the space for the radical transformation of the way we gather racial data in America. One possible outcome of the U.S. Census Bureau's categorical back-and-forth on racial and ethnic classifications is either the dilution of racial data or the elimination of race as an official category. In 2003, Ward Connerly and his colleagues lost the first round in their California Racial Privacy Act (which would have prohibited state government agencies from collecting or publishing data concerning race or ethnicity), but we fear that such initiatives may be successful in other states. Moreover, the attack on affirmative action, which is part of what Stephen Steinberg[36] has labeled the "racial retreat," and U.S. Supreme Court decisions that weakened[37] or struck down race-based criteria to achieve diversity are clarion calls signaling the end of race-based social policy in the United States. In their recent 2007 decision, the U.S. Supreme Court repudiated attempts by the Seattle, Washington, and Louisville and Jefferson County, Kentucky, school districts to reduce the negative educational impact of racially concentrated housing patterns by greater racial diversification of their public schools. Most telling for our discussion was a concluding statement in the U.S. Supreme Court decision by Chief Justice Roberts: "The way to stop discriminating on the basis of race is to stop discriminating on the basis of race" (pp. 40–41)[38] Again, this trend reinforces our Latin Americanization thesis because the elimination of race-based social policy is, among other things, predicated on the notion that race no longer affects minorities' status. Nevertheless, as in Latin America, we may eliminate race by decree and may maintain—or even increase—the level of racial inequality.[39]

A Look at the Data

To recapitulate, we contend that because of a number of important demographic, sociopolitical, and international changes, the United States is developing a more complex system of racial stratification that resembles those typical of Latin American societies. We suggest that three racial strata will develop— namely, whites, honorary whites, and the collective black—and that a central factor determining where groups and members of racial and ethnic groups will fit will be phenotypic, with lighter people at the top, medium in the middle, and dark at the bottom. Although we posit that Latin Americanization will not fully materialize for several more decades, in the sections that follow we examine various objective, subjective, and social interaction indicators to determine whether the trends support our thesis.

Objective Standing of Whites, Honorary Whites, and Blacks

If Latin Americanization is happening in the United States, gaps in income, poverty rates, education, and occupational standing among whites, honorary whites, and the collective black should be developing. The available data suggests this is the case. In terms of income, as shown in Table 3.1, white Latinos (Argentines, Chileans, Costa Ricans, and Cubans) are doing much better than dark-skinned Latinos (Mexicans, Puerto Ricans, and so forth). The apparent

Table 3.1 Mean per Capita Income (in U.S. Dollars) of Selected Asian and Latino Ethnic Groups, 2000

Latinos	Mean income, $	Asian Americans	Mean income, $
Mexicans	9,467.30	Chinese	20,728.54
Puerto Ricans	11,314.95	Japanese	23,786.13
Cubans	16,741.89	Koreans	16,976.19
Guatemalans	11,178.60	Asian Indians	25,682.15
Salvadorans	11,371.92	Filipinos	19,051.53
Costa Ricans	14,226.92	Taiwanese	22,998.05
Panamanians	16,181.20	Hmong	5,175.34
Argentines	23,589.99	Vietnamese	14,306.74
Chileans	18,272.04	Cambodians	8,680.48
Bolivians	16,322.53	Laotians	10,375.57
Whites	17,968.87	Whites	17,968.87
Blacks	11,336.74	Blacks	11,366.74

NOTE: We use per-capita income because family income distorts the status of some groups (particularly Asians and whites), and some groups have more people than others contributing toward the family income.

SOURCE: U.S. Dept. of Commerce, Bureau of the Census. Census of Population and Housing, 2000 [U.S.]: Public Use Microdata Sample: 5-Percent Sample [Computer file]. ICPSR release. Washington, DC: U.S. Dept. of Commerce, Bureau of the Census [producer], 2003. Ann Arbor, MI: Inter-university Consortium for Political and Social Research [distributor], 2003.

exceptions in Table 3.1 (Bolivians and Panamanians) are examples of self-selection among these immigrant groups. For example, four of the largest ten concentrations of Bolivians in the United States are in Virginia, a state with just 7.2 percent Latinos.[40]

Table 3.1 also shows that Asians exhibit a pattern similar to that of Latinos. Hence, a severe income gap is emerging between honorary white Asians (Japanese, Koreans, Filipinos, and Chinese) and those Asians we contend belong to the collective black (Vietnamese, Cambodian, Hmong, and Laotians).

Tables 3.2 and 3.3 exhibit similar patterns in terms of education. Table 3.2 shows that light-skinned Latinos have between three and four years of educational advantage over dark-skinned Latinos. The same table indicates that elite Asians have up to eight years of educational advantage over most of the Asian groups we classify as belonging to the collective black. A more significant fact, given that the American job market is becoming bifurcated (good jobs for the educated and bad jobs for the undereducated), is that the proportion of white Latinos with "some college" is equal or higher than the white population.

Table 3.2 Median Years of Schooling of Selected Asian and Latino Ethnic Groups, 2000

Latino	Median education, y	Asian Americans	Median education, y
Mexicans	9.00	Chinese	12.00
Puerto Ricans	11.00	Japanese	14.00
Cubans	12.00	Koreans	12.00
Guatemalans	7.50	Asian Indians	14.00
Salvadorans	9.00	Filipinos	14.00
Costa Ricans	12.00	Taiwanese	14.00
Panamanians	12.00	Hmong	5.50
Argentines	12.00	Vietnamese	11.00
Chileans	12.00	Cambodians	9.00
Bolivians	12.00	Laotians	10.00
Whites	12.00	Whites	12.00
Blacks	12.00	Blacks	12.00

SOURCE: U.S. Dept. of Commerce, Bureau of the Census. Census of Population and Housing, 2000 [U.S.]: Public Use Microdata Sample: 5-Percent Sample [Computer file]. ICPSR release. Washington, DC: U.S. Dept. of Commerce, Bureau of the Census [producer], 2003. Ann Arbor, MI: Inter-university Consortium for Political and Social Research [distributor], 2003.

Table 3.3 Educational Attainment of Selected Asian and Latino Ethnic Groups, 2000

Latinos	≤ 12 grades, %	College, %*	Asian Americans	≤12 grades, %	College, %*
Mexicans	85.14	14.85	Chinese	50.35	49.65
Puerto Ricans	76.45	23.54	Japanese	40.56	59.44
Cubans	64.99	35.02	Koreans	51.04	48.97
Guatemalans	84.64	15.36	Asian Indians	44.05	55.95
Salvadorans	85.87	14.13	Filipinos	45.86	54.14
Costa Ricans	63.06	36.94	Taiwanese	34.78	65.22
Panamanians	53.90	46.11	Hmong	88.05	11.51
Argentines	51.88	48.11	Vietnamese	67.48	32.19
Chileans	55.56	44.44	Cambodians	82.14	17.87
Bolivians	55.91	44.08	Laotians	88.55	17.45
Whites	60.88	39.12	Whites		
Blacks	72.90	27.10	Blacks		

*Includes "some college," "college graduate," and "advanced degree."

SOURCE: U.S. Dept. of Commerce, Bureau of the Census. Census of Population and Housing, 2000 [U.S.]: Public Use Microdata Sample: 5-Percent Sample [Computer file]. ICPSR release. Washington, DC: U.S. Dept. of Commerce, Bureau of the Census [producer], 2003. Ann Arbor, MI: Inter-university Consortium for Political and Social Research [distributor], 2003.

Hence, as Table 3.3 shows, 35 percent of Cubans, 37 percent of Costa Ricans, 48 percent of Argentines, and 44 percent of Chileans have attained "some college" or higher levels of education—proportions that compare very favorably with the 38 percent of whites. In contrast, the bulk of Mexican Americans, Salvadorans, Puerto Ricans,[41] and Guatemalans (70%) have just attained twelve years or less of education. Likewise, the educational attainment of Asians reveals a similar pattern between elite and collective black Asians—that is, elite Asians substantially outperform their brethren (and even whites) in the "some college" and higher categories. It is worth pointing out that the distance in educational attainment between elite and collective black Asians is larger than that between whites and dark-skinned Latinos. For example, although 50 percent of Chinese, Japanese, and Koreans have "some college" or higher level of educational attainment, more than 80 percent of Hmong, Laotians, and Cambodians have attained a high school diploma or less.

Substantial group differences are also evident in the occupational status of the groups (see Table 3.4). The light-skinned Latino groups have achieved parity with whites in their proportional representation in the top jobs in the

Table 3.4 Occupational Status of Selected Latino Groups, 2000

	Occupational Status, %					
Ethnic groups	Manager and professional related occupations	Sales and office	Services	Construction, extraction, and maintenance	Production, transportation, and materials moving	Farming, forestry, and fishing
Mexicans	13.18	20.62	22.49	14.14	23.76	5.54
Puerto Ricans	21.14	29.46	21.40	8.34	19.01	0.66
Cubans	27.84	28.65	16.09	10.21	16.68	0.53
Guatemalans	9.49	16.13	29.73	14.59	27.55	2.51
Salvadorans	8.96	17.29	32.11	15.44	24.84	1.37
Costa Ricans	23.35	22.76	25.46	11.61	16.27	0.55
Panamanians	31.07	32.82	20.27	5.61	9.94	0.29
Argentines	39.77	24.68	14.84	9.24	10.96	0.51
Chileans	32.12	23.92	20.05	10.32	13.13	0.46
Bolivians	27.20	25.80	23.85	11.19	11.73	0.23
Whites	32.07	27.03	15.02	10.12	14.77	1.00
Blacks	21.48	26.48	23.96	7.57	19.84	0.65

SOURCE: U.S. Dept. of Commerce, Bureau of the Census. Census of Population and Housing, 2000 [U.S.]: Public Use Microdata Sample: 5-Percent Sample [Computer file]. ICPSR release. Washington, DC: U.S. Dept. of Commerce, Bureau of the Census [producer], 2003. Ann Arbor, MI: Inter-university Consortium for Political and Social Research [distributor], 2003.

Table 3.5 Occupational Status of Selected Asian Ethnic Groups, 2000

Ethnic groups	Occupational status, %					
	Manager and professional related occupations	Sales and office	Services	Construction, extraction, and maintenance	Production, transportation, and materials moving	Farming, forestry, and fishing
Chinese	47.79	22.83	15.04	2.77	11.42	0.15
Japanese	46.90	28.05	13.24	4.50	6.70	0.60
Koreans	36.51	31.26	15.65	3.97	12.38	0.23
Asian Indians	55.89	23.39	80.7	2.25	10.03	0.37
Filipinos	34.87	28.70	18.49	4.62	12.35	0.98
Taiwanese	60.96	24.78	8.44	1.34	4.43	0.06
Hmong	14.67	24.14	17.33	4.51	38.57	0.77
Vietnamese	25.21	19.92	19.64	6.03	28.50	0.71
Cambodians	16.66	25.37	17.26	5.45	34.67	0.59
Laotians	12.55	20.60	15.02	6.07	44.96	0.81
Whites	32.07	27.03	15.02	10.12	14.77	1.00
Blacks	21.48	26.48	23.96	7.57	19.87	0.65

SOURCE: U.S. Dept. of Commerce, Bureau of the Census. Census of Population and Housing, 2000 [U.S.]: Public Use Microdata Sample: 5-Percent Sample [Computer file]. ICPSR release. Washington, DC: U.S. Dept. of Commerce, Bureau of the Census [producer], 2003. Ann Arbor, MI: Inter-university Consortium for Political and Social Research [distributor], 2003.

economy. Thus, the share of Argentines, Chileans, and Cubans in the two top occupational categories (Managers and Professionals, and Sales and Office) is 55 percent or higher, which is close to the whites' 59 percent share (Table 3.5). In contrast, the bulk of the dark-skinned Latino groups such as Mexicans, Puerto Ricans, and Central Americans are concentrated in the four lower occupational categories. Along the same lines, the Asian groups we classify as honorary whites are even more likely to be well represented in the top occupational categories than those we classify in the collective black. For instance, although 61 percent of Taiwanese and 56 percent of Asian Indians are in the top occupational category, only 15 percent of Hmong, 13 percent of Laotians, 17 percent of Cambodians, and 25 percent of Vietnamese are in that category.

Subjective Standing of Racial Strata

Social psychologists have amply demonstrated that it takes very little for groups to form, to develop a common view, and to adjudicate status positions to nominal characteristics.[42] Thus, it should not be surprising if gaps in income, occupational status, and education among these various strata are contributing to group formation and consciousness. That is, honorary whites may be classifying themselves as white and believing they are different (better) than those in the collective black category. If this is happening, this group should also be in the process of developing whitelike racial attitudes befitting of their new social position and differentiating (distancing) themselves from the collective black. In line with our thesis, we expect whites to be making distinctions between honorary whites and the collective black—specifically, exhibiting a more positive outlook toward honorary whites than toward members of the collective black. Last, if Latin Americanization is happening, we speculate that the collective black should exhibit a diffused and contradictory racial consciousness as blacks and Indians do throughout Latin America and the Caribbean.[43] We examine some of these matters in the sections that follow.

Social Identity of Honorary Whites

• Self-Reports on Race: The Case of Latinos.   Historically, most Latinos have classified themselves as white, but the proportion of Latinos who self-classify as such varies tremendously by group. Hence, as Table 3.6 shows, although 60

Table 3.6 Racial Self-Classification by Selected Latin America Origin Latino Ethnic Groups, 2000

Ethnic group	White	Black	Other	Native American	Asian
Dominicans	28.21	10.93	59.21	1.07	0.57
Salvadorans	41.01	0.82	56.95	0.81	0.41
Guatemalans	42.95	1.24	53.46	2.09	0.28
Hondurans	48.51	6.56	46.43	1.24	0.29
Mexicans	50.47	0.92	46.73	1.42	0.45
Puerto Ricans	52.42	7.32	38.85	0.64	0.77
Costa Ricans	64.83	5.91	28.18	0.56	0.53
Bolivians	65.52	0.32	32.79	1.32	0.05
Colombians	69.01	1.53	28.54	0.49	0.44
Venezuelans	57.89	2.58	20.56	0.36	0.60
Chileans	77.04	0.68	21.27	0.44	0.56
Cubans	88.26	4.02	7.26	0.19	0.29
Argentines	88.70	0.33	10.54	0.08	0.35

SOURCE: U.S. Dept. of Commerce, Bureau of the Census. Census of Population and Housing, 2000 [U.S.]: Public Use Microdata Sample: 5-Percent Sample [Computer file]. ICPSR release. Washington, DC: U.S. Dept. of Commerce, Bureau of the Census [producer], 2003. Ann Arbor, MI: Inter-university Consortium for Political and Social Research [distributor], 2003.

percent or more of the members of the Latino groups we regard as honorary white self-classify as white, about 50 percent or fewer of the members of the groups we regard as belonging to the collective black do so. As a case in point, although Mexicans, Dominicans, and Central Americans are very likely to report "Other" as their preferred racial classification, most Costa Ricans, Cubans, Chileans, and Argentines choose the white descriptor. These 1990 census data mirror the results of the 1988 Latino National Political Survey.[44]

• "Racial" Distinctions Among Asians.   Distinctions between native-born and foreign-born Asians (e.g., American-born Chinese and foreign-born Chinese), and between economically successful and unsuccessful Asians are developing. Leland Saito, in *Race and Politics,* points out that many Asians have reacted to the "Asian flack" they are experiencing with the increase in Asian immigration by fleeing the cities of immigration, disidentifying from new Asians, and invoking the image of the "good immigrant." In some communities, this has led older, assimilated segments of a community to dissociate from recent migrants. For example, a Nisei returning to his community after years of overseas military service, told his dad the following about the city's new demography: "Goddamn dad, where the hell did all these Chinese came from? Shit, this isn't even our town anymore."[45] To be clear, our point is not that Asian Americans have not engaged in coalition politics and, in various locations, engaged in concerted efforts to elect Asian American candidates. Our point that the group labeled *Asian Americans is* profoundly divided along many axes.

Racial Attitudes of Various Racial Strata
• Latinos' Racial Attitudes.   Although researchers have shown that Latinos tend to hold negative views of blacks and positive views of whites,[46] the picture is more complex. Immigrant Latinos tend to have more negative views about blacks than native-born Latinos. For instance, a study of Latinos in Houston, Texas, found that 38 percent of native-born Latinos compared with 47 percent of foreign-born Latinos held negative stereotypes of blacks.[47] This difference may be related to the finding that 63 percent of native-born Latinos versus 34 percent of foreign-born Latinos report frequent contact with blacks.

However, the incorporation of the majority of Latinos as "colonial subjects" (Puerto Ricans), refugees from wars (Central Americans), or illegal migrant workers (Mexicans) has foreshadowed subsequent patterns of integration into the collective black. In a similar vein, the incorporation of a minority of Latinos as political refugees (Cubans, Chileans, and Argentines) or as neutral immigrants trying to better their economic situation (Costa Rica, Colombia) has allowed them a more comfortable ride in America's racial boat. Therefore, although the incorporation of most Latinos in the United States has meant becoming nonwhite, for a few it has meant becoming almost white.

Nevertheless, given that most Latinos experience discrimination in labor and housing markets as well as in schools, they quickly realize their nonwhite status. This leads them, as Nilda Flores-Gonzales[48] and Suzanne Oboler[49] have shown, to adopt a plurality of identities that signify "otherness." Thus, dark-skinned Latinos are even calling themselves black or African Dominican or African Puerto Rican.[50] For example, José Ali, a Latino interviewed by Clara Rodríguez, stated, "By inheritance I am Hispanic. However, I identify more with blacks because to white America, if you are my color, you are a nigger. I can't change my color, and I do not wish to do to." When asked, "Why do you see yourself as black?" He said, "Because when I was jumped by whites, I was not called 'spic,' but I was called a 'nigger.'"[51]

• Asians' Racial Attitudes.   Various studies have documented that Asians tend to hold antiblack and anti-Latino attitudes. For instance, Bobo, Zubrinsky, Johnson, and Oliver[52] found that Chinese residents of Los Angeles expressed negative racial attitudes toward blacks. One Chinese resident stated, "Blacks in general seem to be overly lazy" and another asserted, "Blacks have a definite attitude problem."[53] Studies on Korean shopkeepers in various locales have found that more than 70 percent of them hold antiblack attitudes.[54]

• The Collective Black and Whites' Racial Attitudes.   After a protracted conflict over the meaning of whites' racial attitudes, survey researchers seem to have reached an agreement: "a hierarchical racial order continues to shape all aspects of American life" (p. 344).[55] Whites express and defend their privileged social position on issues such as affirmative action and reparations, school integration and busing, neighborhood integration, welfare reform, and even the death penalty. Regarding how whites think about Latinos and Asians, not many researchers have separated the groups that comprise Latinos and Asians to assess whether whites are making distinctions. However, the available evidence suggests whites regard Asians highly and are significantly less likely to hold Latinos in high regard.[56] Thus, when judged on a host of racial stereotypes, whites rate themselves and Asians almost identically (favorable stereotype rating) and rate negatively (at an almost equal level) both blacks and Latinos.[57]

Social Interaction Among Members of the Three Racial Strata

If Latin Americanization is happening, one would expect more social (e.g., friendship, associations as neighbors) and intimate (e.g., marriage) contact between whites and honorary whites than between whites and members of the collective black. A cursory analysis of the data suggests this is, in fact, the case.

Interracial Marriage   Although most marriages in America are still intraracial, the rates vary substantially by group. Although 93 percent of whites and blacks marry within group, 70 percent of Latinos and Asians do so and only 33 percent of Native Americans marry Native Americans.[58] Even more significant, when one disentangles the generic terms *Asians* and *Latinos,* the data fit even more closely the Latin Americanization thesis. For example, among Latinos, Cubans, Mexicans, Central Americans, and South Americans have higher rates of outmarriage than Puerto Ricans and Dominicans.[59] Although interpreting the Asian American outmarriage patterns is very complex (groups such as Filipinos and Vietnamese have higher than expected rates in part as a result of the Vietnam War and the military bases in the Philippines), it is worth pointing out that the highest rate belongs to Japanese Americans and Chinese,[60] and the lowest to Southeast Asians.

Furthermore, racial assimilation through marriage (whitening) is significantly more likely for the children of Asian–white and Latino–white unions than for those of black–white unions, a fact that bolsters our Latin Americanization thesis. Hence, although only 22 percent of the children of black fathers and white mothers are classified as white, the children of similar unions among Asians are twice as likely to be classified as white.[61] For Latinos, the data fit our thesis even closer as Latinos of Cuban, Mexican, and South American origin have high rates of exogamy compared with Puerto Ricans and Dominicans.[62] We concur with Moran's[63] speculation that this may reflect the fact that because Puerto Ricans and Dominicans have far more dark-skinned members, they have restricted chances for outmarriage to whites in a highly racialized marriage market.

Residential Segregation among Racial Strata   An imperfect measure of interracial interaction is the level of neighborhood "integration."[64] Nevertheless, the various indices devised by demographers to assess the level of residential segregation allow us to gauge in broad strokes the level of interracial contact in various cities. In this section we focus on the segregation of Latinos and Asians, because the high segregation experienced by blacks is well-known and studied.

• Residential Segregation Among Latinos.   Researchers have shown that Latinos are less segregated from and are more exposed to whites than blacks.[65]
Yet, they have also documented that dark-skinned Latinos experience blacklike
rates of residential segregation from whites.

Logan[66] reports indices of dissimilarity[67] and exposure[68] for the Hispanic–
white dyad in various standard metropolitan areas for 2000. In standard metropolitan areas with high concentrations of Latinos, such as New York, Long
Beach, Fresno, Hartford, or San Antonio, the dissimilarity index is relatively
high and the exposure index is very low. Although the latter index is affected by
the relative size of the populations whereas the former is not, it is worth pointing out that when Latinos have a significant presence in an area (10–40%), the
level of exposure is lower than expected. For example, in Fresno, Long Beach,
and San Antonio, with Latino populations ranging from 44 to 47 percent, one
would expect high levels of exposure to whites. Yet, the index of Hispanic–
white exposure in these cities is 28, 17, and 22 respectively.

In predominantly Latino areas (e.g., Laredo, El Paso, and Brownsville, cities
that are 80% or more Latino) or in white-dominated areas (e.g., Altoona, Mis-
soula, and Madison, cities that are less than 3.5% Latino), the indices seem to fit
the expected pattern.[69] Thus, in cities with few whites, the index of dissimilarity
is relatively low and the exposure index is very low—ranging from about 14
percent in El Paso to 5 percent in Laredo. Conversely, in cities that are dominated by whites, the index of dissimilarity is also low but the index of exposure
is extremely high.

Still, these indices may misrepresent race relations on the ground in these
cities. First, white-majority cities are cities that have not yet reached the "racial tipping point" (e.g., low percentage of Latinos in the cities such as Altoona,
Pennsylvania, with a Latino proportion of 0.51%). Second, in these cities the experiences for white- and dark-skinned Latinos may be totally different. In Madison, Wisconsin, where the first author lived for nine years, white Latinos have a
vastly different racial existence than dark-skinned ones. Last, in predominantly
Latino cities such as Miami, new forms of residential segregation are emerging
(e.g., segregation by streets, segregation by not associating with Latinos even if
living in "mixed" neighborhoods) that are not captured by any of these indices.

• Residential Segregation Among Asians.   Of all minority groups, Asian
Americans are the least segregated. However, they have experienced an increase
in residential segregation lately.[70] In a recent review, Zubrinsky Charles[71] found

that from 1980 to 2000, the index of dissimilarity for Asians had increased 3 points (from 37–40 points) whereas the exposure to whites had declined 16 points (from 88 points to 62 points). Part of the increase in segregation (and the concomitant decrease in exposure) may be the result of the arrival of newer immigrants from Southeast Asia (Vietnam, Cambodia, and Laos) during the past two decades.[72]

Logan[73] also reports the dissimilarity and exposure indices for the Asian–white dyad in selected areas of the United States for 2000. Because of the relatively small size of the Asian population in the United States (less than 4% of the total population), the index is perhaps less useful than for blacks and Latinos. Nevertheless, the observed patterns are fitting of our thesis regardless of whether the proportion of Asians is large, moderate, or tiny. Thus, Honolulu, the only Asian-majority area in the United States, has a moderate dissimilarity index of 40.5 and a low exposure index of 15.6. San Francisco, with a relatively large Asian population (about 25%), has a dissimilarity index of 35.2, which is close to the Latino index of 47.9 but less than the 62.5 index for blacks. These lower dissimilarity indices and higher exposure indices vis-à-vis Latinos and particularly blacks tend to fit our prediction that the bulk of Asians are moving to the honorary white category. More interesting, even in cities such as Beumont-Port Arthur, where Asians are a tiny minority, their index of dissimilarity is substantially lower than that of blacks (54 compared with 71) and their exposure index is much higher than expected vis-à-vis blacks (51 compared with 28).

Conclusion

We have presented a broad and bold thesis about the future of racial stratification in the United States. However, at this early stage of the analysis and given the serious limitations of the data on Latinos and Asians (most of the data are not parceled out by subgroups and hardly anything is separated by skin tone), it is difficult to make a definitive case. It is plausible that factors such as nativity or other socioeconomic characteristics explain some of the patterns we documented.[74] Nevertheless, almost all the objective, subjective, and social interaction indicators we reviewed confirm the trend in the direction of Latin Americanization. For example, the objective data clearly show substantive gaps between the groups we labeled *whites, honorary whites,* and *the collective black.* In terms of income and education, whites tend to be slightly better off than honorary whites, who tend to be significantly better off than the collective black. Not surprising, a variety of subjective indicators signal the emergence of *internal* stratification among racial minorities. For example, although some Latinos (e.g., Cubans, Argentines, Chileans) are very likely to self-classify as whites, others are not (e.g., Dominicans and Puerto Ricans living in the United States). Groups that are more likely to classify themselves as white exhibit a racial attitudinal profile compared with groups that do not classify themselves as white. Last, the objective and subjective indicators have an interactional correlate. Data on interracial marriage and residential segregation show that whites are significantly more likely to live near honorary whites and intermarry with them than with members of the collective black.

If our predictions are right, what will the consequences of Latin Americanization be for race relations in the United States? First, racial politics will change dramatically. The Us versus Them racial dynamic will lessen as honorary whites grow in size and social importance. They are likely to buffer racial conflict—or derail it—as intermediate groups do in many Latin American countries.

Second, the ideology of color-blind racism will become even more salient among whites and honorary whites, and will also muffle opposition or resentment among members of the collective black. Color-blind racism,[75] an ideology similar to that prevalent in Latin American societies, will help glue the new social system and further buffer racial conflict.

Third, if the state decides to stop gathering racial statistics, the struggle to document the impact of race in a variety of social venues will become monumental. Even more significant, because state actions always affect civil society, if the state decides to erase race from above, the *social* recognition of races in the polity may become more difficult. We may develop a Latin American-like "disgust" for even mentioning anything that is race related.

Fourth, the deep history of black–white divisions in the United States has been such that the centrality of the black identity will not dissipate. The research on even the "black elite" shows that they exhibit racial attitudes in line with their racial group.[76] That identity, as we argued in this chapter, may be taken up by dark-skinned Latinos, as it is being rapidly taken up by most West Indians. For example, Al, a fifty-three-year-old Jamaican engineer interviewed by Milton Vickerman stated:

> I have nothing against Haitians; I have nothing against black Americans. . . . If you're a nigger, you're a nigger, regardless of whether your are from Timbuktu. . . . There isn't the unity that one would like to see. . . . Blacks have to appreciate blacks, no matter where they are from. Just look at it the way I look at it: That you're the same.[77]

However, even among blacks, we predict some important changes. Their racial consciousness will become more diffused. For example, blacks will be more likely to accept many stereotypes about themselves (e.g., "We are more lazy than whites") and have a "blunted oppositional consciousness."[78] Furthermore, the external pressure of multiracials in white contexts[79] and the internal pressure of ethnic blacks may change the notion of blackness and even the position of some blacks in the system. Colorism may become an even more important factor as a way of making social distinctions among blacks.[80]

Fifth, the new racial stratification system will be more effective in maintaining white supremacy.[81] Whites will still be at the top of the social structure, but they will face fewer race-based challenges. And, to avoid confusion about our claim regarding honorary whites, let us clarify that their standing and status will be dependent upon whites' wishes and practices. *Honorary* means that they will remain secondary, will still face discrimination, and will not receive equal treatment in society. For example, although Arab Americans should be regarded as honorary whites, their treatment in the post-September 11 era suggests their status as white and American is very tenuous.

Although some analysts and commentators may welcome Latin Americanization as a positive trend in American race relations, those at the bottom of the racial hierarchy will discover that behind the statement "We are all Americans" hides a deeper, hegemonic way of maintaining white supremacy. As a Latin America-like society, the United States will become a society with more rather than less racial inequality, but with a reduced forum for racial contestation. The apparent blessing of "not seeing race" will become a curse for those struggling for racial justice in years to come. We may become "All Americans," as commercials in recent times suggest, but, to paraphrase George Orwell, "some will be more American than others."

Meanings of Skin Color

Race, Gender, Ethnic Class, and National Identities

WHAT IS THE MEANING OF SKIN COLOR for individual and collective identities? What role did the construction of skin color hierarchies play in nineteenth- and twentieth-century colonialism, and what role does it play in contemporary Western-dominated global culture? Conversely, for those who have been subject to colonialism, racism, sexism, and class exploitation, what is the role of alternative skin color ideals in forging identities? These questions require us to look at how meanings of skin color intersect with and interact with meanings of other kinds of difference, including race, gender, class, and nation.

Joanne L. Rondilla and Maxine Leeds Craig explore the meaning of skin color in relation to race and gender identity among those affected by colonialism and racism. Rondilla examines the sources of Filipina's skin color ideals as depicted in skin-lightening advertisements. She recognizes the multiple entanglements of successive colonization in the Philippines, by Spain, the United States, and Japan; the current marginal position of the Philippines in the hierarchy of Asian nations; its role as an exporter of labor to multiple sites around the world; and its exposure to Western media culture in shaping its national identity. Rondilla argues that Filipina's desire for lighter skin is not aimed at attaining "whiteness," but at emulating the ideal of "Asian beauty," an ideal that includes not only porcelain white skin, but also straight black hair and almond eyes. Although in some ways resisting Western standards of beauty, the ideal Asian beauty is one that has been constructed by the white imagination. Craig Limns the continuities and fluctuations in skin color ideals among African Americans by looking at contestants and winners of black beauty pageants, focusing in particular on the Miss Bronze pageant of the 1960s and 1970s. Although, historically, black beauty pageants recruited and crowned only light-skinned winners, the Miss Bronze contest encouraged entries by women of all hues and crowned some darker skinned contestants, especially during the peak years of the Black Movement. Craig's account suggests that during periods of heightened black nationalism, darker or at least medium skin tone may be viewed as more authentically black and thus better representing black America.

In their chapters, Aisha Khan and Christina A. Sue explore the meaning of skin color for individual and collective identities in very different contexts. Khan's study of the Indian community in Trinidad examines the difficulty of placing Indo-Trinidadians within the dominant black–white continuum that consists mostly of "in-between" shades. Even without a black–white binary (which is often seen as excluding groups that are neither white nor black), the Trinidadian case shows that a "mixed nation" that celebrates hybridity can exclude those who are not part of the black–white binary from the national imaginary. By symbolic means, mounting in one case a bright-pink effigy of a traditional Indian deity, Indo-Trinidadians display and celebrate their cultural identity outside the dominant color continuum. Christina A. Sue's fieldwork and interviews in Veracruz, Mexico, illuminate ordinary people's thoughts about skin color as an aspect of personal identity and interpersonal relations. Sue finds that Veracruzenos, who along with other Mexicanos embrace the national ideology of *mestizaje,* readily talk about and characterize themselves in terms of skin tone, but are usually unable or unwilling to place themselves and others racially. Although eschewing "race talk," they are attentive to differences in skin tone within their own families and seek light-skinned partners to whiten their progeny. Furthermore, they deny any knowledge of the intermixture of African heritage within the predominately *mestizo* population, despite the historical importance of the region as the site of entry and incorporation of large numbers of African slaves during the nineteenth century, and instead attribute the darkness of many local people to sun exposure.

E.N.G.

Filipinos and the Color Complex

Ideal Asian Beauty

Joanne L. Rondilla

A PHILIPPINE ADVERTISEMENT FOR A PRODUCT called SkinWhite reads, "Get 99% whiter, better." A 2003 report stated that more than 2 million units of skin-lightening soap are sold annually in the Philippines. Less than a year later, a survey about skin-lightening usage conducted by Synovate revealed that among its respondents in the Asia–Pacific region, the Philippines reported the highest rate of usage, with 50 percent of the respondents stating that they currently use skin-lightening products.[1] In an essay, a second-generation Filipina in her early twenties writes, "A friend of my mother's called me a 'dark beauty.' I was so offended. 'Dark' was a loaded word and she pulled the trigger. . . . The word *dark* and *beauty* just did not go together. *Dark* canceled *beauty* out. Dark meant you were lower class, ugly and unimportant."[2]

This chapter looks at how skin-lightening products are marketed and sold, and what these advertisements say about skin color and beauty. I specifically chose advertisements from the Philippines because skin lightening there is an age-old practice that is rooted in the multiple layers of colonialism the archipelago has had to endure: from Spanish and American colonialism, to the rise of the Chinese and Spanish *mestizo* middle class. Additionally, it is influenced by its proximity to countries such as China, Japan, and Korea, and the various media from these countries that is brought into the Philippines such as TV and film.

Given this, here are some things that need to be clarified. First, people in the Philippines using skin lighteners is not necessarily a move toward whiteness or Europeanness; it is also related to looking East Asian or Chinese. Although the standard of beauty in the Philippines (as seen in these advertisements) is more East Asian or Chinese inspired, it is a very specific kind of beauty consisting of extremely pale skin, straight jet-black hair, and large, double-lidded, almond-shaped eyes. The standard of beauty that we see here illustrates the valorization of East Asian beauty, but how that beauty is defined is according to white standards. In short, it is Asian beauty according to the white imagination. Second, the marketing of skin-lightening products is a reflection of multiple colonizations in the Philippines. Last, although skin-lightening advertisements use different marketing strategies in different parts of the world, the messages they convey are still the same. It is extremely important to examine these various layers because it illuminates the issue of colorism beyond black and white terms. Also, the alarmingly high rates of skin-lightening usage and the strong emphasis of color in the Philippines are too serious to ignore.

This chapter takes an in-depth look at how colorism affects Asians and Asian Americans in the Philippines and the United States. How does colorism operate among Asian and Asian American communities? How are these issues related to the global sale, marketing, and production of skin-lightening products? Colorism is part of a larger and more complex global phenomenon that is carried out through the flow of media. To illustrate this, I will examine how skin-lightening products are marketed by comparing two sets of skin-lightening advertisements from the Philippines and the United States. I am interested in exploring the extent to which perceptions of light skin change or are maintained across national borders and how communications media contribute to the spread of ideas favoring light-skinned images and the use of skin-lightening products.

The notion that those who are white or those who have light skin are superior to those with dark skin has had a profound impact around the world, especially with media technologies such as TV, film, and the Internet. According to Stuart Hall, globalization is part of a longer colonial history that began when Europe encountered the rest of the world. Hall states, "The recent integration of financial systems, the internationalization of production and consumption, the spread of global communications networks, is only the latest—albeit distinctive—phase in a long, historical process."[3] Hall describes globalization as the following:

> The process by which relatively separate areas of the globe come to intersect in a single imaginary "space"; when their respective histories are convened in a time-zone or time-frame dominated by the time of the West; when the sharp

boundaries reinforced by space and distance are bridged by connections (travel, trade, conquest, colonization, markets, capital and the flows of labor, goods and profits) which gradually eroded the clear-cut distinction between "inside" and "outside."[4]

In short, globalization involves the flow of ideas, products, images, and so forth, that, through technological advances in the media, closes the gap between perceived differences among people. Although some may see globalization as positive because it inspires disparate peoples, information, and products to connect, there are also some serious negatives to this, particularly in relation to the beauty and skin-lightening industry. The desire or supposed need for light skin has become a profitable commodity worldwide. Companies such as L'Oreal are able to sell the same skin-lightening products in different countries. Although the marketing strategies may differ, the messages (rooted in colonial thinking) behind what they are selling remain constant. That skin color marks the civilized and modern from the savage and backward, and that one can now invest in changing this marker highlights the connections among colorism, colonialism, globalization, and capitalism.

The Seductive Power of Skin Lightening

It is difficult for one to walk around in everyday life and not be influenced by the images that one encounters—from the ultrabeautiful people on the television and movie screens, the billboard advertisements for beauty products, and the plethora of cosmetics websites. Writer Wendy Chapkis explains: "Indeed, female beauty is becoming an increasingly standardized quality throughout the world. A standard so strikingly White, Western and wealthy it is tempting to conclude there must be a conscious conspiracy afoot."[5] For many Asians, the implicit message that they are fed each day is that they are not white enough. Their noses are not pointed enough, eyes not big enough, and, although pale, their skin is not the right kind of light.

These controlling images are quite compelling. Patricia Hill Collins states that "controlling images are designed to make racism, sexism, poverty and other forms of social injustice appear to be natural, normal, and inevitable parts of life."[6] Although images of lighter skinned successful people (including lighter skinned Asians) continue to grace the covers of magazines, and messages such as "Now lighten your skin from within" travel through the Internet, it is important to note that these messages are instruments of power used, not necessarily to help Asians improve their state of being, but for the ruling class to profit. For example, ten years ago, it was uncommon to see skin-lightening products at local department store cosmetics counters. Today, every major cosmetics company has some form of skin lightener. In the end, the increase in popularity of skin lighteners has less to do with one's actual need for it and more to do with profit a company can make by creating a demand and actually supplying the product to consumers.

Although Asians do not constitute a large sector of the popular media, the beauty pressure for Asian women to lighten their skin is very high. Through independent and ethnic-specific media, there is a growing number of Asian American-specific beauty magazines such as Los Angeles-based *Audrey*. There are large Asian-based cosmetics companies such as Shiseido and Shu Uemura that cater to the specific needs of an Asian clientele. Additionally, smaller, direct-sales companies such as Esolis (which is now defunct), DHC, Pola, and Noevir tout their products and send their catalogs to Asian and Asian American prospective consumers.[7] Each of the cosmetics companies mentioned here has a line of skin-lightening products. These brands claim to target the specific needs of Asian skin. For example, Esolis' primary target market was Asian American women. An introductory letter from Esolis president Tari E. Reinink explained the following:

> Let's face it, there are clear differences between Asian and Caucasian skin, and it's likely you have been frustrated at finding the right skin care products that work for you. . . . Esolis products address the specific needs of Asian skin including dark spots, uneven skin tone, oiliness, breakouts and skin sensitivities. Our products use clinically proven technologies to illuminate and brighten your skin, repair and protect it from the sun, restore moisture and reverse the signs of aging.[8]

In terms of who actually uses these products, there seems to be a divide between immigrant consumers versus nonimmigrant consumers. Nonimmigrant Asian women tend to veer away from skin-lightening products whereas immigrant women tend to opt for them, even looking to use the same skin-lightening products they are accustomed to using in their home country. (It is common to see skin-lightening products in Asian grocery and beauty stores.) I would like to address briefly the issue of the immigrant versus American-born stances toward the color complex. Asian Americans (regardless of whether they would like to recognize it) have a particular privilege within the Asian and

Asian American color hierarchy. Working behind the cosmetics counter and in speaking with numerous clients, I have observed that Asians who seek out skin lighteners are more likely to be members of the immigrant generation. Because they are caught in the middle—between Asia and the United States—they tend to be influenced by the beauty standards from the home country, which, as we have seen in the advertisements, valorize light skin. These ideas travel to the United States when these women immigrate.

The desire for light skin among these women is doubly important. On one hand, light skin is seen as beautiful in the home country. On the other hand, when they come to the United States, the image of a typical American is usually of one who is white and has Eurocentric features. In their study of skin color hierarchy among Asian Americans, Rondilla and Spickard point out that a few immigrant interviewees mentioned that their skin color preference came from their home country. A thirty-six-year-old Cambodian Chinese immigrant woman stated, "I don't think the Cambodians that are born here care about skin color. . . . Only the person that was born in Cambodia. They do care about their color."[9] However, another way that immigrant women are affected by images of Asians in the United States is through their beauty expectations of their children and grandchildren. In the same study, some interviewees repeatedly talk about wanting their children to stay out of the sun or to choose lighter skinned partners to have lighter skinned grandchildren.[10] Immigrant women are definitely affected by various images of Asians in the United States. Although they see few Asians in popular media, they sometimes feel pressure to measure up to such standards.[11]

Kathy Peiss incorporates a similar discussion in her book when she states that daughters of immigrant parents tended to use cosmetics to look more "American." This is because it helps them (in their own eyes) to assimilate and become part of the landscape of the newly adopted home country.[12] I would like to carry this analysis further by considering the power of U.S. colonization in a country such as the Philippines, and how status symbols change depending on locale. Immigrant generations have a particular idea of what success should look like. In the home country (in this case, the Philippines), success is defined by light skin because it illustrates that one is not part of the laboring class and does not have to work under the hot sun. Additionally, the majority of the upper class in the Philippines are lighter skinned mixed-race Filipinos. The look of success in the United States is a different story, because, as an industrialized nation, most people already work indoors. Tan skin in the

United States is a marker of the leisure class, because it implies one was vacationing.[13] This, along with the influences of the black is beautiful, brown pride, and yellow power movements of the 1960s and 1970s make it a little easier for American-born generations not to valorize light skin and other Eurocentric standards of beauty.

Being American in effect lightens one's status regardless of skin color—at least in the eyes of many Asian immigrant women. Although many Asian Americans tend to be perplexed that immigrant members of the community want light skin, they do not recognize that their own desire to be tan or to darken their skin is related to the same colonial process. Hence, many Asian Americans who shun skin lightening may opt for the U.S. beauty standard and invest in tanning. Because tanning involves skin darkening, many believe that the process symbolizes going back to a natural state of being. Tanning may give Asian Americans a sense of ethnic authenticity and can possibly allow them to believe it is natural for them to be tan (even if they obtained the tan through artificial means). While giving a guest lecture in a contemporary issues course, a second-generation Filipino student stated, "I don't understand why my mother tries so hard to be light. She uses tons of skin-bleaching products from the Asian grocery store, while I'm here trying to get a decent tan" (personal communication with author).

A critical look at this complex reveals that tanning and lightening are two sides of the same coin. Beauty is part of one's class identity, but the markers of class identity differ depending on where you are. In the end, the beauty industry profits from the idea that one's class has a particular look, and that look can be purchased.[14] This complex is one that leaves immigrant Asians disadvantaged and longing for a particular class status (which many immediately equate to skin color) and elevates Asian Americans because they have a particular class status regardless of their skin color.

Selling Lighter Skin: The Advertisements in Asia and the United States

In countries such as the Philippines and Thailand, it is quite common to see major advertisements for skin-lightening products. Usually, these advertisements feature Asian women with glowing white skin, jet-black hair, and delicate, almond-shaped obsidian eyes. The message in these ads is clear: It's okay to be Asian as long as you're the right kind of Asian. Meaning, you must be light, have big eyes, and a body that is at least twenty pounds lighter than average. It seems that these are the requirements for entertainers in Asia and, to some extent, people who sell such products.[15] As in advertising in the United States, advertisements in Asia convey the message that Asians are simply one product (or a series of products) away from perfection.

Although these companies are trying to sell whiteness, they are selling a particular kind of whiteness. While many may think that Asian women use skin lighteners to become white or European, this is not necessarily true. As someone who has worked in the cosmetics industry for a number of years now, I have spoken to many women who use such products. Many of them are indeed satisfied with being Asian or having Asian features. In fact, they like being Asian, because it gives them a distinct and unique identity. However, they just wish their features were a little bit "better." Although they wouldn't trade in their dark hair or almond-shaped eyes for blonde hair and blue eyes, they are looking to "clean up" or become "better" versions of themselves.

Given the state of globalization. Scholar Koichi Iwabuchi writes,

> Globalization processes, however, have not simply furthered the spread of Americanized "global mass culture." They have also promoted the flow of intraregional media and popular culture within East and Southeast Asia. These popular cultural forms are undoubtedly deeply imbricated in U.S. cultural imaginaries, but they dynamically rework meanings of being modern in Asian contexts at the site of production and consumption. In this sense, they are neither "Asian" in any essentialist meaning nor second-rate copies of "American originals." They are inescapably "global" and "Asian" at the same time, lucidly representing the intertwined composition of global homogenization and heterogenization, and thus they well articulate the juxtaposed sameness and difference among contemporaneous indigenized modernities in East and Southeast Asia.[16]

With respect to Asia, Iwabuchi points out that it's not just about whiteness, it is also beyond whiteness; it is global and fraught with its own set of issues and intricacies. *Time Magazine* writer Hannah Beech explores the idea of Eurasians as "a global progeny of an increasingly global world." It seems that mixed-race Asians are the new faces of Asian marketing. In Bangkok, 60 percent of the entertainment industry are mixed race. Chinese Dutch American actor/producer Declan Wong states, "When I think of Asia, I don't necessarily think of people who look like me. . . . But somehow we've become the new face that sells the new Asia."[17]

The connections between Asians and Asian Americans and skin lightening are carried to the international sphere when we examine the correlation between the skin-lightening market abroad targeted at Asian women and skin lightening in the United States targeted at Asian American women. To help us look at these connections, we will be comparing a series of skincare advertisements. The first is from two L'Oreal products from the Philippines: a sunscreen called UV Perfect and an exfoliating mask called White Perfect. The second is from a catalog by a now-defunct company (as mentioned earlier) called Esolis. Based in the United States, this company's target audience was Asian American women. We will be looking at the section of the Esolis catalog called "For women who are serious about brightening their skin," which focuses on the Sol Brightening System.

See the Philippine advertisement for L'Oreal's UV Perfect (Figure 4.1) is a two-page spread featuring a Portuguese Chinese movie star from Hong Kong, Michele Reis. The left side of the advertisement features her covering part of her face, as if she is blocking something. The right side of the advertisement shows a photo of the actual product (the product is about a quarter of the size of Reis' face on the opposite page) and the text reads as follows:

Technological breakthrough in UV Protection: For the first time in a daily care regimen, the ultrapowerful association of Mexoryl SX + XL against harmful

Figure 4.1 Philippine Advertisement for L'Oréal's UV Perfect

UVA and UVB to prevent skin darkening. Activa cell to stimulate skin's natural repairing process. Maximum pleasure: Ultralight and quickly absorbent UV Perfect creates an unnoticeable screen on your skin leaving it soft, smooth and matte. Dermo-Expertise. From research to beauty. Because you're worth it.

This ad focuses on the actress' face and less on the product. Reis' look is racially ambiguous. To advertisers, she is white (with some exotic features). To audiences in the Philippines, she is Asian (with some European features). This allows the L'Oreal advertisers to believe that they are embracing a new kind of beauty—one that is not Eurocentric—and allows women in the Philippines to relate to her Asian face and at the same time aspire to her measure of whiteness. Her face or her beauty represents a type of *relatable ideal*. With this, advertisers can claim that Reis' beauty is universal and speaks to many women because she is racially ambiguous. Using mixed-race models is common in advertising all over Asia because such models are seen to have global appeal and inspire sales. Yanto Zainal, president of Macs909 advertisement agency in Jakarta, explains, "Indos [mixed-race people] have an international look but can still be accepted as Indonesian." Along those same lines, Widarti Goenawan, publisher of *Femina,* a popular Indonesian women's magazine, claims, "Indonesian women see these girls as exotic, but not exactly threatening. . . . It is an ideal to which they can aspire." [18] Given this, advertisers can claim that Reis represents sameness, not difference. However, in a commentary about Saira Mohan, a Punjabi Irish French model who was deemed the "new global beauty" by *Newsweek* magazine, scholar Margaret Hunter states,

> The paradox of purporting "global" beauty to a woman who could be mistaken as "European, European, or European" seems an obvious contradiction. But this is the paradoxical discourse of the new beauty regime. It is simultaneous inclusive, multicultural, and new, while remaining exclusive, Eurocentric and old. The "new global beauty" as Mohan is called in the article is in fact old-fashioned, white beauty re-packaged with dark hair. This means that beauty, and thus capital, is still elusive for many women of color as it continues to be defined by primarily Anglo bodies and faces. [19]

Hunter's remarkable point is reflected in this advertisement and L'Oreal's deliberate positioning of Reis as the representative for their product. Reis is beautiful enough to be marketable, yet exotic enough for the everyday woman in the Philippines to identify with her. In Reis, they see an Asian women they can identify with and hope to be like.

What advertisers do not realize is Reis does not represent sameness. Rather, she symbolizes a skin color hierarchy that has existed for hundreds of years. In her discussion of the beauty queue, Hunter explains,

> The beauty queue explains how sexism and racism interact to create a queue of women from the lightest to the darkest, where the lightest get the most resources and the darkest get the least. The lightest women get access to more resources because not only are they lighter skinned and therefore racially privileged, but their light skin is interpreted in our culture as more beautiful and therefore they also are privileged as beautiful women. The conflation of beauty and light skin is part of how racial aesthetics operate—lighter-skinned people with more Anglicized features are viewed by most in American culture (either consciously or unconsciously) as superior.[20]

Although advertisers try to position Reis as a relatable ideal, they instead reveal a power dynamic that is prevalent in the Philippines: Light skin is indeed a marker of higher class, but light skin is not necessarily limited to European or American definitions. Light skin because one is (in part) Chinese (or East Asian) is also a marker of higher class. Hunter's notion of the beauty queue, translated to the Philippines, is not limited to just a black–white spectrum. It also includes East Asians as lighter skinned and more racially privileged than darker skinned Filipinos. This dynamic can also explain why many public figures (entertainers, politicians, and so forth) in the Philippines tend to be light skinned and look like they are of part East Asian or European ancestry.[21]

Judith Williamson explains, "Our culture, deeply rooted in imperialism, needs to destroy genuine difference, to capture what is beyond its reach."[22] Reis' face does exactly this for the L'Oreal ad; because she is Asian, it is assumed that women in the Philippines can relate to her features. Reis symbolizes the ideal that women should strive for by investing in these beauty products. When they invest in these products, consumers are in turn investing in the idea of what they fantasize they might become, regardless of the actual result of the products. In a recent survey of the popularity of skin-lightening products, 41 percent of respondents who reportedly use such products stated that they have noticed little or no difference in their skin as a result.[23] Despite this, consumers continue to invest in the idea of having lighter skin. On the other hand, some consumers may claim that skin-whitening products do work, and that they are worth the money they invest in them. For these people, they indulge in obtaining the type of beauty they have always desired. It makes them feel more accepted. "I . . . go to the store and get a skin lightening to get more of an even tone. But I would like to be lighter. I think it looks better."[24]

In comparison, the Esolis catalog section, "For women who are serious about brightening their skin," also features a racially ambiguous model (see Figure 4.2). Although she could pass for Asian, she has slightly darker skin than other models in the catalog. Also, the other models have features that are more distinctly Asian. Unlike the UV Perfect ad, the Esolis catalog focuses more on the product, and makes it so that the product and text are the relatable elements, and the model's face presents the problem as opposed to the solution.

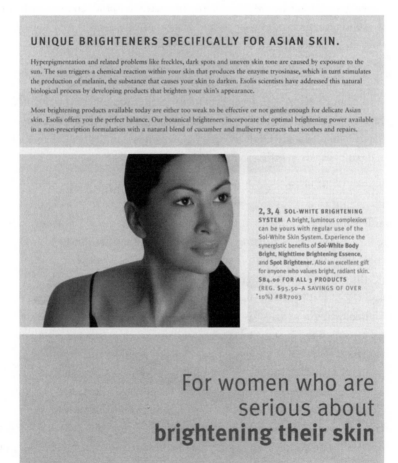

Figure 4.2 Excerpt from Esolis Catalog

The model is slightly darker skinned and is looking up; she represents the consumers who, as the caption states, are "serious about brightening their skin." It seems that her racial ambiguity marks her inauthenticity. Hence, if she brightens her skin, she could possibly be "more Asian" than she already is.

This catalog excerpt emphasizes the uniqueness of Asian skin and the need for products that specialize in such areas. Like the UV Perfect ad, the problem posed in the catalog is hyperpigmentation:

> Unique Brighteners Specifically for Asian Skin. Hyperpigmentation and related problems like freckles, dark spots, and uneven skin tone are caused by exposure to the sun. The sun triggers a chemical reaction within your skin that produces the enzyme tyrosinase, which in turn stimulates the production of melanin, the substance that causes your skin to darken. Esolis scientists have addressed this natural biological process by developing products that brighten your skin's appearance.
>
> Most brightening products available today are either too weak to be effective or not gentle enough for delicate Asian skin. Esolis offers you the perfect balance. Our botanical brighteners incorporate the optimal brightening power available in a non-prescription formulation with a natural blend of cucumber and mulberry extracts that soothes and repairs.[25]

Both advertisements position darkness as a problem, even though the Esolis catalog recognizes hyperpigmentation as a "natural biological process." Regardless of whether these products use botanical or scientifically developed ingredients, both see whitening or brightening as the solution to preventing darkness. Hyperpigmentation is simply a pseudoscientific euphemism for the skin getting darker, particularly through sun exposure.

The UV Perfect product in the Philippine advertisement is sunscreen. In the United States, when a sunscreen is advertised, the product is usually positioned as something that protects the skin. For example, an advertisement for a sunscreen called UV Plus, by Clarins, claims that it leaves the skin "strongly protected against UVA and UVB infrared rays, skin's youthful appearance is preserved." An equivalent sunscreen in the Philippines is marketed in a very different way, because instead of focusing on protection from harmful sun rays, it centers around the ideas of correcting and repairing bad skin. The UV Perfect ad focuses on skin darkening as a problem that needs to be fixed. Hidden behind this text is the notion of saving these consumers from their fate of being dark and savagelike. Aging is not their problem; skin cancer is not their problem. Skin color is their problem. In typical colonial fashion, it takes science to right the wrong of their skin color. By using mostly pseudoscientific jargon such as the new and innovative ingredients "Mexoryl XL Filter + Activa Cell," the product is used to "prevent skin darkening" and "stimulate skin's natural repairing process." The advanced, scientific ingredients are used to lighten dark-skinned consumers, and Reis poses as an example of that possibility. Ultimately, women in the United States use the Clarins sunscreen to be protected and women in the Philippines use sunscreen to be perfected.

The Esolis catalog emphasizes the uniqueness of Asian skin and the need for products that specialize in such areas. Like the UV Perfect ad, the problem posed in the catalog is also that skin gets darker. The text is deceptive, because it softens its pseudoscientific jargon to emphasize the unique and delicate nature of Asian skin. It seems that the Esolis catalog positions science as an inadequate means of addressing the delicate nature of Asian skin, because to treat Asian skin, one must use methods that are naturally and spiritually sound. Although this may seem reasonable to some, what this really does is reiterate stereotypical Orientalist thinking, which sees Asian women as delicate lotus blossoms; situates Asian culture as meditative, at one with the earth; and uses ancient medicinal practices. Both advertisements position darkness as a problem and both see whitening or brightening products as the solution to preventing darkness. Regardless of whether these products contain botanical or scientifically developed ingredients, using them is a justifiable solution to a process that occurs naturally in the body.

The next product we will look at is featured in a two-page L'Oreal advertisement from the Philippines for a "deep whitening mask" called White Perfect (Figure 4.3). The ad reads as follows:

Innovation: Triple Melanin Block Concentrate. The expert whitening mask for bright skin, like glowing from within. White Perfect. A cream mask for a complete action on skin fairness, radiance and transparency. 1) Intense whitening mask: triple concentrated Melanin Block helps regulate melanin production. 2) Facial Massage: Microbeads help exfoliate dark dead cells from skin's surface to boost skin brightness. Instant proven results: More radiant + transparent skin. 97% of women agreed. Smoother, more even skin tone. 93% of women agreed.

In this ad, the racial connotations are quite blatant:

1. Darkening can and must be stopped.
2. Lightness is more than just skin deep and must come from "within."

Figure 4.3 Philippine Advertisement for L'Oréal's White Perfect

Lightening is not limited to the skin; it must come from other facets of one's being.

3. Lightening can happen instantly and is something that many women aspire to and can achieve.

These are all assumptions that go unquestioned.

That a major worldwide company such as L'Oreal can sell an "expert whitening mask" clearly illustrates that race does matter. The quest to erase one's racialized features has become a profitable commodity. I do not wish to imply that everyone has fallen into the trap of desiring light skin. However, for some, the social, economic, and political benefits of light skin are too difficult to pass up. This is reflected in an editorial featured in the *Philippine Daily Inquirer* titled, "Whiteners Won't Transform 'Morena' into 'Mestiza.'"[26] Writer Lora Gahol begins, "No amount of whitening cream will turn caramel tint into milk." What starts as a realistic and progressive view on skin lighteners takes an unexpected turn when she attempts to make the distinction between bleaching and lightening:

Bleaching is designed to make the skin lighter than its original color, thus the need for strong chemicals. Whitening, on the other hand, only tries to bring back the skin tone you had as a baby. . . . Morenas and true-blue Pinays, though they may have to give up dreams of alabaster skin, reap considerable benefits from whitening preparations. The products help to improve dramatically skin texture and generate glow. Whitening is for everybody. And the great news is everybody can find a product to suit her budget and skin type. Local manufacturers and affiliates of high-end international labels have released their own versions of the highly popular skin-care preparation, giving consumers more and more choices.[27]

Gahol's commentary illustrates how light skin has become a marker of success and a worthwhile investment. Her writing uses some of the same tropes the ads use, such as the notion of light skin signifying a journey back to one's "natural" state. Promoting the idea that lightness is natural is how some companies and consumers can justify using a skin lightener. As Gahol explains, whitening is natural, for the process entails bringing "back the skin tone you had as a baby." On the other hand, bleaching is unnatural because it alters one's original skin tone. Hence, this process should be shunned. One must pose the question: Is there really a difference between whitening and bleaching? If one were to compare the ingredients in whitening and bleaching products, one would find the same types of ingredients.

Catherine Lutz and Jane Collins, explain how racist assumptions have become a part of popular belief: "Like other forms of essentialist reasoning, racist thought has the appeal of simplicity, and it draws authority from invoking biology and nature."[28] Unfortunately, this seems to be the popular sentiment regarding skin lightening, especially in the Philippines, other parts of Asia, and among Asian Americans of the immigrant generation. As mentioned earlier, skin lightening is a multimillion-dollar industry in the Philippines and other areas of Asia. However, the false notion that Filipinos should desire white skin was created by more than 500 years of Spanish and American colonial history. This idea is so ingrained that it becomes accepted as if it were a cultural norm. Many cosmetics companies have taken advantage of these ideas and have turned them into an entire industry. David Gosling, president and managing director of Avon India Beauty Products, states, "Fairness creams are trendy throughout the Asia–Pacific. People here basically want lighter skin. Culturally, fair skin is associated with positive values that relate to class, lifestyle and beauty."[29]

Gahol's previous commentary also celebrates the accessibility of light skin: Regardless of income level, one can reap the benefits of going back to a natural state of lightness. Deborah Root notes that, "Consumption is power, and the ability to consume excessively and willfully becomes the most desirable aspect of power."[30] Along similar lines, Williamson states that capitalism creates the idea that everything (including one's social position) can be bought and exchanged.[31] The power of consumption is something to consider because possessing light skin alone does not symbolize power. That one can buy light skin and even be excessive about the buying is another symbol of power. I mention this because we cannot assume that only dark-skinned people use skin lighters—especially when these products are advertised so widely—to the point where light skin becomes a common desire for *everybody*. Peiss explains,

> Beauty may have been considered the birthright of only wealthy or fortunate women in the nineteenth century, but cosmetics advertising sold the idea than an attractive appearance was an accomplishment all could easily achieve. Mail-order and tabloid-style ads promised cheap, instant beauty to working women unable to afford the time and money leisured women spent on beauty culture.[32]

Even if one was not born into money, one could appear to be of a higher social standing by simply looking the part. Although this may not actually change your social standing, it allows the working class to feel as if they have escaped their social station (even if it is only temporary).

Finally, the type of language used to promote skin lightening does not limit its market only to dark-skinned consumers. This can be seen in the White Perfect ad's usage of key phrases such as "bright skin," "radiance," and "smoother, more even skin tone." Peiss explains that the use of a word such as *bright* implies changing the skin's condition by smoothing out its texture, as well as turning a dark skin into a lighter shade of brown.[33] In her excellent essay, Amina Mire states, "When catering to the needs of White women, pharmaceutical/cosmetics industries put greater emphasis in their advertising on how their products will make their consumers attain 'beautiful,' 'pure,' 'translucent,' 'healthy looking skin.' I argue that these adjectives signify whiteness."[34] Some of the key terms used in the text—*flawless, radiance, purify, brightness, clarity, perfection, luminous, even, softer*—imply a Eurocentric beauty standard that is imposed on Asian and Asian American women.

The meanings differ according to where particular advertisements are featured. In taking a closer look at the text, the Philippine ads use *whitening* as a key marketing phrase, the U.S. ads replace it with *brightening*. In this way, U.S. advertising can incorporate the same racially charged messages, but in a more covert way. According to the advertisements, Asian women in the United States do not "whiten" their skin (to do so would be to insinuate that they were participating in some type of ethnic cleansing ritual). Instead, they "brighten" to improve radiance and to prevent aging and hyperpigmentation (these are the same key phrases that are found in most skincare literature in Asia). Peiss states, "This use of the word *bright* [italics added] had a double meaning: By smoothing rough or uneven skin, creams did brighten, in a sense, by improving the reflectivity of light, but among African Americans the term had a distinct connotation, that of light brown skin."[35] Again, although the idea of having radiant and luminous skin is appealing, one must ask: What are the racial implications behind such terms? In truth, to brighten and to whiten are different sides of the same coin. Advertisers have just learned to adapt the jargon to the population they are targeting.

Striving for ideal beauty is always a complicated issue, because notions of beauty are constantly changing. This is, in part, to satisfy market needs and demands, and to affirm the powerful. In the past when Filipinos would strive for ideal beauty, it meant that they wanted more European or Spanish (given Philippine colonial history) features: pointed noses, lighter skin, larger eyes, and so forth. Today when these same women strive for ideal beauty, they look to a different set of standards—one that is influenced by the Chinese *mestizo* ruling class in the Philippines and its proximity to East Asia. This shift in East Asian beauty *seems* to acknowledge elements of Filipino beauty. However, these seemingly new standards are not new at all. Instead, they are intertwined with East Asian values that have a Westernized underpinning to them. This is what makes the color complex among global Filipino communities unique. When these women want to embrace dark hair and almond-shaped eyes, they seem to challenge Eurocentric ideals. When taking a closer look, Eurocentric standards are being masked by what Hunter refers to as "global beauty"—the notion that diverse beauty standards are actually repackaged values that reflect current power dynamics.

In her study about mixed-race people, scholar Kimberly DaCosta quotes a casting agent who explains that images of mixed-race people "conjures up an immediate sense of both globalization and technology. The blended look says 'we're all in this together' and that 'the world is getting smaller.'"[36] DaCosta's discussion resonates in this essay, especially with respect to models in these cosmetics advertisements. Although advertising and popular culture at large seem to move toward greater diversity by casting more entertainers of color, these entertainers are only appealing as long as they remain racially ambiguous. Advertisers do this as a way to try to erase racial and color lines. However, these global faces do the opposite by pointing to difference as opposed to universality. Rebecca King-O'Riain states: "The mixed-race body then does not destroy race, but leads to a repoliticization and problematization of race."[37] Last, although skin-lightening advertisements attempt to cater to specific markets, the messages and products are all the same. While the world may be changing, notions of skin color remain constant.

The Color of an Ideal Negro Beauty Queen

Miss Bronze 1961–1968

Maxine Leeds Craig

THE SUREST GENERALIZATION THAT CAN BE MADE about black beauty contests before the 1960s is that the winners usually had light skin tones. This pattern reflects what has been called *colorism,* or the longstanding and frequently institutionalized African American practice of reserving positions of social privilege for light-skinned blacks. A closer look at early black beauty pageants suggests, however, that colorism was never universally accepted.

For example, in 1914, a widely read black newspaper, the *New York Age,* invited its female readers to send their photographs to the paper's New York office for inclusion in a contest to select the fifteen most beautiful black women in the United States. When a panel of judges chose only light-skinned women as winners, a reader from Tuskegee, Alabama, wrote to the editors to ask how women who looked more "Nordic" than "Negro" could serve as representatives of the race. In 1927, the *Western American,* a black newspaper published in California, organized a beauty contest and informed its readers that they wanted colored contestants of all hues. Although a light-skinned woman ultimately won the contest, black women of a range of shades entered it, and journalists covering the contest commented on the issue of color as a source of potential controversy. Two decades later, the Miss Fine Brown Frame contest was held at Harlem's Golden Gate Ballroom in 1947. When, at the end of an evening of entertainment, the judges awarded the title to a light-skinned woman, a sizable portion of the audience, who preferred a dark-skinned contestant named Evelyn Sanders, was outraged. The organizers attempted to mollify the crowd by splitting the title from the cash prize, a tactic that only increased the audience's collective anger. In the end, the crowd prevailed and Evelyn Sanders was crowned Miss Fine Brown Frame.[1]

These examples demonstrate both institutionalization and popular contestation of hierarchies of color. Popular awareness of colorism within black communities is not new, nor is black denunciation of it. Sometimes as lone voices of protest and sometimes collectively, African Americans questioned, rejected, and directly challenged preferences for light skin. Rather than being an uncontested constant within African American life, the force of colorism has vacillated in response to changes in the political climate. As an example of the variability and complexity of black practices, discourse, and preferences surrounding skin tone, this chapter looks at how skin tone mattered within Miss Bronze, a black beauty contest that took place between 1961 and 1968, a period when Civil Rights and Black Power Movement activism inspired widespread black cultural reassessment.

Miss Bronze was a beauty contest for black women that began in southern California in the late 1950s. It expanded into a statewide contest in the years 1961 to 1968 with the establishment of the northern California Miss Bronze contest, a lavish preliminary event that included celebrity entertainers such as singers Nancy Wilson and Lou Rawls, program endorsements from local white politicians, major corporate sponsorship, and military honor guards. Winners of Miss Bronze in northern California flew to Los Angeles to compete with contestants from the southern part of the state. In this chapter, I examine how black women, in the midst of transformations in both national and black cultures, encountered and responded to the changing social meaning of their own color and the color of others. I look at women who competed in a beauty contest because this setting, which is so explicitly about outward appearance, brings questions related to color sharply into focus. I interviewed nine Miss Bronze pageant contestants, including two winners of the northern California Miss Bronze title. A tenth contestant sent me her memories of the pageant via e-mail. I was able to gain insight into the perspectives of the organizers through an interview with the northern California pageant's principal producer, Belva Davis, one of the pageant's financial supporters, and through examination of program books, promotional materials, and 141 articles about and images of the pageant that were published in San Francisco Bay Area newspapers.[2] One year's program book bears a record of the impressions of its original owner, in the form of handwritten judgmental notes under contestants' portraits that were presumably written while he or she watched the pageant as a member of the audience.

The word *bronze* in the pageant's title suggests both a color and a valuable metal associated with statues. In the 1950s, when Howard Morehead established the original Miss Bronze pageant in Los Angeles, the name may have signified both a specific skin tone as well as the sturdy elegance of the metal. Throughout the 1960s, however, black women of a range of shades entered the Miss Bronze pageant and won the title. Apparently, in those years, bronze signified race but not a specific color. Color mattered in the Miss Bronze contest, but not in the predictable way that it had in earlier black contests. In many past contests, winners were chosen on the basis of beauty criteria that excluded dark women. Women with dark skin tones had little or no chance of winning and may have been discouraged from even entering such contests. In contrast to past practices, the organizers of the Miss Bronze contest actively recruited women of a range of shades.[3] During the contest's brief existence, light-skinned women, brown-skinned women, and dark-skinned women wore the Miss Bronze crown.[4] In the mid 1960s, the racially integrated Civil Rights Movement that had focused on ending discrimination declined as a variety of black organizations that strove for black autonomous power emerged. Alongside these political developments, blacks inside and outside of social movement organizations examined the meaning of black identity and its relationship to Africa, everyday black practices such as hair straightening, and the significance of and meanings attributed to skin color.

Color's Meaning

Rather than being a constant in African American life, the extent of privilege granted to those with lighter skin has varied. The variance is best understood as having two dimensions: salience and meaning. Both the extent to which skin color mattered and the meanings attached to different skin tones have shifted throughout time.

Sander Gilman has argued that features of bodies are given meaning by culturally diffused "systems of representation."[5] My studies of black beauty contests demonstrate the presence of fluid and competing systems of representation. One system was a nationally dominant system of representation corresponding to dominant standards of beauty. These beauty standards were a complex set of tastes and judgments promoted by a vast array of what were, through the first half of the twentieth century, white institutions such as the Miss America pageant and Hollywood film studios. These standards circulated within black communities alongside a complex and contested yet identifiable set of specifically black tastes and judgments.

It is useful to combine Gilman's systems of representation with the popular concept of "type" as it has been theorized by historian Kathy Peiss. Peiss has argued that as early as the end of the nineteenth century, cosmetics manufacturers incorporated racial and ethnic difference into their advertisements by using the language of "type," a frame that had, and continues to have, popular resonance.[6] Cosmetics industry beauty typologies not only define physical types but link such assemblages of physical features to moral and psychological types. Advertisements and popular media cast women as "wholesome girl-next-door" types or "exotic" types based on, among other things, skin color.

The concept of systems of representation can be used to theorize the ways that popular typologies perpetuate systems of inequality. In a system of representation, assemblages of different characteristics are presumed to constitute types of persons. These types become linked in the popular imagination with racial identities, class positions, and degrees of sexuality. Drawing on racist, sexist, and elitist systems of representation, popular images of types give continued life to racist, sexist, and elitist ideology. Historically white systems of representation disparaged black women in general, but positioned some light-skinned women as exotic types. Exotic, when associated with women's bodies, connotes a fusion of beauty, sexual availability and difference. The difference inherent in the label *exotic* is difference from the unmarked, white woman's body. Historically, within black systems of representation, light skin was considered beautiful and was associated with economic and social privilege. However, light-skinned women were not exotic within a black context; they were the daughters of the solid middle class.

Two systems of representation circulated within black communities: one nationally dominant and the other specifically black. W. E. B. Du Bois' concept of double consciousness provides a useful way to think about the interrelationships between white and black systems of representation.[7] One way of understanding double consciousness is that blacks must see themselves and judge themselves as whites see them. In this sense, double consciousness is a way of describing the internalization of racist systems of representation. However, Du Bois also describes double consciousness as a gift. It is the gift of second sight. I understand the gift of second sight as an ability to recognize the presence of racism. The experience of living behind the veil of darkness denaturalizes hierarchies of color and, thus double consciousness implies a critique of the social hierarchy. Double consciousness then is simultaneously an internalization of dominant views of oneself and a critical awareness of the structure of racism. I found the contradiction of double consciousness within black beauty contests. Acceptance of the color hierarchy and rejection of it, preferences for light skin coupled with an awareness of the racism of the preference created a pattern of recurring tensions and conflicts in black beauty contests.[8]

These tensions were present as the Miss Bronze contest sought to select a woman to represent the race. When the Miss Bronze producers placed advertisements in black newspapers calling for contestants, they stated, "Our purpose is to select a representative Negro beauty queen." Beauty queens are almost always called upon to represent some entity, be it a nation, a region, or a race.[9] They have been cast as symbols of national unity in times when national identity is contested, have been used to claim recognition of citizenship by groups that racism sought to exclude from national membership, and have stood as emblems of the high value of a group that is disparaged by a structure of inequality. Existing in the context of a racist society that either excluded blacks from representation or included blacks through a disparaging set of stereotypical images, black beauty queens became important symbols of black worth. African Americans challenged the whiteness of existing all-white beauty contests and the selection of light-skinned beauty queens in black beauty contests because something more than an individual woman's attractiveness was at stake in the selection of a queen. At a national level, black women had been excluded from the position of the popularly glorified, chaste but alluring beauty queen. Miss Bronze was organized at a historical moment when the popularity of beauty contests was at a peak. In 1960, 85 million television viewers watched the Miss America pageant.[10] In an era in which women were celebrated for their beauty far more often than they were valued for their accomplishments, celebrating black beauty was a way to demonstrate the value of black people in general. Who could embody the representative Negro beauty queen? Miss Bronze pageant producer Belva Davis explained, "We used the pageant to make political statements about segregation, being left out, and about complexion and all of that."[11] Her words suggest that Miss Bronze was selected as a symbol for two different audiences. As a representative whose presence could constitute a statement about segregation, Miss Bronze was a symbol who would represent black women to whites. Her attractive face and body could refute disparaging representations of black women, and her cultivated bearing could prove wrong white segregationists' claims of white social superiority. This orientation is evident in promotional material for the pageant. The writers of the 1966 Miss Bronze Pictorial Review said Miss Bronze contestants "entertain, innovate and they integrate. For as they project poise, personality, talent and ability, many doubts are dispelled; there is no barrier that can withstand their charming challenge."

Although the contest was a black institution, Davis used it as an instrument of racial integration. Each year she recruited whites to join the predominantly black selection panel, including persons who were involved in contests, such as Miss California, that served as gateways to the historically all-white Miss America pageant. Promotional material for the Miss Bronze pageant boasted of the entrance of former Miss Bronze contestants into the historically white Miss Oakland, Miss San Francisco, and Maid of Berkeley contests as evidence of its own success.

Miss Bronze was also a symbol for black audiences. She was chosen to represent black women to other black women and to black men at a time when class, color, privilege, and racial authenticity were divisive issues that intertwined in black popular consciousness. As quoted earlier, Davis said that the pageant was useful for making a political statement about complexion. This statement would have had the greatest meaning for black audiences because they, more than whites, were attuned to distinctions among black women and were personally invested in the reassessment of black systems of representation. In a 1963 interview, Davis described the kind of young woman sought by the Miss Bronze pageant: "We try to avoid those who are too Caucasian in feature. And skin color varies, but I might tell you this—the fairer she is the less chance she seems to have of winning! The girl should look like a Negro."[12]

The record of Miss Bronze shows neither a disappearance of colorism nor a reversal of values, but rather a period of heightened contestation that opened new possibilities for the ways beauty would be defined. A cultural climate in which systems of representation were in flux is visible in the hand-written annotations of an audience member who jotted his or her assessment of the contestants on a copy of the evening's program. "Too fat" is scrawled underneath one woman's image, "dress was too old-fashioned" under the portrait of another. "BLA" begins another judgment, written under the photograph of a dark-skinned contestant, and then, in the same ink, an attempt to cross out the comment. Presumably the beauty critic began to write *black,* a negative judgment regarding the appearance of the contestant, and then, uncomfortable with his or her own comment, stopped midstream. Before *black* became widely adopted as the term used to describe all people of African descent, it was used primarily in a narrower sense to describe persons with dark complexions. The partially effaced comment on the Miss Bronze program captures a moment of double consciousness in which a black person rejected dark skin and then self-censored the judgment.

American blacks usually divide the range of complexions into three parts: light, brown, and dark. Studies that have been attentive to this categorization, rather than discussing colorism in terms of the two categories of light and dark skin, have found that the colorist hierarchy is not a simple one. Privilege within black communities was not distributed in steadily increasing increments according to skin tone. A recent study by Edwards, Carter-Tellison, and Herring based on 1992–1994 survey data found that medium-brown African Americans, regardless of gender, had spouses with higher incomes than dark-skinned or light-skinned African Americans.[13] The incomes of the spouses of brown-skinned persons, however, were only slightly higher than the incomes of spouses of black persons with light skin. Dark-skinned men and women were unlikely to be married to spouses with high incomes. This pattern points to an often overlooked finding of earlier research on skin color, the popularity of the middle brown position. Drake and Cayton's classic study of a black Chicago community in the 1930s documented a widespread rejection of dark skin yet noted the popularity of medium-brown skin.[14] Light women won the beauty contests, and they were most certainly favored in mass-produced entertainment, but medium brown was a popular color in everyday African American assessments. The concept of double consciousness, when interpreted as a conflicted acceptance and critique of a color hierarchy, can explain the popularity of brown skin tones. Brown is neither the most disparaged position in the color hierarchy nor the position that is closest to white.

The tension of double consciousness also manifests itself in a system of representation in which dark skin represents authenticity and light skin represents privilege.[15] Thus, double consciousness sets up two competing hierarchies: one that values light skin for its closeness to whiteness and another that values dark skin as a more authentic form of black embodiment. To some extent, these meanings rest on biologically based understandings of race in which dark skin represents genetic racial purity. They also rest, however, on longstanding patterns, with origins in the slavery era, during which whites granted greater privileges to black persons whose lighter skin spoke of their white ancestry.[16] After slavery, lighter skinned blacks often consolidated and perpetuated their light skin privilege through processes of social exclusion. Arising from this history and its perpetuation in contemporary black social life and social institutions, conflicts surrounding skin color in black beauty contests were often framed in terms of the tension between light-skinned privilege and dark-skinned authenticity.

Complexion and Conflict in Miss Bronze

When the Miss Bronze judges selected the dark-skinned Cynthia Badie as the first northern California Miss Bronze in 1961, they signaled that the colorist regime had ended. Badie entered the contest after a black photographer noticed her and encouraged her to join. She guessed that he had invited her because he wanted dark women to be included in the contest. I asked her if she had any trepidation about entering a contest in which most of the other women would have lighter skin. She answered that she "never even thought about it. No. Never did." She had grown up with an awareness of skin color hierarchies and was even teased by family members about her dark skin. She said, "I used to be called 'Blackie' and all of that. And it didn't bother me because it was done in a joking way." But she also heard, within her family, that she was good-looking. "My aunt used to say, 'Oh you're black, but you're so cute!'" Furthermore, as a young woman, she took modern dance lessons from Ruth Beckford, a regal and dark-skinned woman. Beckford gave her an image of dark-skinned beauty.

The 1961 contest challenged colorist hierarchies, but after this beginning, the contest returned to the long-established pattern of crowning light-skinned winners in black beauty contests. The winners in 1962, 1963, and 1964 had light skin tones. Each contestant in the Miss Bronze pageant knew that skin color was an important element of her appearance that could lead her to being judged as beautiful or flawed, a perfect representative of the race or not. They stood before an integrated panel of judges and a primarily black audience and made their own estimations of how they would likely be assessed by dominant and African American beauty standards. In the 1960s, in nationally dominant typologies, light-skinned black women were exotic types. We can see how this system of representation worked in the life of Janice Scott, a black woman with a light complexion who competed in the Miss Bronze pageant.[17] A child of a solidly middle-class Bay Area black family, Scott had ballet and piano lessons throughout her childhood. As a teenager, her social activities were strictly supervised by her parents. Scott became a model who received bookings for lunch-hour fashion shows through a modeling agency that hired her as its only nonwhite model. The agency assigned her to clients who requested models with sex appeal. Scott explained, "I guess more than anything I wanted to be the All-American ingénue type, but my look was not that." A designer told her to "stop trying to be something you're not. . . . Accept your look and go with it because that's you." In an all-white context, positioned by a white system of representation, her tan skin color signified racial mixture and meant that the strictly raised, hometown young woman was not All-American. She was exotic. In the context of the Miss Bronze contest, however, light skin was not exotic. Instead, it spoke, correctly or not, of her class position and of privileges associated with her status, and threw into question her authenticity as a representative black beauty queen. Scott was comfortable onstage and felt that it was possible that she would do well in the contest. The night of the pageant she was stunned and furious when a darker woman was crowned the winner. In the weeks before the contest, the press had described the winner as "lovely," but Scott could only describe her as "the least attractive girl in the contest."

> I had been out there and I knew [balls up her hand into a soft raised fist] that this Black Power thing was in . . . and that they had made that decision because they thought that was the right thing to do. . . . My mother . . . and my father and all my friends, they all thought, "Well, this is a rip-off because they didn't pick the prettiest person." . . . I knew that there were other factors involved.

Scott had internalized a colorist hierarchy that had long benefited women like her, yet during the mid 1960s, colorism was increasingly the focus of public critique. While Miss Bronze contestants wearing formal gowns rode in motorcade parades through the black neighborhoods of Berkeley, California, Black Panther Party members sold newspapers on the same thoroughfares proclaiming "black is beautiful" and helped to transform the way many would see beauty. In this context, white judgments of beauty were increasingly irrelevant, and traditional black standards were contested. This contestation formed the context in which the judges made decisions, audiences viewed the contest and supported or were angered by its outcome, and contestants anticipated whether they would be selected to be a queen. Beliefs that light skin was the prettiest were directly challenged by celebrations of dark skin as not only the most authentically black skin tone, but the most beautiful.

Linda Jones was a very light-skinned woman who entered the Miss Bronze pageant in the mid 1960s with confidence. She did not win. I asked her if she was surprised by the outcome. She was somewhat surprised, but conceded that the winner was "the perfect Miss Bronze."

"She was a kind of a pretty color . . . nice figure and nice smile. And so she just kind of fit a Miss Bronze image on the outside," remarked Jones.

"Pretty color?" I asked. "Was she a brown-skinned girl? Lighter skin?" She described the winner to me by matching her skin tone to that of an earlier winner. Her skin color was light, but she was darker than Jones. She continued,

> I guess if you're going to pick a Miss Bronze winner I—for me, I mean, I didn't, I never felt it should be judged on color. I feel like a Miss Bronze could be any color. But if you're getting really technical, I guess they felt she reflected the right color to represent Miss Bronze.

Jones saw herself as too light to have been considered the perfect Miss Bronze. Seeking to explain the outcome of the contest, she reached for the word *technical*. Technically, she seems to suggest, a representative black beauty queen should meet certain physical specifications of beauty and of blackness. Another very light former contestant described herself as a "tragic mulatto" in the contest who could not win because of the pale color of her skin. By the mid 1960s, beauty's definition had expanded to include a range of skin tones. Light-skinned women continued to be identified as beauties, but especially light-skinned women were unlikely to be chosen as black beauty queens. In an era of heightened black consciousness, a woman who could be mistaken for white could not be celebrated as an ideal representative of the race.

Complexion (and All of That) and Conflict in Miss Bronze

Belva Davis noted that she developed the contest to address issues of "complexion and all of that." Color is one element or signifier in a system of representing race, gender, and class and, within black communities, skin color is seen and read alongside a woman's hair texture, hair length, body type, and style of moving in ways that mark her racially and position her socially. Just as light skin could call into question a black women's black racial authenticity, hair textures, body types, and ways of moving that were associated with whites could lead others to see her as less black. This section continues to look at color, but views it in the context of two bodily characteristics that a woman could control: her hair and the way she moved.

In African American neighborhoods in the 1960s, small charm schools opened that offered young women lessons in the techniques of middle-class feminine deportment. Historian Laila Haidarali argues that the demand for black charm schools coincided with the growth of opportunities for black women in formerly white female occupations that resulted from Civil Rights Movement victories against discrimination in employment.[18] The Miss Bronze pageant organizers sent all contestants to a charm school to learn the arts of middle-class female embodiment. Davis' vision of the pageant was that it could be both a showcase for beautiful black women and an institution that transformed black women by giving them what she called "basic life skills . . . how to walk, how to sit, how to eat in a restaurant." In her view, this mode of deportment had no necessary relationship to race or to color. Miss Bronze contestants were trained to be what Julie Bettie has described as middle-class performers.[19] The acquisition of these skills became problematic for a few contestants. Given that multiple obstacles prevented most blacks from acquiring the economic foundation of middle-class status, there was a great deal of ambivalence among blacks regarding middle-class performances. In the 1960s, black working-class consciousness found frequent popular expression through ridicule or disparagement of "bourgeois" or "bougie" blacks.[20]

The charm school short course required that the Miss Bronze contestants master a new way of walking. At first, the walk felt unnatural to each one who learned it, although almost all accepted it, in the end, as a more sophisticated way to move. It was, in the context of its period, a stylized performance of middle-class femininity, taught as a skill that was necessary for black women who were being groomed to enter formerly white glamour positions. The walk distinguished the polished Miss Bronze contestants from their peers outside of the contest. This became problematic for one contestant, Carol Johnson.

Johnson was a brown-skinned woman whose father was a manual worker. She was in the audience at a Miss Bronze pageant, witnessed the crowning of a dark-skinned Miss Bronze and was astonished. She had never seen a public celebration of black women of all shades. She later entered the Miss Bronze pageant as a contestant. She described what she felt was the ease with which some of the light-skinned contestants performed the beauty queen role and described, by way of contrast, her own awkwardness performing the motions required of a beauty pageant contestant. She described the charm school lessons as excruciatingly difficult and recalled, "I wanted to cry because I kept saying 'I can't do this. This is unnatural for me! I'll never be able to do this . . . .' I just thought it was torture."

We can trace a colorist, raced, classed, and gendered economy of symbols in Johnson's experience of learning to walk for the pageant. The pageant, she said, required that "I had to now have this poise and posture of 'everyone look at me' . . . and the scariness was, could you do it? And would people think that you were being pretentious and as the word back then 'bourgeois.' . . . Were you now being 'bougie?'" As she explained her experience of learning to walk like a beauty queen, she mentioned that at the same time, and as a consequence of having acquired a new walk, she cut off her long hair. Johnson's hair grew long and thick. She did not, in her words, have to straighten it. Straightening hair was so normative for black women of her era that women whose hair had natural tight curls "had" to straighten it. Her hair texture and length was rare among black girls. Long wavy hair, a characteristic associated with light-skinned, mixed-race women, was a mark of distinction for a brown-skinned young woman. Partly because black women whose racial mixture was recognizable in lighter skin or longer wavy hair, were often wealthier than those with darker skin or short, tightly curled hair, and partly because, regardless of wealth, black women with lighter skin or longer, wavier hair had more status within black communities, light skin color and wavy hair texture were associated with prosperity.[21] A history of an unequal distribution of wealth and status shaped the black public meaning of light skin, long hair, and wavy hair. Long hair diminished Johnson's working-class black authenticity. Her newly acquired stylized walk put further distance between Johnson and her friends. To minimize that growing social distance, she cut her hair. Common short hair could compensate for her extraordinary new walk.

Johnson was aware that walking smoothly in high heels was associated with a middle-class performance, a performance that conflicted with her actual social position. It was also a performance that she assumed lighter skinned women accomplished with greater ease. She described the apparent comfort of women whose color destined them to be "somebody." "It was your destiny to be somebody," she said. "And you were somebody because you were light skinned, unfortunately."

I asked Stephani Swanigan, a light-skinned woman from a middle-class background who was crowned Miss Bronze in 1963, about the experience of walking in heels for the contest. "Walking prissy down a ramp," she recalled "was not in my tool kit at the time." Like Johnson, Swanigan acquired the skill as part of her training for the contest. I asked if it was in any way problematic for her to acquire these new skills of self-presentation. "I really didn't think much of it," she said. "For me, that's what went along with being a participant." Several of her closest friends were in the contest and they acquired the new walk along with her. She left no group behind as she perfected the new walk.

Johnson could see the ease with which contestants like Swanigan stepped into the role of beauty queen and attributed it to skin color. What I see is that class and color were often intertwined and provided a readily available frame for black women to understand their experiences. Historically, colorism determined the actual distribution of wealth in black communities. By the 1960s, color was no longer as determinative of class, and light-skinned beauty contestants did not always win beauty contests. Nonetheless light-skinned women, especially middle-class ones, could easily assume that they would be perceived as attractive, and color and class continued to be connected in popular interpretive frames. The Miss Bronze pageant organizers attempted to uncouple race from beauty and color from class. They succeeded in producing pageants in which women of a variety of shades were recognized as beautiful and they taught all of them to walk like beauty queens. As I have shown, the contestants took up the role of beauty queen with varying degrees of comfort, and their degrees of comfort were in some, but not all, cases affected by the color of their skin.

Although few of the Miss Bronze participants or organizers that I interviewed actively participated in organized black political activism, all saw themselves as integrationists committed to ending racist barriers through collective efforts to support individual achievements. During the contest's question-and-answer segment, Swanigan was asked about her hopes for social change. She thought her response contributed to her success in the contest. She said that she hoped for a day when there would not have to be a separate contest for black women. Her sentiment aligned with beliefs held by the organizers of the contest, who established Miss Bronze as a challenge to segregation. Belva Davis always included whites among the judges. Her motives for recruiting white judges were both practical and ideological. The presence of white judges ensured that contestants would meet representatives of white beauty contests and white-owned media, and thus she created opportunities for participants in Miss Bronze. Yet Davis also saw the integrated composition of the judging panel as a model for the white contests. Although she sought to include white judges, Davis did not capitulate to nationally dominant standards when she and her staff recruited women for the contest. The Miss Bronze pageant did not end the black beauty contest pattern of crowning black women with light complexions, but it shook its foundation by expanding the definition of black beauty. Women with dark skin were actively recruited to enter the contest, dark and medium-brown women wore the crown, and women who might not be recognized as black never won.

Conclusion

When Belva Davis built the northern California Miss Bronze contest, she hoped to challenge racial exclusion outside of the contest and colorism within it. The transformation in black consciousness that emerged from the Civil Rights and Black Power Movements made it possible for her to realize that goal in part. By crowning dark-skinned beauties, she enabled dark-skinned women to see themselves as others saw them, and to see themselves as beautiful. Audiences watching the pageant, especially during the years when dark women were crowned, saw a system of representation that challenged traditional color hierarchies. Black was beautiful, elegant, poised, and wholesome. At the same time, a stage full of African American women of a variety of shades also challenged the system of representation that excluded light-skinned women from authenticity. The contest provided a showcase for new ways of thinking about the meaning of skin tones.

During the early decades of the twentieth century, Marcus Garvey's massive Universal Negro Improvement Association not only challenged white racism, but encouraged blacks to celebrate the beauty of dark skin. The Civil Rights and Black Power Movements of the 1960s and early 1970s similarly stimulated popular black discussion of black beauty standards and created the climate in which dark-skinned women could win the Miss Bronze title as both the popular and the judges' favorite. Regardless of whether social movements engage in deliberate cultural work, they almost always have cultural consequences, reshaping the meanings associated with racialized and gendered bodies. When social movements decline, the meanings that they supported weaken or perhaps are retained in partial or distorted forms. Changes in preferences for skin color within black communities have not proceeded in a linear fashion, from an unquestioned disparagement of dark skin to a privileging of dark skin tones. Nor has there been a steady diminution in the significance of skin tone. Instead, African American skin color preferences have vacillated over time and have been shaped, to a significant degree, by social movements. Black women's bodies have been the focus of this long-running and ultimately unsettled African American debate about the meaning and significance of the color of skin.

6 Caucasian, Coolie, Black, or White?

Color and Race in the Indo-Caribbean Diaspora

Aisha Khan

IN CHAGUANAS, TRINIDAD, THERE IS NOW A PERMANENT SITE called the *Divali Nagar* (Divali Village), erected in 1986 as a temporary exhibition to commemorate Indian culture in and contribution to the Caribbean. Each year the Nagar has an exhibition theme. In 1987, when I first visited it, the theme was the Ramayana, the ancient Hindu epic of the trials and adventures of the prince, Rama, his wife, Sita, and the arch-demon Ravana. This choice of theme was not surprising, because "Ramleela" plays have been reenacted throughout Trinidad soon after indentured Indians arrived there in 1845. As with all culturally distinguished groups in Trinidad—Indian, African, Levantine (Syrian-Lebanese), Chinese, Amerindian, "French Creole," "Spanish," and British descent—the public presentation of selected cultural traditions (typically music, arts, and certain religious practices) has constituted, since the postwar nationalist period and political independence (in 1962), the mainstay representations of group identity, uniqueness, and political constituency. In short, the definitive delineation of "we culture," as local parlance phrases it, is in part the basis upon which the state defines its national identity, and also partly the basis upon which voting blocks, organized according to cultural heritages that indicate racial–ethnic ancestries, press for the resources and opportunities of state patronage.

In accordance with its Ramayana exhibition theme, this particular *Divali Nagar* boasted a giant effigy of Ravana, "Rawan" in Trinidad, waiting, as the epic tale goes, for his final comeuppance. Although neither this theme nor the effigy of Rawan were surprising in themselves, what I found particularly striking about Rawan, besides his size and high-top tennis shoes, was his color. In classical Indian color classification, Rawan is said to have dark skin. He is

95

Figure 6.1 Effigy of Rawan, Chaguanas, Trinidad
SOURCE: Photo by author.

conventionally portrayed as black, dark blue, dark green, or some combination thereof. This contemporary Trinidadian Rawan was *pink* (Figure 6.1), and
quite deliberately so. Pink is certainly not the only color in the many generations of portraying Rawan in Trinidad, but it signified for this Rawan a neutral racial identity. Although other colors—even shades of brown—might be
chosen, his portrayal as black would have the possibility of conveying highly
charged, preferably avoided racial messages in this former British colony, with
its still-vigorous ideological legacy of a color–race hierarchy dividing European
"white" from African "black." The structure and meaning of race has had a great

deal of interdisciplinary scrutiny by scholars of colonial societies and of post-colonial conditions, but the problem of color, its meanings, and its hierarchical arrangement have not had equal scholarly attention, especially considering the relationship of color to the concept of race.

Considering color in the Caribbean's South Asian diaspora directs us not to rest with a discussion of "Why rarely, if ever black?," but also to ask, "Why pink?" It is these two queries that this chapter pursues. My argument is that color categories applied to human groups in colonial societies of the Americas necessarily are institutionalized into practices of colorism that cannot be distinguished from racism in terms of the ideological work that colorism performs. This is the case even when color is ostensibly decoupled from race. Yet, as this example from Trinidad will show, the power of color to convey particular messages can come as much from color's variable meanings including ostensible neutrality, as from its definitiveness. Our contemporary Rawan's coloring in pink both skirts and underscores a broader, abiding discourse about shades of difference in diaspora.

Indo-Trinidadians and the African/European Axis of Race and Color

From the earliest days of colonial rule in many societies of the Americas, the social and moral order was based in part on ranked gradations of attributes such as skin color, hair texture, and facial features that embodied the right as well as the might of rule. In most cases, the intention of those who devise color and race categories is to present fixed and indubitable identities as a means of maintaining social order (assigning certain qualities and proclivities, legally and socially disciplined, to each racial and color segment of the society). However, these descriptions and presumptions in fact fluctuate according to particular moments in political and social history. Hence, such terms as, for example, *mestizo* ("mixed") in Peru, *black* in the U.S., *indio* (*Indian*) in the Dominican Republic, and *branco* (*white*) in Brazil, take on different meanings in different historical and cultural moments. They can invoke immutable or mutable traits, negative or positive valences. Yet each particular context of use generally establishes a hegemonic interpretation that prevails as the authoritative mode of expression. In other words, in any given circumstance, not all fluctuations and variability are equal.

Indian immigration to the British West Indies began in 1838 and lasted until 1917, as part of the British colonial government's post-emancipation indentured labor scheme. Indentured ("coolie") laborers were shipped from India and contracted to work on Caribbean sugar plantations. The greatest number, approximately 239,000, went to what was then British Guiana (Guyana today) and the next greatest, about 144,000, went to Trinidad (today Indo-Trinidadians constitute about 40% of the population). By the time the first indentured laborers arrived in Trinidad (on May 30, 1845), a local system of stratification was already in place, organizing social classes and the majority "races," European and African, along with the "colors" of persons these "races" generated, into a hierarchical social, legal, and moral order. The model is an ideological grid in which race-based and color-based identity categories are concurrent: Cultural citizenship, or modes of belonging in both colony and independent nation-state, have been based to a significant degree on ideas about biological inheritance, in which founding ancestral progeny are viewed as springing from African and European progenitors, and a vertical color continuum lexically marks gradations of shades of black–white mixes, notably "brown" and "red." Indeed, there is, for example, no local race or color lexicon for mixed offspring of Indian and European parents, and there is only one term—*dougla*—for Indian-African offspring.[1]

In Trinidad, then, as in much of the Caribbean, race is both biologically heritable (insofar as it represents, and is represented by, family lineage) and socially heritable (insofar as it represents, and is represented by, class position, which in turn is ascertained in part by particular kinds of behavior and values). Hence, for Afro-Trinidadians, the color term *brown* historically has served as both a category of racial identity and a category of middle-class status. For Euro-Trinidadians, what I have called the "ethnic modifiers"[2] *French Creole* and *Trinidad white* historically have served as categories of racial identity (in this case, not-quite-white, as in mixed somewhere along the genealogy) and also as categories of class status, in which contemporary French Creole and Trinidad white can (although not always) signal downward mobility over time. Downward mobility, in turn, may have cultural implications for being associated with certain kinds of lifestyles (e.g., dissipation) or membership in the lower class.

These examples show the ways race, color, and culture (through notions of class and its presumptive values and behaviors) are articulated in reference to Trinidad's two ancestrally foundational populations. Under colonial rule, European (British, French) cultural hegemony predominated, where, if *Creole* meant originative peoples, it also meant peoples ideally guided by and measured against the principles and assumptions of European bourgeois cultural standards and values—in theory, adoptable by properly assimilated (brown) Afro-Trinidadians (as opposed to black, who historically have been indexical of the working class). Under the 1962 postindependence flag of the republic, these bourgeois standards and values essentially remained intact, although wielded by an Afro-Trinidadian middle-class intelligentsia who assumed governing authority from the British. The precepts of the racial foundational axis and the color terminology of the preindependence era continued to marginalize postindependence Indo-Trinidadians. As late additions to the new forms of diversity that Caribbean colonial labor projects were viewed as setting in motion, as lexically elided in terms of belonging based on racial and color categories, and as culturally "foreign" in terms of ancestral heritage and worldviews, Indo-Trinidadians face a particular kind of political and social challenge.

Concerned with establishing an international presence free of subaltern associations, the first postindependence government as well as the governments of today grapple with ways to project national identity through ideologies that valorize appropriate (hence, selected) cultural traditions. Although things European have gone the way of the white population (currently, 0.6 percent of the total)—that is, giving way to postindependence emphasis on things Afro-Trinidadian, especially such defined Afro-Trinidadian traditional heritage as calypso and steelpan music, Carnival celebration, and Orisha religion—things Indian have had a more precarious place in the nationalist narrative.

As a lexically unmarked, culturally foreign, relatively new addition to the Creole society, Indo-Trinidadians' presence, paradoxically, is registered, in a sense, by their absence: They are figured into the mix that is the Trinidadian nation as a juxtaposed element, rather than an amalgamated one. So, for example, although Carnival symbolizes authentically merged African and European traditions and is thus a germinal dimension of this "rainbow" country, Indo-Trinidadian contributions to the rainbow are typically seen as externally rather than locally generated. The state's embrace of Hindus' Divali and Phagwa religious festivities, Muslims' Eid religious festivities, Indian Arrival Day celebrations, and bhajan music (Hindu hymns) figure in the national portrait, but as adjunct practices rather than progenitor practices. The conventional representation of Trinidad's foundational axis has ruled out Indo-Trinidadians being true Creole (originator) members of Trinidadian society and relegates them, even today, in terms of state management of the cultural heritage that represents the Trinidadian heterogeneous, *callaloo* nation, to the simultaneous status of both culturally foreign and excluded, and culturally familiar and included.

This phenomenon of absent-presence means that Indo-Trinidadians are necessarily a part of the Afro-Euro race and color hierarchy. Although distanced from it, Indo-Trinidadians are still implicated within it because hierarchies are defined according to what and who they leave out as much as what and who they enclose within. In other words, visibility can be apparent in a number of ways. Their ideological exclusion from the foundational moment of Trinidadian society removes them from the racial equation of Trinidadian nationalism (Afro + Euro = authentic, Creole Trinidadian); however, they are not shorn of the meaning of, nor outside the consequences of, color and race. Indians' long association with color hierarchies and racial identities, on the subcontinent and in the diaspora (evident in colonial reportage, academic scholarship, and contemporary diasporic imaginaries as well as perhaps in their own indigenous texts), lend color and race an ambiguity rather than an absence. The elastic quality of color and race as it has been associated with Indians allows Indo-Trinidadians to claim, reject, and revise simultaneously the racial hierarchies that continue to undergird Trinidadian society as they struggle for rights and recognition as a constituency that matters in national representation. When applied to the Indo-Caribbean, as elsewhere, the problematic of color is that color designations can confirm, deny, or equivocate about the racially charged contexts that give color meaning. We must, then, understand the pink color of our *Divali Nagar's* Rawan within a particular sociohistorical and cultural moment, which includes creative symbolic imagery on the part of those who designed this particular effigy. Pink in this context is able to express a desire to avoid association with key ideological legacies: the colonial legacy of the inferior blackness of Africans and Indians, and the postindependence legacy of the ascendance (superiority) of the blackness of contemporary rule. Expressed, as well, is a desire to mediate for themselves, the ancient legacy (claimed and denied) of images of dark (black, blue, green) demons and other disrupters of social and moral order.

Emigrating from the subcontinent, Indian indentured laborers understood themselves, and were understood by others in British West Indian former slave plantation societies, in accordance with identities significantly characterized by certain tropes about ancestry, notably caste and other aspects of religion, and language. Although Indians, Africans, Europeans, and the rest did not possess identical images about each other or the same forms of cultural understanding of each other, certain themes were dominant in the racial discourse and cultural capital of colonial Europe with which everyone in a given society, like Trinidad, would have had a degree of familiarity—through conversation, moral codes, newspapers, laws, and instruction from the church. Informing the monumental tropes of caste, religion, and language, and thus contributing to representations of Indian identity, was the valorization of Indian "Great Traditions" and "high culture" that contradicted, and thus complicated, images of the subaltern "coolie" laborer. The perceived contrast (in the colonial gaze) between the two—the people and civilization that produced Great Traditions and high culture, and the people of the "loin cloth and a pot of rice"[3]—created an ideological binary that arguably produced more puzzles about the identity, character, and capabilities of Indians, a binary between what I describe as lofty versus base.

Last, although observers of India under the British Raj were no strangers to calculations about Indians' place in cultural evolution, and hence their location in racial and color typologies, in colonial societies in the Americas, where phenotype was a key element of rule, racial and color types (of group and person) took on a certain urgency as Indians, and then Indo-Caribbeans, competed with various sectors of labor, primarily formerly enslaved Afro-Caribbeans, partly on the basis of character distinctions ostensibly reflected in racial and color ancestries. Levels of capability, skill, stamina, and suitability to a form of labor were parsed by colonial authorities and sugar estate owners according to perceived distinctions in appearance and behavior among Indian indentured laborers, and between them and Afro-Caribbeans. For example, although these nineteenth- and early twentieth-century discourses generally marked Indians as less able to endure hard physical labor than Afro-Caribbeans, Indians were nonetheless contracted to perform the agricultural work of a sugar colony; the darker and more "African-like" Madrassis were often unfavorably contrasted with Indians from Calcutta to the north who were, according to some, lighter in color and more tractable. The simultaneous appellations of *Aryan*-although-not-necessarily-Caucasian, *Caucasian*-but-generally-not-white, and *coolie*-frequently-black, were variously used to characterize Indian and Indo-Caribbean peoples.

To examine the meaning and significance of color, and color and racial hierarchies as they have been applied to and deployed among Indians in Trinidad, three interrelated contexts need to be explored: scholarly interpretations of ancient subcontinental forms of hierarchy, notably caste and what it might reveal about South Asian color ideologies; colonial discourse about the color of the colonized, notably Afro- and Indo-Trinidadians, in late-nineteenth-

and mid-twentieth-century Trinidad; and contemporary Indo-Trinidadians' engagement (and disengagement) with color hierarchies as they pursue the politics of cultural production and cultural citizenship, with, for example, such representations as our pink Rawan described earlier.

When we approach ambiguity and elasticity as a way of thinking about things that possess a logic and produce consequences rather than as passive or ineffectual conditions, ambiguity and elasticity render color a kind of floating signifier, a flexible symbol that is widely recognized but interpreted in different ways because of its capacity to deliver multiple messages and to be put to many uses. The logic, terms, assumptions, and ideologies that produce *color* (and *race, gender,* and so on) over time freight them with particular significance according to context and to the practices by which *color* is made intelligible and forceful. It is by now well recognized among scholars (including those in this volume) that hierarchical arrangements of phenotype categories are often an important element of the ideological apparatuses according to which unequal relations of power have been institutionalized and rationalized in stratified societies. Indo-Caribbeans, who constitute what I will call the *twice-colonized*— in India under the British and then in the British West Indies—present a rich case for examining the ways that a feature of identity (in this case, color), and related metaphors that code color, such as *coolie, Aryan,* and *Caucasian,* are categorized and interpreted as social facts with particular power to both assert and explain larger questions about cultural identity, history, and race.

When we return to our pink Trinidadian Rawan at the end of my discussion, we will have considered some key factors that might have prompted the message this effigy sends about not being black, and how the significance of this message came to be in this part of the world, not the least of which is the paradox of absence positing presence. As Sidney Mintz[4] observed half a century ago, perceptions of color in the Caribbean do not merely reflect observable phenotype; observed phenotype necessarily works in combination with many other factors. My aim is to show that (1) registering color is never based simply on empirical observations (the social value of color defines what we "see" and what it means) and (2) that although color hierarchies must work in tandem with other forms of hierarchy, such as race, color categories may in some cases be the principle idiom through which hierarchy is affirmed or denied, especially when direct reference to certain ways of thinking or speaking are socially stigmatized.[5] In sum, and perhaps counterintuitively, being left out of the Afro-Euro axis of Trinidadian society's ancestral origins and lexical mapping does not make color (or colorism) less significant among Indo-Trinidadians. The elasticity and ambiguity of Indo-Trinidadians' history of color and race has placed them in varied and shifting social locations. This does not represent vagueness in the sense of absence, but equivocation in the sense of multiple presences. *Caucasian, coolie, black,* and *white* each has its color codes which have shaped the varying criteria for Indo-Caribbeans' valuation and whose referents some scholars and broader communities trace back centuries.

Indian Ancestry, Type, and Phenotype

In the social science scholarship on South Asia there has been increasing attention to race and, to a lesser extent, color. As Susan Bayly recognizes, the "major element in the portrayal of colonial thought about Indian society is the theme of race . . . debates about the definition and significance of race were applied to an extraordinarily wide range of issues in contemporary science and social theory" (p. 167).[6] Scholars have posited that the exchanges between South Asian colonized and European colonizer fostered mutual co-optations and appropriations of one another's lifeworlds, if not regimes of rule.[7] John Rogers argues about early modern Sri Lanka:

> [N]ineteenth century racial ideology introduced striking changes, but it was not built on a blank slate. Ideas of difference with a quasi-biological character were already prevalent before the beginning of British rule, and many of the symbols and labels propagated in the name of racial ideology were drawn from earlier periods. On the other hand, modern racial ideology was selective in its appropriation of existing symbols and labels, and often used them in ways that fundamentally altered their meaning.[8]

Unequivocally phrased by Peter Robb, the question is whether Western race theory was potent among South Asians at home and abroad "because the theory was hegemonic, or because it fitted like a virus on the host cell, caste" (p. 44)?[9] In the Indo-Caribbean/Indo-Trinidadian context, these perceptions and the ideological work they undertake have always been conversations between colonizer and colonized, rather than simply invidious distinctions emanating from the subcontinent or superimposed onto "Indian reality."

Embedded in these questions is the evidence, and its interpretation, of racial and color thinking among precolonial South Asians. At the heart of this matter is the nature of the denotation *Aryan* and its categorical contrasts. Romila Thapur argues that the earliest distinction Aryans made between themselves and others was linguistic and, to a lesser extent, physical.[10] In the *Rg Veda*, the earliest of the Vedic texts (circa 1500 BCE), references to the *Dasa* or *Dasyu*, the local tribes conquered by Aryan speakers who viewed them as barbaric, are compared with demons, have black skin and flat noses, practice "black magic," are treacherous, do not perform the expected sacrifices, and speak an alien language. However, far from a dualistic model, degrees of variation in differences were important, such as political status, ritual status, and economic power.[11] Thapur concludes that "it is doubtful that the term *arya* was ever used in an ethnic sense."[12]

According to D. D. Kosambi, in Sanskrit the term *Dasyu* referred to "a hostile, non-Aryan people," whose *varna,* or "color" (only later coming to mean "caste") was *krsna,* or "black." This "distinguished them from the Aryans, and hence can only refer to their darker complexion, as contrasted with the lighter skin-colour of the newcomers [the Aryans]."[13] Taking the Harappan civilization as the harbingers of "civilization" in India, some scholars have suggested that "proto-Australoids" ("Mediterranean," "flat-nose and thick lips") mixed with indigenous peoples, "thus creating the Dravidians."[14] If Dravidians, through these ancestral origins, are dark, Aryans then represent subcontinental lightness. On the other hand, although the outstanding Aryan feature is linguistic, there is also "some doubt as to whether there were really Aryans at all."[15] Despite these dueling claims and interpretations, the legacy that their many centuries of study, by easterners and westerners alike, has been the creation of a veritable tradition of bipartite division of light/civilized/northern Aryan versus dark/uncivilized/southern Dravidian.

The concept of race itself changed dramatically from the late eighteenth century, "when theorists speculated about the distinguishing political and moral character of the so-called 'Aryan' and the non-'Aryan' races . . . rather than in predominantly evolutionary terms."[16] A Western version of the Aryan concept gained popularity in Europe in the nineteenth century because it was conducive to a scientific approach and was congruent with burgeoning nationalisms.[17] In developing what Tony Ballantyne calls "Company Orientalism," a "detailed and organized body of knowledge," the British East India Company fostered the work of such scholars as Sir William Jones, Max Muller, and Samuel Laing. Influential Victorian popularizers of "Aryanism," they shifted from classical sources for Indian historiography to local Indian texts, promoting the idea of a common Indo-European cultural heritage as well as a "Sanskritocentric" vision of Indian culture that "celebrated Sanskrit and the Vedas but decried contemporary [Indian] culture as debased and backward."[18] In India, Indians whose vested interests lay in British colonial rule relied on Aryanist ideology for their own advantage. Ballantyne quotes a Bengali journalist who wrote in 1874 in the *Indian Mirror* about the impact of scholars of Aryanism on Indian society: "[W]e were niggers at one time. We now become brethren."[19] Although I think we must allow the possibility that this writer was speaking ironically, in any case his remark underscores an additional point significant for our discussion. The "Hindoo" might be comparable with other Aryans in some fashion, but nineteenth-century British scholars reified differences between Indians and "other peoples under white domination"—for example, "Negroes," "Red Americans," and Australians, who could not possibly attain the accomplishments, as Laing put it in one 1862 lecture, of having produced the *Ramayana* or *Mahabharata*.[20]

Old World Discourse and New World Race Science

As Ballantyne observes, British colonial interpretations of India became increasingly racialized during the nineteenth century, but it was contested and reshaped to fit a number of other agendas. The theory of Aryan origins has been so powerful "because of its generality and flexibility."[21] In the early- to mid-twentieth-century United States, the legal system has been ambivalent about the correlation among Indians, whiteness, and Caucasian. In the Bhagat Singh Thind case of the mid-1920s, "Justice George Sutherland ruled that being Caucasian was not enough to be white."[22] At times when citizenship was considered favorable, the courts ruled that Indians were white because they were Caucasians and, therefore, naturalizable.[23] Even when citizenship was not viewed in positive terms, such as in a 1922 decision to deny citizenship to a Japanese national, the U.S. Supreme Court argued that *white* was synonymous with *Caucasian*. After decades of debate, in 1975 the U.S. Federal Interagency on Culture and Education classified people from the Indian subcontinent as "Caucasian/white," distinct from such "oriental Asians" as Chinese and Japanese. The next year, in 1976, the U.S. House of Representatives shakily concluded that "some Indians are Caucasian, and others are not," and that "not all Caucasians are white."[24] This resolution helped to preserve, among other things, the ambiguity and elasticity among Indians that race and color possess, both in diaspora and, by extension, in the "homeland."

Trinidad's frequently asserted population heterogeneity, along with its "types," have roots long before Trinidad's mid-twentieth-century struggles over political independence, nationhood, and citizenship. In his discussion of race "from Columbus to hip hop," Gary Taylor suggests that "modern whiteness began on July 31, 1498," when Columbus found in Trinidad "white people where he did not expect to find them." In this "Trinidadian moment [of] modern whiteness," Columbus wrote that "in contrast to Ethiopians" (sub-Saharan Africans), who were "black" and had hair "like wool," "these people of the island [Trinidad]," despite belonging to the same "clime" (latitude) as the Ethiopians, "are white, with long hair, and of yellow color." In the 1630s, a Spanish missionary in what is either present-day Panama or Colombia described Indians who were as "white and blonde" as Belgians. Regardless of whether this missionary also saw for himself what he described (possibly only on the hearsay of others), the apparent certainty on Columbus' part in identifying as "white" Amerindians in Trinidad and the wider Caribbean (he perceived white populations throughout the region) suggests that during this early period of New World colonization, "white" was a less exclusive designator of population type than it would be two centuries later when it became reserved for certain "northern" lineages of phenotype, language, and custom. During the sixteenth century, the Amerindian "complexion" was a "puzzle" that Columbus and his contemporaries like historian Peter Martyr felt needed to be explained.[25] By the eighteenth century, those other "Indians" would pose a puzzle about whiteness that continued to stimulate colonial attempts at typological solutions.

Generally speaking, by the nineteenth century, the puzzle about Caribbean racial and color categories was more or less solved. As part of a racial accounting schema with which we are familiar today, race and color categories organized the social order and the relations (at least ideologically, if not always in practice) between the two most salient founding ancestral "types" in the region—Afro and Euro—and these designations gave meaning and justification to local social hierarchies. Europeans were clearly owners of the category of whiteness, yet they were divided into various gradations of white that were mediated by class distinctions. Hence, authentic "whites" in Trinidad were British, Spanish, and French; suspect "whites" (that is, those tainted by proximity, both sexual and social, to nonwhites) were labeled "Trinidad white" or "French Creole." Continuing this logic of class signification, authentic "blacks" clearly belonged to an African heritage but, by definition, also to a grassroots heritage (poor and working class). Because color categories are social symbols rather than literal descriptions, those persons of African heritage who were able to claim membership among the middle class and elite were not "black" but "brown," regardless of whether they were genetically mixed with European ancestry. In both Euro and Afro cases, color comprised a readily recognizable palette according to which identity types were assigned, and at the same time each was mitigated by class. By contrast, the color and race, and thus identity of Indians in Trinidad (and the wider Caribbean) were more ambiguous, and, as explained earlier, to this day do not belong to the tripartite pyramid of white–brown–black, race–color–class arrangements constituted by Afro and Euro.

When Indians' point of reference is India, they are not "white," they are "Aryan," they are "Caucasian," they are "Asiatic." Caucasian/Aryan/Asiatic are associated with Brahmanical (that is, high-culture) Hinduism. As indentured immigrants, however, Indians are in the colonial gaze even further from "white," becoming, as "coolies," increasingly "black," both because of and irrespective of their claims to Hinduism, in the estimation of bourgeois sectors of Trinidadian society. In India, colonial racial designations were varied and shifted with locality and religious practice, the latter representing level of development, or civilization. On Caribbean plantations, even with acknowledgment of the "multiplicity of Indian languages" there,[26] the classificatory diversity of the subcontinent was collapsed into a minimum of identities—notably, variations on an oppositional contrast between Calcutta/Madras, north/south, Aryan/Dravidian, elite/peasant, docile/wild, enlightened/superstitious. These identities reflected the organization of plantation production and its need for justification; they thereby emphasized the blackness and precarious barbarism, if not savagery, of the coolie laborer. Notwithstanding the distinctions British colonizers in India made between Hindus and Muslims, these stereotypes would follow both (as "coolies") onto the plantations of the Caribbean. In this context of labor tensions and subordinate class position, religious belief and practice in Trinidad take on both pejorative associations and alleged subversive qualities, significantly displacing any residual admiration of Indian high culture. And it is this loss of culture that darkens.

Once in the Caribbean, a lofty Hinduism became the base *Hindoo.* Although Indo-Trinidadians were not specifically presented as distinguished by class position, their perceived industriousness, restrained temperament, and incongruous, "oriental" clothing of turbans, *orhni* (women's head scarf), and *dhoti* (men's pantaloons), for example, all spoke to an exoticism that, if inferior to European civilization, still managed in the colonial gaze to evoke some measure of cultural accomplishment. By 1931, reports like that of A. Hyatt Verrill could still affirm that "many [Hindus] still adhere to their native customs and costumes, and add a most picturesque Oriental touch. . . ."[27] As coolie laborers or their agricultural progeny, Indo-Trinidadians did not possess quite sufficient picturesqueness to claim unambiguously the high culture and lofty genealogy of genuine "orientals." Commentaries from outside observers generally reflect an implicit comparison between Indian immigrants and what is imagined about the Indian subcontinent; the foil is another (better) kind of Indian rather than another (similar or worse) kind of uncivilized laborer in the New World.

The articulated discourses of class and race are interwoven such that few observations of these sorts can be taken at face value, given the multiple implicit assumptions they contain. In his 1887 "Caribbees" travel memoir, for example, William Agnew Paton says, "Certainly, everything and everybody I beheld were strange enough to warrant such a confusion of [East and West] localities in my mind. The cooly men . . . except for their blackness, their faces are characteristically European. Their features are the features of thin and emaciated Italians, Frenchmen, Englishmen—in a word, Caucasians."[28] Once again, this time in the New World, we see the enigma of Indians' disconcerting cultural exoticism, palpably conspicuous in phenotype, for Paton and many others both reassuring and incongruent. Culture and phenotype or race are mutually shaped, with Western European types constituting a touchstone; as culture becomes stranger, cultural affinities can also be renounced. For example, referring to Indo-Trinidadians' general comportment, late Victorian traveler Alfred Radford writes of coolies in Trinidad, "were they not black, I could easily have taken them for great gentlemen." Clearly not Caucasian, or even near Caucasian in Radford's estimation, it could not matter how "proud" and "civilized" these "coolies" also seemed to him.[29] *Black* bespeaks of their social position (disdained immigrants) and their social class (unlettered laborer); thus, they are walking contradictions of their cultural accomplishments. Local nineteeth- and early-twentieth-century discussions of Indo-Trinidadians, for example in the press, tended to highlight the negative not only by implicitly emphasizing their alien appearance, but by using such imagery as "dark" and "uncivilized," thereby underscoring either Indo-Trinidadians' inferiority to (middle class, brown) Afro-Trinidadians or the commonalities between them. Whether Indo-Trinidadians were worse than Afro-Trinidadians or equivalent depended on the social class of the Afro-Trinidadian referent, as well as the particular issue or controversy at hand. Labor and immigration, for example, were for decades particularly heated issues between Indo and Afro, stoked by the divide-and-rule tactics of British colonial authority.

The Past in the Present?

Indians have been characterized, and have characterized themselves, as having carried their cultural heritage with them in diaspora, at the same time as they have been charged with leaving it behind in the homeland or bringing with them inauthentic versions, diluted by imperfect memory and unfavorable conditions for proper cultural practice. This mode of thinking has shaped other, more local, scholarly discourse and analysis. Explanations for the antagonism between Indo-Trinidadian and Afro-Trinidadian has crossed two centuries, but essentially form one consistent, if broad, narrative of cultural necessity. Trinidadian historiography and received wisdom draw from an array of hegemonic cultural motifs that constitute the building blocks of ideologies.

In preindependence Trinidad, Indo-Trinidadians' denotation as plantation labor underscored both the baseness and the loftiness of their authentic exoticism. In postindependence Trinidad, when cultural performance has become the modus operandi for "racial" groups' competition for state patronage, Indo-Trinidadians' authentic exoticism has been fraught with contradictory pressures: their need to belong appropriately to a Western, Afro-Christian nation while at the same time maintaining a sufficiently distinct (and thus perhaps dangerously extraneous) cultural profile. As a final consideration, distinctiveness begs the question of selection. Which versions of history and culture should represent the community, and who, then, is "the community"? Traditions of all sorts are, after all, not merely unearthed, they are also (more frequently) created. Indo-Trinidadians have taken these issues into their own hands for about a century, principally in the Indo-Trinidadian press and religious–cultural organizations, where "the enigma of arrival" (to borrow from V.S. Naipaul) has been solved—over and over again.

When Indo-Trinidadians are depicted in romantic imagery that emphasizes their superior evolution, or quaint customs, picturesque clothing, and spiritual propensities, the portrait is one that transcends daily life, suggesting a people not quite real, but more appropriate to storybooks. Subsumed within Trinidadian racial and color ideology, Indians became increasingly epitomized by the colonial hierarchy as coolie and as black, as opposed to the noble (or at least with majestic lineage) subcontinental Aryan or Caucasian, even as observers continued to notice "Caucasian" features. The cultural symbols of class position came to the fore, distinguishing Indo-Trinidadian from Afro-Trinidadian in structural as well as phenotypic terms. The closer to manual labor and economic fragility Indians/Indo-Trinidadians have been, the greater their similarities to grassroots Afro-Trinidadians (the "folk," the "black"), and thus the greater their differences from the ideal Afro-Trinidadian—middle class and refined (and, historically, "brown"), or at least further along the way toward those states.

Rarely, if ever, using the term *Caucasian,* Indo-Trinidadians today might certainly be heard discussing historical or religious subjects where the word *Aryan* comes into play. However, like other delicate matters in public discussion, connections between Aryan and whiteness, if made, would be qualified in favor of the national rhetoric of a *callaloo* modernity: tolerance of diversity, forward thinking, and democratic representation. More likely, *Aryan* would arise in discussion about ancient religious and linguistic history. The term *white* is a slightly different matter. It is typically treated with care in order to avoid what are today decried as colonial remnants of bigotry and backward thinking, but it is also common in everyday conversation. Among the most frequent contexts where "white" arises is in commenting on someone's appearance—phrased, for example, as an allegedly objective point of fact or humorous teasing, as when people from my field site in southern Trinidad emigrated in the 1990s to North America and returned after spending a period of time there without engaging in outdoor work, looking or behaving "white–white," as family and friends would note (that is, phenotypically lighter in shade and/or behaving in a more cosmopolitan, "modern"—read, upwardly mobile—way).

White, like all colors in color and race hierarchies, is cultural—in the sense of being a socially constructed interpretive category, in being a gauge of behavior and values, and in symbolizing the physical appearance of skin. In Indo-Trinidad, "light" or "clear" skin color are descriptors that do not necessarily raise questions about Indian cultural identity. In fact, many Indo-Trinidadians quietly prefer "light" or "clear" skin if an aesthetic choice must be made, but "Indianness" nonetheless must ideally be kept intact. Much like the prized color for a mate listed in personal ads for contemporary South Asian marriage arrangements is "wheatish" (see this volume), which asserts an Indian value system and is a hedge against dark-skinned respondents, many Indo-Trinidadians have stated to me that if given a choice, they would prefer an Indian (subcontinent or diasporic) partner to a white partner, and yet that person should be "light" or "clear." *Whitening* comes with class mobility and immigration; "white" is not unequivocally desirable because of what it represents for many Indo-Trinidadians: culture loss.

The position taken by Indo-Trinidadians today, by and large, is that "we culture," as it is locally phrased, has sustained the community in trying circumstances. The position taken by other Trinidadians, by and large, is that it is this culture that has insulated Indo-Trinidadians and thereby hindered their assimilation. However, these debates are not simply a matter of a neat cleavage into two stances. When engaging both colonial and postindependence discourses, Indo-Trinidadians began to place new kinds of emphases on the high culture of their ancient civilization, Great Traditions, authentic heritage, and the contentious interplay among *Caucasian, coolie, black,* and *white.* The importance of the distinctions among these, and *laborer* and *elite,* took on a different sort of insistence than it had on the subcontinent, despite the pervasiveness of the British Raj.

Summing Up: Ideological Hues

In his novel *The Enigma of Arrival* Naipaul[30] addresses a mystery of sorts, embarking on a quest for self as an Indo-Trinidadian in diaspora—that is, as a displaced person living abroad in England. The dilemma of diasporic liminality has raised existential questions for a number of Indo-Caribbean thinkers. As a stock Indo-Caribbean conundrum, Naipaul's arrival enigma resonates with another key form of Indian arrival enigmas. Not self-reflexive, but arguably still part of a quest for knowledge about the human condition, this form of enigma has to do with colonial representations of indentured immigrants and their progeny. Ideologies about the ways color, culture, and race are connected to form specific types, and the ways each particular type represents a kind of "Indian," both solidify and destabilize the certainty and singularity of a *coolie* identity. *Coolies* were not quite *white,* even if occasionally *Aryan,* and were not quite *black* when compared with Africans in Africa and with grassroots Afro-Caribbeans, and were not quite dismissible as *coolies* when linked to Great Tradition heritage, yet were primarily *black* and *coolie* when linked to indentured labor.

Although discussing a case far distant in time and place from contemporary Trinidad, Romila Thapur makes an interesting observation that is apropos of the Indo-Caribbean. She observes that "the most significant clue to assimilation lies not so much in the loss of ethnic identity as in participation in the sense of the past. There is the mutual appropriation of the past on the part of two groups where the group with the weaker historical tradition accepts the stronger tradition."[31] Living in a society riven with contests over the preeminence of particular cultural-historical traditions, and still steeped in the ideological legacy of colonial racial foundations based on African and

European forebears and a color hierarchy based on the permutations of black–brown–white that an Afro-Euro foundation generates, Indo-Trinidadians lie simultaneously both within and outside these social frames. The ambiguity of their own, ostensible colors in their New World history gives them certain relationships to the pink that was chosen to represent Rawan mentioned at the beginning of this chapter. This pink is elastic and ambiguous, and like all symbols, represents more than one message. Using this color, Indo-Trinidadians can communicate their racial neutrality and tolerance of difference with the message: We are not portraying villainous Rawan as black, nor as white, both of which carry their share of locally politicized ideological baggage. Rawan's pinkness can be, on the one hand, an announcement that Indo-Trinidadians are *outside* the Afro-Euro color hierarchy of black/white and its articulated hues. But this comment on their exteriority is not defeatist; rather, it agentively conveys a message of mediation (not being "racial") through the untypical linking of pink with the figure of traditionally black/dark Rawan. On the other hand, at the same time Indo-Trinidadians announce their *belonging* in the national portrait of callaloo rainbows by deploying this color as racially neutral, staying outside of the fraught legacy of color yet employing a temperate alternative color which creates a space for them in the discourse of nation and national identity.

Thus it is not the end of the story that Indo-Trinidadians are absent from the foundational image of Trinidad. Their lexical (color terminology) elision, along with alleged cultural exoticism, mean that they can engage this absence in ways that make their presence visible, by creating, if you will, a pink space—neither "Caucasian," "coolie," "black," nor "white"—for themselves where marginality can highlight what is not at the center. If this pink effigy were associated with Afro-Trinidadian cultural production (or Euro-Trinidadian, for that matter), the color would take on a different ideological hue, so to speak. It would recall the connection that pink has to white and black (as a variation of whiteness), because Afro-Trinidadians and Euro-Trinidadians are forever memorialized in Trinidad's racial accounting of Afro-Euro foundations. Connected to things Indian, this pink effigy conveys several messages: We Indo-Trinidadians will avoid possible charges of insensitivity and "being racial" by not portraying Rawan as black (despite his traditional, subcontinental depiction); we can choose pink as an alternative color because our being external to the Afro-Euro axis lends pink a symbolic neutrality when deployed by Indo-Trinidadians that it is not likely to possess in conjunction with African or European forebears; and we can, simultaneously, both comment on our absence from the Afro-Euro foundational axis of the Trinidadian nation and assert our presence within it. Paradoxically, Indo-Trinidadians can affirm their social belonging with the reminder that they are, in the terms of color and race, outside of that belonging.

7 The Dynamics of Color

Mestizaje, Racism, and Blackness in Veracruz, Mexico

Christina A. Sue

THE LITERATURE ON RACE RELATIONS HAS SHOWN that racial and color categorization, racial consciousness, national ideologies, and patterns of discrimination have developed very differently in Latin America than in the United States. The distinction has been characterized as a system based on a "mark of color" versus a "mark of origin."[1] Yet, despite the supposed importance of skin color gradations in Latin America, we know little about the discursive and analytical meaning of color on an everyday level. In the case of Mexico, scholars have noted sensitivity to color differences only in passing. Moreover, when the issue of discrimination is addressed, the focus is on the division between whites, *mestizos* ("mixed-race"[2] individuals), and Indians. This divide homogenizes *mestizos* at the expense of analyzing the dynamics of color *within* this population. Given the fact that racial dynamics in Latin America largely manifest in terms of color differentiation, the analysis of color dynamics within the *mestizo* category is of utmost importance.

In this chapter I discuss Mexicans' everyday conceptions of color as they relate to the national ideologies of *mestizaje* (race mixture) and race blindness,[3] as well as conceptions of blackness. My analysis draws on ethnographic fieldwork, 112 semi-structured interviews, and five focus groups conducted during 2004–2005 in the twin cities of Veracruz and Boca del Rio. Veracruz was the major port of entry and incorporation of African slaves to the plantations in Mexico.[4] In these urban cities, there is a broad range in phenotypic characteristics and diversity among the *mestizo* population. These factors make it an ideal site for studying the intersecting issues of race, color, race mixture and blackness.[5] For my sample, I selected respondents who varied in terms of color, class, and gender. After observing how Veracruzanos use color descriptors in everyday discourse, I classified the respondents into the color categories of *güero/a* or *blanco/a* (white), *moreno claro/a* (light brown), *moreno/a* (medium brown), *moreno oscuro/a* (dark brown), and *negro/a* (black). When possible, in the text, I use the Spanish version of the intermediate color terms (*moreno claro, moreno, moreno oscuro*) to retain the original meaning because the English translations are mere approximations. However, to provide for smoother translation, I do translate the terms *blanco* and *negro* to *white* and *black,* respectively.

National Ideology of *Mestizaje*

During the presidential regime of Porfirio Díaz (1877–1880, 1884–1911), racialized categories were incorporated into the nation-building process and the *mestizo* was deemed the national symbol of Mexico. After the Revolution, the ideology of *mestizaje* was further explicated and popularized by José Vasconcelos who, in response to Eurocentric racism, which proclaimed the racially mixed countries of Latin America to be doomed to third-world status, privileged mixture over purity. Since then, it has been widely assumed that this ideology has generated a national pride of mixed-race status among the citizens of Mexico, although we have little empirical research to support this assertion. Therefore, my aim in this section is to detail the contemporary popular understandings of the ideology of *mestizaje.*

Veracruzanos have appropriated the ideology of *mestizaje* as a strategy to whiten themselves within the mixed-race category. As opposed to viewing mixed-race status as an end in and of itself, individuals strive to lighten the skin color of future generations by choosing lighter-skinned partners. To demonstrate how central the idea of whitening through race mixture is to the culture, one only need focus on the colloquial phrase *limpiar* or *mejorar la raza* ("to clean" or "to better the race"), a term that embodies the whitening sentiment. This phrase is used to describe the seeking out of lighter-skinned partners so that the next generation will come out lighter—a motivation that can be seen in comments made by Jose,[6] a sixty-three-year-old *moreno oscuro* taco vender with African-origin features, who takes the idea of "bettering the race" very seriously. Jose openly expressed his preference for white women and, when asked if race mixture is a good or bad thing, replied as follows:

> Jose: Well, here in Mexico we do not consider it to be a bad thing because, as I told you before, my wife's color is "cleaning the race" a little bit, right? The children of my children will be white. They will not be my color.

Christina Sue (CS): But does this bother you?

Jose: No, of course not.

Similarly, his daughter, Vanesa, a *morena* with African-origin features, referred to how the need to "clean the race" affected her choice for a partner: "You have to clean the race, right? You need to lighten a little bit. That is why my partners have always been white." She even made similar comments about the inter-color status of her parents: "Sometimes we joke and tell my dad, 'With my mom, you refined your race because mom is white with a delicate nose.'"

As these examples demonstrate, much of the justification for avoiding darker-skinned partners lies in the hope of whitening the next generation. However, this avoidance is also constructed as a more immediate concern of personal preference. Maria, a fifty-four-year-old *morena oscura* daycare worker with African-origin features, who sometimes self-identifies as black, insisted that she accepts her color but is opposed to marrying a "very, very black" individual: "I am not racist, but people who are very, very, very black, very *morena,* I have found, do not share my pH [laughs], my chemistry." Although she referenced personal preference, she also shared her worries about the potential color of her offspring if she were to marry someone who was "black": "Yes. If I had a child, and the father was black and with me being black, how would the baby come out? I thought about that. . . . The poor babies would be called blackies. It happens with everyone in the daycare. One little one tells another, 'Get away blackie—you are very black, get away from here.'" Maria's concern may be rooted in her own childhood experience and her reported recollection of being repeatedly told she was an "ugly black."

In another middle-class family, the father is *moreno oscuro* with African-origin features, and the mother is *morena clara.* Their twenty-six-year-old daughter, Marisa, resembles her father. During a conversation among Marisa, her mother, and myself, when it became obvious that Marisa knew little about the slave history in the region, Marisa's mother intervened in the conversation. She lowered her voice substantially and began to educate Marisa about the history of the African-origin component in the local population. It appeared to be the first time this history had been discussed between them. As her mother finished, I asked Marisa if she would marry someone of another race. She paused, "With the exception of a black, right? [laughs] Because the children would come out—well, they would come out black . . . [short pause]." She continued, "If someone with unrefined features marries a black, who in general has a flat nose and thick lips, that is too much." Throughout our conversation, Marisa referred to her own features with disdain. Although Marisa falls on the dark end of the color continuum and has African-origin features, she spoke of "blacks" as a group of which she is not a member, and consistently made her negative feelings about blackness and her desire to not be associated with blacks evident.

When I asked Marisa her thoughts on the next generation (her children), and whether she would support them marrying someone darker, she responded with a hesitant "Yes," but when I asked if she would *prefer* they marry someone lighter (most people would not outwardly say they would reject a darker person but, overwhelmingly, people would say they prefer a lighter person), she quickly said "Yes . . . because if one is a descendent from dark people and marries a person who is dark, the children aren't going to come out very attractive, shall we say. They are going to have very flat noses, or in other words, be very unrefined." She explained that:

> Marisa: For example there are *morenos, morenos* with very fine features, like a pointed nose, thin lips, small eyebrows, a face that isn't very round, but instead, oval. They are still accepted. But the majority of the *morenos* have flat noses, are dark [lowers voice], have thick lips, and round faces . . . even though they are thin, they have chubby cheeks. Is it that kind of face, right? They are not appealing.
>
> CS: It doesn't look good? You don't like that look either?
>
> Marisa: No.
>
> CS: Do you like your own features?
>
> Marisa: No. I would like them if they were more. . . . The truth is no. . . . I would have liked to have my mom's nose, because hers is not very, very wide.

Notice the importance placed on markers of blackness, other than skin color alone. Marisa sees herself as the product of *mestizaje,* but laments the features inherited from her father's side and wishes that she had the more "refined" features of her lighter-skinned mother. Not only is Marisa not accepting of her own features, she hopes to erase such traits in her children by finding a partner who is lighter and who has more "refined" features.

Opinions about *mestizaje* can be largely driven by the phenotypic appearance of the individual. Those who inherit more European traits tend to be very positive about the benefits of *mestizaje* whereas those with more indigenous or

African-origin features seem more frustrated, or even bitter, about the prospects of whitening through *mestizaje*. In the following examples, observe how the phenotypic "outcome" of individuals largely determines their position on *mestizaje*. Yessica, a twenty-one-year-old white university student with blonde hair and green eyes, described her views on race mixture:

> Yessica: Well, it is a good thing for me because I got the good side of the situation. If in my family my ancestors had been indigenous or slaves or something like that, I would have come out *morenita*,[7] right? But in my family, what predominates is the European *mestizaje*. Obviously many people say, "Oh, I am of European descent," but from way, way back, right? Ultimately there was mixture between the indigenous, *morenos*, and everyone. . . . But, my mixture was more directly from Europeans, whites, a pure race.
>
> CS: Do you feel that if you were *morena*, you would consider [*mestizaje*] to be a good thing?
>
> Yessica: The truth is no. . . . If I had grown up *morena*, I would have seen it as something normal. But right now if you ask me, "Would you like to be *morena*?" I would say no.
>
> CS: Do you like to be blonde?
>
> Yessica: Yes, I love it.

Compare Yessica's statement with that of Martín, a sixty-year-old *moreno oscuro* navy captain: "My dad was tall and dark skinned. My mom was white, but short. So, I got what I didn't want to get: shortness from my mom and dark skin from my dad. I should have gotten whiteness from my mom and being tall from my dad, right?" Although Martín is slightly bitter about his own personal phenotyptic outcome, he nevertheless married a tall, light-skinned woman, likely in hopes that his children would come out lighter. The high rate of race mixture in society seems to foster the idea that "I could have come out lighter," as is the case with Rosa, a thirty-four-year-old *morena* lower-class housewife: "I would look at the white people and they would catch my attention. My mom is white but my dad is [dark] like my husband. So I wanted to be white. I would say, '. . . Mom, why didn't I come out like you?' I would tell her, 'I want to be white.' Because being white was really more attractive to me."

In another case, Belinda, a forty-six-year-old *morena oscura* lower-class housewife with indigenous features, described why she has always longed for whiteness: "Well, all of them were white; all of my sisters and brothers were white. I was the only, the only *negrita* and I felt like they paid less attention to me. It was like they rejected me or made fun of me because I had this skin color." In the case of Belinda and others who come from mixed-race families, the possibility of coming out lighter or inheriting European characteristics leads to a focus on what "could have been."

If the goal is to whiten, one may wonder about the views of the people who marry individuals darker than themselves. Respondents who stressed that love is color blind acknowledged there are barriers to overcome. For example, Lupe, a forty-one-year-old middle-class housewife who was dating a Cuban man of African descent, asserted that color is not important in a relationship. However, she spoke of constantly having to endure the critical looks of outsiders and rejection by her family. In another case, Rosa, the thirty-four-year-old *morena* lower-class housewife married to a *moreno oscuro* man with African-origin features, told me that love is blind, but admitted that, as a child, she had insisted she would never marry a "black" person. She shared that her family still teases her, reminding her how determined she had been to marry someone lighter. Similarly, Esteban, a twenty-nine-year-old white computer technician, who is partnered with a *morena* woman, shared with me that he used to date white women and that white women are still his preference. Therefore, even among many of those who date or marry darker partners, the preference for a lighter partner persists. Sometimes individuals dating or married to darker partners react by dismissing or lightening their partner's color. Judy, a thirty-five-year-old university professor who is partnered with a *moreno oscuro* man of obvious African origin, struggled with this tension:

> For me, if he was green or had purple hair, I would not care. I don't know how to explain it, but I don't like him because he is the color he is. I mean, I don't care about that. I have never liked men with dark skin. I have never seen a person of the black race that I can tell you . . . I like him. I am attracted to him . . . Never. I could tell you the partners I have had were generally light skinned with dark hair and dark eyes, because that is what I like the most. But, well, it would be the same to me if I had a boyfriend who was green or whatever, right? That is not important to me.

Despite the fact that Judy has a partner who is darker than herself, she still holds on to her ideal of whiteness. Instead of critiquing the idea that whiteness is desirable, Judy emphasizes that color is not important. After Judy made the previous remarks regarding her distaste for black men, I was a bit confused because her boyfriend has prominent African-origin features, self-identifies as black and is referred to as *negrito* by others. So, for clarification, I asked Judy how she describes her partner's color, and she replied as follows:

> He comes from a family that is Mexican. They are *morenos claros*. His siblings are a little bit less dark and since he studied in a military school and was doing so many things, well obviously he has had more sun exposure than the rest of his family, right? [laughs]. But I know his family and well, they are not a family of blacks to put it like that, right?

Intermarriage is not a random phenomenon. In the United States and Brazil, a "status exchange" sometimes occurs when an individual marries someone with lighter skin or from a higher-status racial group by offering other valued attributes such as economic status, education, or power.[8] Similarly, in Veracruz, it is much more socially acceptable for an individual to marry someone darker if the partner is of a higher SES.

This perception of a status exchange dynamic was pointed out to me by Claudia, a forty-eight-year-old *morena clara* high school teacher, regarding our mutual friend, Sergio, an African American man living in Veracruz who is partnered with a *morena* woman. One afternoon, after a chat involving all four of us, Claudia shared with me that she thought Sergio's girlfriend was jealous of the friendship we had with Sergio. She then said, "She is stupid to think that someone would take him away from her, as ugly as he is. I don't like blacks. I wouldn't marry a black person." She later told me his girlfriend is with him only for his money because she obviously is not with him for his looks. Oftentimes, people interpret inter-color relationships through the lens of status exchange; people become puzzled if they cannot identify a "logical reason" (such as money, status, etc.) for a lighter individual to choose to be with someone who is darker.

It is important to mention the gendered pattern of *mestizaje* in Veracruz. It is much more common and acceptable for a man to marry a woman who is lighter than himself than vice-versa. Well-off or high-status *moreno* or *moreno oscuro* men often have partners who are lighter than themselves. In a patriarchal society such as Mexico, there are many more single men than women with high SES, allowing men more opportunities to trade their status for a partner's more desirable color. Furthermore, not only are single women with high SES rare, they are generally not *morena, morena oscura,* or *negra*. Lastly, because beauty is seen as a more valuable trait for women to possess, a woman's skin color is less likely to be overlooked than that of a man's.

Veracruzanos do not embrace their mixed-race status in and of itself; instead, they strive to "whiten" themselves and their progeny. This dynamic is not to be interpreted as people trying to cross racial group boundaries or "pass." Instead, individuals seek to whiten *within* the mixed-race category. Because physical features as opposed to ancestry are privileged in Veracruz, the emphasis is placed on being phenotypically white, not racially "pure."

Race-Blind Discourses on Racism

An offshoot of Mexico's national ideology of *mestizaje* is the belief that racism cannot exist in a racially mixed society. Given this belief, Mexico has long held a race-blind ideology in which race talk and racial classification are deemed inappropriate, and merely noticing racial differences is seen as a racist act. At the national level, the race question has not been included on the census for nearly a century.[9] This may help explain the discomfort that I encountered when talking to Veracruzanos about racial classification.

Although Veracruzanos are extremely reluctant to talk about race, racial differences, or a racial hierarchy, they readily use a proxy discourse based on color to incorporate such distinctions into everyday conversation. Although talking about someone's race is seen as racist, talking about someone's color is seen as commonplace and appropriate; the former violates the race-blind ideology, whereas the latter does not. Individuals are highly uncomfortable using racial terms, yet are at ease when referencing color distinctions. Thus, the color discourse allows Veracruzanos the ability to talk about race, or at least something like race, in a way that does not conflict with the national race-blind ideology.

The distinction between the social meaning of race and color became quite clear when people were asked to self-identify using an open-ended format. When asked what racial category they belong to, respondents usually showed confusion, discomfort, or an inability to classify themselves racially. However, when I asked people to self-classify in terms of color, such requests received a very different reaction. People answered without hesitation and their responses seemed much more "natural" than the forced classification by race.

The view that classifying by race is racist does not generally apply to classifying by color. Therefore, many of the contradictions that an outsider may perceive in Veracruz (hearing that race talk is taboo, but simultaneously hearing constant references to people's color) are not seen as contradictions by Veracruzanos. Simply put, race and color are viewed as distinct folk categories. Color is seen as a descriptive marker whereas race connotes both categorization and the creation of a hierarchy. This is not to say that color discourse is not related to categorization or a hierarchy, and one could even argue that, on a theoretical level, color is simply a proxy for race.

Turning to data excerpts that demonstrate the difference between responses to questions of race versus questions of color, observe how Rodrigo, a thirty-seven-year-old *moreno oscuro* fisherman, responded to my question about his racial identification: "Well . . . mmm, how could I say it? . . . Racially I consider myself . . . well, a dark-skinned person, normal, without discriminating against anyone." Rodrigo's response was very typical. First, he hesitated, responding as if he was caught off-guard and unsure of what to say. He then ended up giving a response that could be interpreted as a reference to color (dark-skinned) as opposed to race. Moreover, when I requested that he self-identify by race, he evoked the idea of discrimination. Aracely, a forty-eight-year-old *morena clara* lower-class housewife, had similar difficulties with classifying herself racially, but oriented very quickly to my question on color.

CS: And what race do you consider yourself?
Aracely: Well, I don't even know.
CS: So, you don't identify with any race?
Aracely: Well speaking of race, now that you mention it . . . yes, yes, I saw something about that in my daughter's textbook, but I don't remember right now. I saw all of the races of the towns here in Veracruz. Yes, something like race but I don't remember the name; I don't remember right now.
CS: And what color do you consider yourself?
Aracely: Well I consider myself to be *morena*.

Aracely tried to recall her race as something that she may have learned or possibly seen in her daughter's schoolbook, although she was not able to remember the "correct" answer to the race question. Although the examples used here are generally from people who are lower to middle class, I found equivalent conceptualizations of race versus color from the upper class as well, with the exception being highly educated individuals who seem slightly more accustomed to the idea of racial classification.

The next examples demonstrate Veracruzanos' expressed discomfort with identifying racially, their association of the term "race" with racism, and their use of a color discourse to escape this association. To begin, observe how Javier, a twenty-eight-year-old *moreno claro* army employee, reacted when I asked about his racial category: "Mmm. Well I am not racist, I don't like to be racist. I see the whole world the same, everyone. *Morenos,* blacks, whites, I see them all the same." Notice that the very mention of racial classification evoked the idea of racism. Interestingly, though, Javier did in fact acknowledge distinctions "*morenos,* blacks, whites," but also suggested he is blind to such differences, a contradiction made by many respondents.

In this next example Sara, a sixty-three-year-old *morena* secretary, discussed her definition of racism: "I understand it to be the classification of races, right? . . . To classify the black, classify the white, and classify the Chinese and all of that." For many, the act of classification in and of itself constitutes racism. Another woman, Beatriz, a fifty-three-year-old *morena oscura* lower-class housewife, made a similar association when I asked her to self-identify racially: "Well, what can I tell you? I am a person who does not feel superior nor inferior to anyone, right?" Although Beatriz did not mention racism directly, she clearly associates racial classification with a racial hierarchy. In the following conversation, I asked Carmen, a nineteen-year-old *morena clara* shoe store employee to discuss her views on what racial category she felt she belonged to: "Well . . . what racial category? Well no . . . Well I am probably . . . in the category . . . well right now I am. . . . I am . . . how can I tell you? . . . Well the truth is, I don't, I don't consider myself to be racist or anything like that. I classify people based on what they are like. . . . I don't pay attention to color or race. I am not like that. . . ."

At first, Carmen struggled to respond and then opposed classification on moral grounds after she could not supply an answer to the question. Like many others, when she found racial classification to be difficult, she resorted to the rhetoric of the race-blind ideology. Although she mentioned that she does not "pay attention to color or race," later on when I asked about her color, she responded, "*Morena clara,*" with no apparent discomfort in making such a classification.

Others, such as Franco, a sixty-four-year-old *moreno oscuro* fisherman, objected to classification by race more quickly: "I don't like that racial stuff because they say there is a god, and God made all of us. I imagine there does not need to be a division of races like there is a division of beliefs. That is not necessary either." Not only does Franco's passage reveal the association of racial classification with racism, it also highlights the evocation of religion in defense of the race-blind ideology. Many of my respondents objected to racial classification under the justification that "God meant us all to be equal," "God created us equal," or "we are all the same before God," although the reaction was not the same for color classification. In fact, when I asked Franco about his color, he very comfortably answered "*Moreno*" without mention of divisions, racism, or religion. Color talk, in its descriptive nature, does not violate the race-blind ideology.

Distancing from Blackness

During the sixteenth and seventeenth centuries, Mexico and Peru were the largest importers of African slaves in Spanish America and, by 1600, people of African origin clearly outnumbered those of European origin in Mexico. When the slave system collapsed in the early 1700s, the biological integration of the African population increased and by the time of independence, the African element was believed to be fully integrated with the rest of the population as a result of "race mixture." However, the supposed "disappearance" of the African-origin population was questioned when, during the 1940s, Aguirre Beltrán located and studied a "black" population on Mexico's southern coast.[10] Since then, scholars have begun to focus on studying contemporary populations of African descent throughout Mexico.

Given their historical tie to a large population of African descent, it is perhaps surprising that so many Veracruzanos distance themselves from the category "black," and conceive of blackness as something foreign to the Mexican nation. Furthermore, Veracruzanos oftentimes attribute the darker phenotype of the local population to sun exposure, thereby negating any possible African heritage. The focus on sun exposure allows many an "escape hatch"—a way to avoid identifying themselves or others who are part of the local population as black. For example, when I asked Lilí, a forty-seven-year-old white upper-class housewife, if there are "black" people in Veracruz, she responded, "Well, I do not know if [they are black] because of their race or because of the sun. I don't know." Although Lilí did not give a definitive answer, she used the idea of the sun (and its effect on skin color) to open up the possibility that there are no "racially" black people in Veracruz.

Even today, blackness is associated with slavery in the region, as can be seen in this example provided by Julieta, an upper-class *morena clara* student who is fond of sunbathing: "Here people are, to a certain point, racist. They care a lot about the color of your skin. There is a person I know who says, 'Blacks are used for slaves.'" Julieta recalled that this same person asked her, "Why do you sit out in the sun? Why do you want to be black?'" This statement demonstrates the emphasis on skin color from a different angle. Not only is a darker skin tone undesirable, but, it still has strong associations with slavery. In this next case, Roberto, a twenty-three-year-old *moreno oscuro* upper-class college graduate, demonstrated how focusing on a color continuum can minimize the emphasis on blackness:

> I think that people here are called "black" to give them a name. But people don't realize that in other places, there are people who are black, black. I mean purple. You could say it like that, right? So for me, for example, in school they say, "Hey, blackie" or whatever, to be affectionate and it does not bother me. . . . But when they see a person who is really black, black, black, they say, "Wow! You are white compared to him." So what we see here are people who are *moreno* and called "black," but they aren't blacks; they are *morenos*.

The use of a color discourse based on the idea of a color continuum allows Veracruzanos to distance themselves (both at the individual and regional levels) from blackness. Roberto referred to people as "black, black" or even "black, black, black"—a common practice that translates to "really black" or "very, very black." Again, if there are people who are "really black," individuals who are *moreno oscuro*, such as Roberto, feel that they do not qualify as being black. Similarly, Rodrigo, a thirty-seven-year-old *moreno oscuro* fisherman asserted: "But we are not black, black. We are a mixture of races with slightly darker skin. I can tell you that 80 percent, the majority, have brown skin because of their job." Rodrigo attributed skin color to "the job," which is an indirect reference to sun exposure.

In another case, Ana, a forty-four-year-old *morena oscura* teacher and independent business owner, and her sister Laura, a forty-three-year-old *morena oscura* newspaper stand worker, also made references to the sun when talking about the color of the local population:

> Ana: Eh, well there are *morenos* and there are blacks. On the coast there are *morenos*.
> CS: Here, on the coast?
> Ana: Yes here, yes. . . . Yes, there are more blacks here because of the sun. . . . Because of the sun, because. . . . I mean, even though oftentimes we are white, normally there is always sun and since we are always in the sun, our skin always gets a little bit darker.

When I asked Ana and Laura about blacks in the Mexican population, they responded as follows:

> Ana: Where are there more blacks? . . . It would be in . . . we have traveled to many parts of the republic . . . but no, not here.
> Laura: In Mexico [City].
> Ana: Only in Mexico City, right? In the federal district, yes.
> Laura: There are all kinds of people.
> Ana: There are more blacks than here. Here there aren't any. Here there are *morenos,* but no blacks.
> CS: Would you say that there are *morenos oscuros* here?
> Ana: Mmm, *morenos—.*
> Laura: *Claros.*
> Ana: *Morenos claros.* . . . Yes, here.
> Laura: And blacks because of the sun.

Again, both Ana and Laura denied the presence of blackness in Veracruz and instead referenced other regions such as Mexico City which they considered to have a black population. They emphasized that Veracruzanos are not that dark-skinned, and Laura ended the conversation by saying that there are blacks in Veracruz, but only because of the sun. At the extreme, any differences that exist in the population are attributed solely to sun exposure, as is demonstrated in the following remark made by Ana: "Economically, the people who are lighter belong to the upper class. . . since normally they don't get sun tanned. They are only in their vehicles, with air-conditioning or are in the malls or always in the shade. . . . And that is how they take care of their skin. That is why the upper class has the white people." Not only does Ana's explanation have the effect of negating or minimizing any racial or color differences by class, she attributes all differences in skin color to sun exposure.

In another example, Cesar, an eighteen-year-old *moreno* student from a lower-class household, when asked if he felt there are more people with "black" features in Veracruz than in other parts of Mexico, described his understanding of race as it relates to the region as follows: "Yes, I think that it is because here there is more heat. In Jalapa, which is the capital of Veracruz, it is cold . . . but the sun here is hot and you get burned, but there you don't." Although Cesar initially said that, in Veracruz, there are more people with "black" features, he quickly shifted to the sun explanation, thereby taking the focus off other phenotypic markers such as hair and facial features, and placing strong emphasis on only one marker of blackness: skin color.

Being black in Veracruz, of course, is not simply a matter of skin tone, but also involves markers such as hair and facial features. When such features were noted, they usually were referred to at the individual, as opposed to the group, level. In other words, it was very uncommon to hear discussions about Veracruzanos generally having very curly hair. Instead, specific individuals who have curlier hair or other features that could be interpreted as representing blackness were commented on. Furthermore, "black" features are believed to be foreign to Mexico and, therefore, a person with such markers is usually assumed to be of Cuban (often a synonym for black in Veracruz) or otherwise of non-Mexican origin.[11] I suspect that such markers are acknowledged less than skin color, because a focus on a broader range of physical markers of blackness in Veracruz would make it much more difficult to minimize the existence of individuals of African origin in society. I was often told that if people in other parts of Mexico were to live on the coast, they, too, would be dark like Veracruzanos. Therefore, the focus on skin color, which involves the discourse of "the sun," allows Veracruzanos to address this phenotypic distinction and, at the same time, absolves them from having to differentiate themselves racially from other Mexicans.

Conclusion

Through my research I have attempted to understand the folk concept of color in Veracruz as it relates to the national ideologies of *mestizaje* and race blindness. I have also sought to understand the distancing from blackness in the region. In all three of these cases, my data have shown that skin color is a variable of everyday importance. In relation to *mestizaje,* I found that people strive to whiten themselves and the next generation within the racial category of *mestizo,* as opposed to trying to cross racial-group boundaries altogether. Because the *mestizo* is not stigmatized in Mexico as a result of a national ideology that equates a Mexican identity with mixed-race status, the focus is on being phenotypically white as opposed to racially "pure." However, racism has not been cast aside with the creation of this national ideology. Instead, the two seemingly contradictory forces of racism and *mestizaje* have worked together, creating a society in which people simultaneously laud their racial mixture and strive for phenotypic whiteness.

Regarding discourses of racism, I found that everyday "color talk" is acceptable in a society that scorns race-based classification. The color discourse allows Veracruzanos to make and act upon such distinctions without feeling their acts constitute racism. The broader lesson here is that race-blind policies have not rid Mexico of such classifications or related discrimination. Finally, in relation to blackness, Veracruzanos distance themselves from the region's African heritage by focusing on sun exposure as a justification for the presence of dark-skinned individuals in the population. Skin color is strongly emphasized when discussing blackness, or the lack of it, in Veracruz; other physical markers of blackness are largely ignored. What can be seen from the data is the way in which a racial hierarchy and related racism can be maintained and even reproduced when emphasis is placed on skin color. As we can see, skin color plays an essential role in the racial dynamics of Mexican society.

Consuming Lightness

Modernity, Transnationalism, and Commodification

III

HAVING ESTABLISHED THAT LIGHTNESS OF SKIN confers advantages and that it is widely valued and desired, we can now look explicitly at skin color as a form of symbolic capital that has exchange value. The first two chapters in Part III examine the symbolic value of skin tone in two very different markets: in assisted reproduction and in marital matching.

Charis Thompson finds that skin tone has remarkable salience in commercial egg donation. A gamete does not have skin, let alone skin tone, so the donor's skin tone is viewed as the best predictor of the skin tone of a resultant child, despite the widespread acknowledgment that the passing on of specific characteristics from biological parent to child is highly uncertain. Skin tone, or complexion, along with race and ethnicity, are among the most common kinds of data solicited from potential donors and displayed for potential recipients. Thompson argues that the perception of skin tone is imprecise and contextually specific, involving other characteristics such as hair texture and facial features. Furthermore, the meaning of skin tone references and reproduces larger historical and transnational patterns of race, class, and national relations.

Jyotsna Vaid's study of Indian matrimonial ads examines skin tone as a form of gendered symbolic capital resulting from the importance of skin tone to perceived attractiveness and desirability in women. Analyzing the frequency and content of references to skin tone in Indian matrimonial ads in a major Indian newspaper and on two Internet sites, Vaid finds that "fair" or "wheatish" skin is frequently mentioned as desired in a potential wife by men, and is mentioned as a positive characteristic by women (or their parents) when describing themselves. Although Vaid refers to traditional cultural and religious sources of

Indian preferences for light-skinned mates, perhaps her most striking finding is that skin tone is mentioned as often or more often by presumably Western-acculturated Indians residing in the United States.

This finding is consonant with Evelyn Nakano Glenn's study of the segmented nature of skin-lightening markets and Lynn M. Thomas' study of skin-lightening practices in South Africa, which indicate that urban, more modernized women are fueling the growth in skin-lightening products in the global south. Glenn contends that transnational pharmaceutical and cosmetic corporations are creating the desire for lighter skin through print, Internet, and television ads that link light skin with modernity, social mobility, and youth. Although global in scope, the skin-lightening market is highly segmented by nation, culture, race, and class. Transnational corporations have responded by offering multiple product lines targeted to specific segments of consumers, and by designing ads and publicity that incorporate local cultural themes and concerns. Thomas' historical study of skin lightening in South Africa also emphasizes the transnational entanglements involved in the proliferation of skin lighteners there, beginning with the introduction of African American lightening products in the 1920s and '30s, and continuing with the increase of a local white controlled lightening industry in the late 1930s. By the 1940s, South Africa became the trading center for the circulation for skin lighteners throughout Africa and even across the Atlantic—a market that has expanded even more since the 1970s. Thomas conceptualizes skin lighteners as a technology of the self—a technology aimed at modifying one's body and other aspects of the self to attain a higher state of happiness, purity, wisdom, and perfection. She views skin lighteners as technologies of the self simultaneously constituted through personal fantasies and structural forces. Thus, the most frequent users of modern skin lighteners from the 1970s onward have been young urban women, often migrants from rural areas seeking to better themselves.

E.N.G.

8 Skin Tone and the Persistence of Biological Race in Egg Donation for Assisted Reproduction

Charis Thompson

THE IDEA OF BIOLOGICAL RACE IS BOTH dead by consensus and very much alive, and the salience of donor skin tone in U.S. infertility treatment involving donor eggs is one site where this state of affairs is manifested. When a donor egg pregnancy is established, a single cell, a gamete, moves from the donor's to the recipient's body. In the United States and elsewhere, practitioners, donors, and patients attribute a plethora of qualities to this single cell, many of them ethnoracial, and most of them routed via qualities attributed to the donor herself, and believed to be carried somehow in the genetic code that the egg will contribute to a resulting child. Thus, if skin tone is salient in choosing an egg donor, it reveals hope for or belief in some kind of biological preservation of skin tone. It also suggests that it makes current "common sense" to tie that which is preserved through the genetic contribution of the egg to phenotypic skin tone in a resulting child in a way that correlates to the socially meaningful categories of race and ethnicity used to sort donors by skin tone in the first place.

Egg donation in the United States is a largely privatized business, setting it apart from the state-sponsored social engineering aspirations of the heyday of eugenics and race science. This crucial difference means that donors and recipients alike find important kinds of subjectivity, empowerment, and agency in these new articulations of biological race. It should not surprise us, however, that the ways in which skin tone features in egg donation reflects and in turn reproduces evolving logics of race and ethnicity that are far from restricted to the realm of the private. Skin tone only makes sense as it is used in egg donation when situated in historically and collectively salient patterns of race differentiation, stratification, and discrimination.

I urge, as I have elsewhere, that the question inherited from the nineteenth and first two thirds of the twentieth century—(How) is race biological?—be replaced by a nonessentialist focus that better captures the dynamic aspects of biological racialization.[1] If instead one asks, "How and by whom and for what purposes is race biologized and biology racialized?" the continued intertwining of evolving understandings of human biology with social categories of people-hood can be seen. The most pressing political questions facing us with the new sites of biological racialization involve understanding the connections between the historical patterns that the logics of race come out of and in turn reproduce, while understanding the kinds of agency that come from being able to assert individual and collective biological identity. In this chapter I begin this task by discussing a number of examples of egg donation from my fieldwork in which skin color was salient.

Skin Tone Perception

In this chapter I adopt a particular theoretical orientation to skin tone percep-tion that I believe to be empirically grounded. Adult humans generally attend to and perceive absolute color and tone poorly, and most need training to do it with any degree of reliability. This is true even when we view objects that are the same except for their color or tone, under constant lighting conditions, from the same perspective. When the things whose color one is comparing are not otherwise identical, it is even harder. Consider how hard it is to match a color swatch to the color of one's walls when touching up an already painted room. Color matching and comparing, no matter the domain, takes training and skill, and is not a pre-given perceptual capability.

I further contend that the kind of training one receives implicitly by inter-nalizing meanings and hierarchies that attune one to socially relevant differ-ences in skin tone are not the same as training in color perception that a painter or artist might cultivate. The artist seeks to perceive differences in a property known as color or tone that can only be arrayed on a spectrum when under-stood in a form that is highly abstracted from its instances. By contrast, people learning to see socially relevant skin tone differences perceive the shade of skin embedded in other ethnoracial marking systems such as hair, language, dress, age, gender, season, type of work, posture, and so on. Perceiving skin tone al-ways involves its intersection with these other attributes and their wider mean-ings and histories. This means that skin color is an index of legibility whose chromatic properties are deeply relative.

Although there are real differences among skin tones, it can be notoriously hard to compare absolute skin tone between individuals who self-identify as belonging to particular ethnoracial groups, even when those groups are designated by color terms such as *black* and *white*. Even *within* the same socially relevant group, the intersecting indices of legibility (some of which are mentioned earlier) such as hair, sun exposure, dress, age, or gender can make skin tone comparisons among members about more than color or tone. Many social and political skin tone terms have powerful significance based on their functioning in social and historical contexts as an either-or binary, rather than a spectrum, further complicating skin tone perception. Consider the notorious "brown paper bag test" among African Americans before the Black Power Movement; in this case, as in many other cases of skin colorism, lighter skin signifies a morass of complex hierarchies to do with inter- as well as intragroup class, gender, and other dynamics.

Perhaps most important (and a product and cause of the theoretical points in the preceding paragraph), skin tone is complexly interwoven with transnational and historical signification. Among well-known examples, *black* refers to different groups in Britain than in the United States. In some parts of the world, the association between paleness and aristocracy still exists, sun-tanned darker skins being supposedly indicative of peasants who spend their lives working in the sun, and residues of these logics can linger even after land reform, urbanization, and other societal changes have largely abolished clearcut aristocracy/peasant distinctions. All these observations about the complexities of skin tone perception suggest its intersection with other perceptible attributes and its inextricability from historical social hierarchies.

I come to the topic of skin tone, then, from a perspective that questions the assumption that skin tone is a given phenotypic attribute, perceptually available to anyone who sees the skin in question. In the research I present here, this questioning of assumptions about skin tone is taken one step further, showing the persistence of these complex interactions of tone, hierarchy, and history through a biological reduction from donor to haploid egg cell to resulting diploid child. I begin with a brief discussion of the use of skin tone in egg donor databases, and then discuss four cases in which patients, donors, and practitioners discussed skin tone in cases in which they were involved. Because donor eggs (and sperm) are cells and not whole organisms, they do not have skin or skin tone. Social and biological assumptions about the heritability of skin tone, its modes of transmission, and the social matrices of reproductive desire of which it is an integral part come to the fore in these cases, revealing the ways in which biological race is still very much alive.

Skin Tone in Egg Donation Advertising and Structuring

The egg donation databases and cases being discussed here all involve so-called "commercial" egg donation, when egg donors are recruited by clinics and a particular donor is chosen by the infertile woman or couple, and the donor is then compensated for her donation. These cases are centered in medical facilities in the United States and all require the intended parent(s) to choose a donor from among a database of available donors. (In the interest of privacy, the clinics from which each database is drawn are not specified.)

Skin tone is one of the categories that some egg donor databases use to characterize and differentiate their donors. For example, one facility with centers in the Southwest, Mexico, and the West Coast, uses skin tone as a heading in classifying egg donors. The skin tones on offer are fair, medium, olive, and black. This purported skin tone spectrum, apart from being composed of rather different kinds of words as the points on the spectrum, is closely tied to affiliations listed in a separate column, under the heading "race/ethnicity." In this database, *black* is tied with the label African under race/ethnicity, whereas *olive* is paired with a Mediterranean or Southeast Asian or Latin American country of ethnoracial origin. *Fair* is restricted in this database to those classified as Caucasian, whereas *medium* is used for mixed, Latino, and some Caucasian donors. Although details vary, this pattern is not unusual; connections among skin tone, nation, ethnicity, religion, region, and race are the order of the day, rather than an exception, suggesting that even at its most descriptive, skin tone needs sociohistorical and geopolitical contexts to make sense. When *skin tone* is not used, a quasisynonym, such as the gendered *complexion,* might be used. One California egg donor database, for example, offers under "complexion" nearly the same choices: fair, medium, and olive. The omission of the option black may signal a belief that the term is a political rather than a descriptive term and thus not a shade of complexion. Omission of an implied darkest category is, however, a characteristic of some egg donor databases, which itself seems implicitly to acknowledge a history of racism based on darker skin tone (as described in a later example).

Although the first database described here paired particular racial/ethnic terms with particular skin tone terms, other databases relativize skin tone to a particular ethnoracial group so that donors listed as Caucasian or African

American, for example, might additionally be listed as fairer or darker skin tone, relative to that group. The second database mentioned earlier, which uses the quasisynonym *complexion,* makes the following kinds of links between its race entry and its complexion entry: Donors with complexion listed as olive include donors whose race is listed as Philippino (sic), Thai, Chinese, African American, and Caucasian. *Medium complexion* is attributed to donors listed as Caucasian and African American, and fair complexion is attributed to Caucasian and Japanese donors. Likewise, a large East Coast egg donor database classifies its donors as light, medium light, medium, and medium dark, and uses each of these skin tones within its different ethnoracial groups, so that there are medium-dark Caucasians and light-skinned Asians and African Americans listed. In this particular database I was unable to find any egg donor listed as dark within any group, providing another example of the logic of the omitted darkest category mentioned earlier.

When neither skin tone nor a synonym is used, various combinations of race, ethnicity, and nationality are used that mix color terms with names of nations, religions, and ethnicities. I have yet to find a U.S. egg donor database or sperm catalog that does not classify donors/specimens by nation, race, and/ or ethnicity in one form or another, although there are regional and other differences in which categories are used.[2] Frequently, there is space on listings to include more than one race/ethnicity, and frequently the race/ethnicity is divided into maternal and paternal contributions, as is typical for donor sperm. From my limited ethnographic experience, where skin tone is made explicit, it is supplied by a combination of self-identification on the part of donors and staff corroboration. Identification is usually also restricted to the listed categories. In this, it departs from the race/ethnicity data, for which the onus is on self-identification.

A second source of skin tone signaling in the advertising and structuring of commercial U.S. egg donation occurs visually, in the form of donor photographs and biographical detail. In sperm donation, photos of the donor as a child rather than as an adult are the most common visual representation. By contrast, adult, not baby, photos of egg donors are almost always given. The visual gestalt of the donor's adult form, including her skin tone is thus integral to the presentation of the egg from the beginning.[3] Eggs are almost always used fresh, on a particular cycle in relation to a particular donation effort by the donor and a particular attempt to get pregnant by the recipient. This means that in egg donation, one chooses a donor, not a batch of available banked and screened gametes, as in sperm donation. The salience of an egg donor's adult phenotypic characteristics frequently needs management.

Both sperm and egg donation require recipients to guess across the four major causal gulfs of popular and scientific understanding of inherited variability: What is the contribution of this half of the genetic complement as opposed to the contribution coming from the other gamete? In a given epigenetic environment, which of the egg's and the sperm's genes will be expressed? What is the role of the gestational environment and subsequent environment of rearing? What relation do the kinds of complex social and physical traits and credentials that correspond to hierarchies of social significance have to genetics in any case? Causal agnosticism along these axes, then, is part of common understandings of genetics and trait inheritance, and is commonly expressed in both sperm and egg donation. The rationale of choosing a donor at all goes something like this: Some of a donor's characteristics may be passed along somehow or other, at least as potential expressed relative to the general population, or relative to a randomly selected donor, so it is worth choosing one donor over another. This is weak causally, but strong enough to support market differentiation of donors, which in turn overemphasizes socially stratifying characteristics. In choosing an egg donor and during treatment, the donor is to the fore, and so is easily elided with her eggs. Because of this, it is hard to separate the donor from the complex, interactive, and underdetermined role of one of her eggs in making a future child.

The fact that egg *donors* are chosen, rather than banked eggs, situates the discussion of egg donor skin tone and other weakly transmissible donor qualities in specific ways. In particular, it is not unusual for egg donation information to include warnings and/or reminders to those choosing an egg donor about the indeterminacy of the relation between a donor's qualities and the qualities of a future child to which the donor's egg contributed. Consider the following passages, from the "Do's" and "Don'ts" page of an egg donation "concierge" company that helps infertile women find matched donors from multiple databases around the country.[4] From the list of "Do": "Remember that blending the genetics of any two people will bring about a wonderfully unpredictable outcome of a child you will cherish regardless of their hair color or their ability to play pro sports."

And from the list of "Don'ts": "Forget that even when dealing with your own genetics you never know what characteristics your child will have." These reminders both celebrate the underdetermination of heritability in egg donation (the "wonderfully unpredictable outcome" of the first quote) and try to avert false expectations (and lawsuits and custody disputes?) by pointing out that even were you able to get pregnant using your own eggs ("your own genetics"), the future child's characteristics would be unknown. All families can point to the variations in such things as hair color and skin tone within them. In the case of skin tone in the United States, this kind of "expected but unpredictable" variation is the subject of a history and a literature of racial discrimination and passing. Egg donation, then, does not erase these histories, but is rather their latest instantiation.

As just mentioned, however, this kind of disavowal of a knowable link between donors' characteristics and future offspring—a quasilegal "truth in advertising" disclaimer—is only one side of the story. Choosing among egg donors at all implies a belief in some kind of causality. Even more telling, perhaps, are some of the market dimensions of the social hierarchies that the characteristics tap into. One egg donation practice based in California advertises to potential egg donors by describing the rewards young women can expect from becoming egg donors:

> Compensation. Donors with our program receive letters and gifts from their recipients and our donor program, as well as knowledge of the results of their donation cycle. Donors are well compensated for their time according to their qualifications. We generously compensate donors to reward them for their job. Please call us to discuss the fees. Premier donors also receive massages, flowers and other gifts from us.[5]

We find from this short passage that egg donors receive nonmonetary as well as monetary rewards for their participation. They stand to receive letters, gifts, and other in-kind rewards from recipients and from the clinic. An interesting emphasis is also placed on knowledge: They will be informed of the success or otherwise of the donation procedure, which might additionally reassure the donor about her own fertility, as well as allow her to infer that she has a genetic child in the world. It also affects her chance of working again and increasing her fees at that clinic. We learn that donors are not only to be compensated, but they will be compensated well. The use of the word *compensation* rather than *payment* underlies the point that donors are remunerated for their time and effort rather than being paid for the eggs, per se, which in turn highlights the gift relations of the procedure that manages cultural queasiness about buying and selling babies. Although fees are thought to be key to donor motivation, and donors are requested to call for more information regarding fees, the gift language underlines the affective premise that donors don't do it only for the money, and it allows donors to rehearse presentation of self in this regard.[6] Crucially, this brief passage also indicates that compensation stratifies egg donors and vice versa. Donors are compensated "according to their qualifications," and there is such a thing as a "premier donor." *Qualifications* corresponds to the qualities according to which donors are listed, and donors are paid more if they have qualities prospective parents turn out to want. In other words, *qualifications* is a constantly self-calibrating combination of recipients' reproductive desire with the parameters of societal success as reflected in the categories according to which donors are differentiated. Being a premier donor combines this eugenic calibration between success and desire with practical assets related to treatment ease and success: being "easy to work with," being a repeat donor, and having been successful in initiating a pregnancy in the past.

Skin tone is just the kind of thing that demonstrates both sides of this egg donation aporia: Donors are chosen and compensated on the basis of desirable qualities, but many such qualities, especially ones like skin tone, are known to be highly unpredictably inherited. I turn, now, from examining formal aspects of skin tone in egg donation—that is, advertising and informational, structural, and procedural materials—to ethnographic examples that extend this initial analysis.

Skin Tone in Practice: Ethnographic Cases

Skin Tone and Whiteness

During the course of my ethnographic work at assisted reproductive technology clinics and with patients, staff, and donors, donor skin tone was occasionally raised. For recipients of different races and nationalities, I have heard skin tone referred to when it seems to be a match with the infertile women's skin tone or, occasionally when the donor's skin tone is like the skin tone of a relative of the recipient. This sometimes occurs when the recipient herself, or the relative in question, has what the recipient considers an attractive or a high-status skin tone. Making the match with one's own skin tone or that of a relative makes a kind of biological claim to the skin tone in question. I have also heard individuals and couples explicitly reject matching their own skin tone in choosing a donor, using the same logic of wanting a donor with whom they consider attractive and/or who has a high-status skin tone. Even explicit nonmatching,

however, can coincide with wanting a future child to be not too markedly superior to themselves (again, as they see it). There is also still often a desire to bring
about some kind of phenotypic "plausibility," some kind of legibility between
mother and child of plausible biological descent. Illustrative of this, one white
woman considering egg donation told me: "I have always hated how pale my
skin is. . . . I'll be covered in wrinkles by the time I'm fifty. I'd love if my egg
donor had skin that was more tan than mine . . . , but I don't want people to
think the child isn't mine or to not give me credit for the child if they are too
different or too beautiful really to be mine."

In this quote, the woman articulates her dislike of her own skin tone in a
manner that connects her pallor to pervasive gendered, racialized, classed stereotypes in the United States of, and rehearsed by, professional white women
fearing showing age ("covered in wrinkles"). In wishing to avoid passing on pale
skin that will wrinkle to a future child, this professional white woman shows
that concern about skin tone is present in groups that have not historically been
discriminated against on the basis of skin tone. Similarly, it reinforces the point
that skin tone concerns have a profound within-group as well as between-group
dynamic, and that the two are in tension. Being less pale seems to need to be
balanced with a risk of a too "tan" child who might look racially other, and so
not look "really" hers.

The salience of skin tone in whiteness in this example can be compared with
the different role of skin tone in gamete donor choice for three gestating women
with whom I spoke who were in mixed-race couples. One, a white woman,
wanting to reflect what she thought of as "believable" skin tones for her child,
considered donors who would help her and her partner have a child who would
likely reflect the appropriate mixed-race phenotype for their respective groups.
In this case, the woman claimed to dislike her own pallor, much as the woman
mentioned earlier did. However, she felt that her husband's sperm would mitigate her own pallor because of his different race, and so she didn't worry about
accepting an egg from a donor who was less pale than her. She also repeated the
common stereotype that mixed-race children are beautiful; but, for this couple,
mixed-race appearance in a future child stood to confer rather than negate belonging. Two other mixed-race couples, lesbians using a sperm donor and a
heterosexual married couple using both egg and sperm donation, chose not to
match the white partner, instead picking donors that emphasized the minority
racial identification of the other partner. The heterosexual mixed-race couple
cited the difficult conditions of identity in the United States for mixed-race

children as the basis for their decision, and the lesbian couple cited the good home that they could give to a strongly racial minority-identified child.

Egg donation is still new enough that there is by no means a consensus about whether to tell others, and who to tell, about having used egg donation. There was a general presumption in my fieldwork, however, that other people "would not be able to tell just by looking," and that the decision of what and to whom to disclose this information would be just that: a decision. It is beyond the scope of this chapter to do justice to the parallels and differences between the signification of skin tone throughout the history of adoption and skin tone in egg donation, but the comparison is revealing nonetheless. Transracial and transnational adoption, especially, tend to be highly legible based on racialized skin tone difference. The difference shows up starkly in the visual logic of gamete donation websites versus adoption websites. There are frequently white couples—straight and gay—shown with nonwhite children in the images adorning adoption websites, reflecting a racist history of nonwhite children being "de-kinned" at high rates and thus being made available for adoption by white parents in this country, and hardly ever the reverse.[7] Gamete donation sites, on the other hand, signify their approximation to genetic parentage by showing parents and children who are matched in racialized skin tone.

I turn, now, to another example in which skin tone in egg donation is narrated and negotiated in practice. In the next example it is U.S. blackness, rather than whiteness, that is at stake. Again, I pay particular attention to the coconstructions of race and skin tone when conjoined in ideas about heritability in egg donation.

Skin Tone and Blackness

In one U.S. egg donation clinic, I was leafing through a binder of egg donor profiles. Most of the donors had a single photograph of themselves—smiling, attractive pictures every one. One donor, however, had the pictures of two adorable children next to her own appealing photo. At first glance, I thought the child photos were earlier pictures of herself, but on closer inspection it was clear that one child was a girl and one was a boy. I asked a staff member about the pictures and was told that they were, in fact, the donor's children. I speculated that the donor's children's photos served to show how cute children from this donor's eggs turned out to be, that they proved her fertility, and that they indicated that her own childbearing was over. These are all attributes in a donor that can be valued by prospective parents and clinics. The staff member agreed that these things are desirable things to signal, and that they are the kinds of things donors, including this one, might say about themselves in their personal statements and that clinics might use to select suitable donors with whom to work. She gave me a different reason for the presence of these photos of the donor's children, however.

The donor, an African American woman, had herself suggested including photos of her children. Apparently, she wanted patients who might select her in part on the basis of her skin tone to see that one of her children is considerably darker than the other, and, as far as was discernible from the photos, darker in skin tone than her as well. The children's photos functioned as a break in a too-easy elision from donor to offspring attributes and as an immediately on-hand visual reminder of the vagaries of genetics. According to the clinic coordinator who discussed this case with me, the woman did not want recipients to choose her as their donor for her lightness of skin, forgetting that it would not necessarily be passed on. Instead, she felt that her children's photos more accurately suggested the idea of a range of possible skin colors that could be expected among offspring born from her eggs.

This woman's innovation in her presentation of self can be considered in relation to the overall argument of this chapter about the relevance of skin tone in egg donation to the logics of race. It is likely that the donor in question felt it important to underline the unpredictability of transmission of skin tone because of the specificity of the freighted history of kinship, inheritance, and skin tone in relation to slavery and blackness in the United States. It is striking how much the addition of the children's photos resembles the logic of racial passing, whereby skin color can reappear in later generations, "outing" the mother and potentially driving out the mother and/or child from the family.[8] Given the fundamental connection between U.S. citizenship and antimiscegenation laws, it is perhaps not surprising that residues of this logic would resurface in the context of a field fraught with its own contestations of legitimate kinship.[9]

I turn, now, to two more cases in which skin tone was salient in contemporary U.S. egg donation practice. In this pair of cases, ethnorace and skin tone logics from other national contexts interacted with the regulatory, pricing, and donor availability and choice structures of U.S. egg donation. Both cases involved reproductive tourism, or the travel of patients from one jurisdiction to another—often one country to another—for reproductive treatment purposes. Domestic and global patterns of racialization and skin tone perception interact around the nexus of reproductive desire that is materialized in reproductive tourism involving egg donation.

Difference Despite Sameness in Skin Tone

At one U.S. clinic I visited, a Japanese couple had recently completed an egg donation procedure. They had traveled to the United States for treatment because egg donation was not legal in Japan. This kind of regulatory gradient, where patients and practitioners move from areas that have more restrictive policies to areas that have less restrictive ones, is a common "driver" of reproductive tourism.[10] The couple communicated to facility staff that they wanted an Asian donor. Asian and Asian American donors, in fact, are heavily recruited by U.S. egg donation companies. The wife also mentioned that light skin was a desirable quality. After perusing donor profiles, she found a donor whose photo and brief self-description she really liked, and she requested more information about the donor.

When she received the longer donor record from the clinic, however, she changed her mind regarding the desirability of this donor and began her quest anew. The reason she gave for ceasing to consider this donor desirable was the information that the donor was of Korean ancestry, rather than Japanese. Anti-Korean prejudice continues in Japan despite the so-called "Korean wave" and the popularity of Korean male soap opera stars among Japanese women. This woman, at least, did not share the recent popular cultural romanticism about Korea or, if she did, romantic desire did not extend to reproductive and genealogical desire. When the Japanese woman found out that the Asian American donor's parents came from Japan's former colony Korea, rather than from Japan, the skin tone and other attributes no longer had the same meaning. The donor's light skin tone ceased to be attractive and desirable if it was not embedded in Japanese ancestry that gave the skin tone hierarchical meaning in the first place.

In addition to illustrating the ways in which skin tone meanings and perception are always intertwined in other histories and hierarchies, this case illustrates something important about what recipients believe donors will pass on to future offspring. In other words, this intertwining reveals something about lay theories of heritability. The woman originally thought that the donor looked right, in part because of her skin tone. She wanted to give that kind of skin tone to a future child. Her reaction to finding out that the donor was of Korean ancestry suggests that what she believed to be passed from a donor through the egg cell linked skin tone inextricably to national and colonial history.

Sameness Based on Difference in Skin Tone

My final example, also involving the complex dynamics of reproductive tourism, concerns a white German couple who came from Germany to a U.S. clinic for egg donation. After perusing donor profiles, they initially chose a donor of South Asian descent. This case was recounted to me by the clinic director in the context of explaining the clinic's orientation to donor choice. Her practice, she said, was to allow infertile couples and single infertile women to choose their own donor from the list of available donors, without intervening in any way. This was consistent with reproductive choice—an example of which she considered her practice in general—and also promoted both donor and recipient satisfaction. This case, however, was the proverbial exception that proved the rule. The director talked with the German couple to understand why they had chosen a South Asian donor, and ultimately ruled against it, offering only to work with the couple in brokering their egg donation if they chose a donor that better approximated a phenotypic match with them.

Why did the couple want a South Asian donor and why did the clinic refuse to oblige them? The couple had recently converted to what the clinic director described as "New Age Buddhism." When they thought about which donor to choose, they thought about what mattered to them, and the donor was, from their point of view, a religious/cultural match precisely because she was differently racialized and had a visibly Asian, non-European skin tone. The likelihood that the donor was in fact Buddhist is probably fairly low, given that Buddhists are considered only to account for between 1 and 2 percent of the Indian population. The couple, citing India as the birthplace of Buddhism, however, found the donor's Indianness to have a kind of primordial ethnic authenticity. They were thus excited about the possibility of having a child who "looked Indian," and felt that a child made from Indian eggs and the husband's sperm and gestated by the wife would be a child truly chosen by them, and thus would be wanted, loved, and so on. The child's phenotypic difference would reveal that the couple had used egg donation to build their family, but an Indian-looking child would also attest to the importance of and simultaneously naturalize and authenticate their new religious affiliation.

Speaking as someone familiar with U.S. racialized reproductive politics, the clinic director thought it unacceptable to bring into being a child who would unnecessarily endure a racial mismatch in its own family—something that battles over multiracial adoption suggested was not in the best interests of the child. The director appreciated that domestic multiracial adoption and transnational adoption are very much better than no adoption at all. However, she felt that actively choosing to add this extra burden to a child just for the sake of bringing some strange primordial biological and genealogical authenticity and legibility to the parents' new, and thus suspect and superficial, affiliation was unacceptable.

The donor request was denied, and during the process the couple's attempt to bring their own series of elisions between class, religion, nation, race, biology, and desire into practice was rejected. The egg donation facility in question was a small operation that prided itself on its humanity toward both donors and recipients, and on working to the highest ethical standards, particularly with regard to making sure that everyone they worked with was involved, because they believed in helping women who could not otherwise have children experience that joy. As far as they were concerned, the German couple's reasoning did not fit honorable reproductive motives and narrative templates, and if the clinic had indulged the couple they would have impugned their own integrity in the process.

Discussion and Conclusion

When I began fieldwork on egg and sperm donation in the 1990s, phenotypic, personal, and cultural matching—seeking donors who had similar ethnoracial identification, personal qualities, and phenotype—between egg donor and recipient or sperm donor and infertile male partner was common, and explicitly and implicitly condoned. Matching seemed both to keep assisted reproduction as "natural" as possible, and to aid families in domestic decisions about disclosure and secrecy regarding donor use, by producing offspring who looked enough like recipient parents to be plausibly "theirs." Matching always had flexibility, however, with recipients seeking to match some but not other of their characteristics, and with gay and lesbian parenting with donor gametes disrupting the gendered matching logic of replacement. Although it is at best anecdotal, in my own data I have come across a willingness to forego matching of one intended rearing but nongenetic parent in the United States, but only when the unemphasized intended parent is the nongestational partner and only when the emphasized race/ethnicity is nonwhite (as exemplified in my earlier discussion of mixed-race couples). The one attempt to forgo matching completely that I discussed earlier was denied, suggesting a persistent attachment to matching logics and their racialized histories. By comparison, the clinic in the second case, involving an African American donor, felt that the donor was being proactive and was actively anti-eugenic in reminding prospective recipients of skin tone unpredictability. The clinic in the Japanese/Korean example thought the patients were being "discriminatory" but "still permissible" under the rubric of choice when they decided not to work with a Korean American donor.

Infamous cases of assisted reproductive technology around the world have reinforced this presumption of ethnoracial matching. An African Italian woman who wished to use a white donor to give her child(ren) a life free of racism was excoriated. A Dutch woman who gave birth to in vitro fertilization (IVF) twins, one of whom was black and one of whom was white, was taunted by her neighbors for the evidence of promiscuity they seemed to imply (she must have had a black lover on the side), until she confessed to all that she had used IVF and sued the clinic for the mistake by which one of her eggs ended up getting fertilized by sperm that did not come from her husband.

A recent well-publicized case, that of the Duncans' from the United Kingdom, however, suggests that a time may be approaching when matching will be replaced or augmented by other rationales for donor choice, and connections among permissible choices and skin tone and race/ethnicity/nation will alter accordingly. The Duncans, tired of waiting for treatment in the United Kingdom, went to India for IVF with egg donation that was both cheaper and easier to attain than had they remained within the European Union. The remarkable aspect of their case was that the Indian ethics committee of the hospital in question agreed to allow the Duncans to receive eggs from an Indian donor. This was the first time this had been permitted, and the birth of the Duncans' visibly (within U.K. race perception categories) mixed-race child after egg donation was also a first. Expanding networks of reproductive tourism and a dramatic increase in egg demand; a growing concern about aging and declining populations and the resultant embracing of reproductive technologies in nationalist and economic pronatalist rhetoric; and the greater familiarity of these procedures might all be leading to a greater acceptance of egg donation using whatever eggs are available. Egg donation that defies a parallel with "normal" heterosexual reproduction in terms of lay understandings of the transmission of race and ethnicity and skin tone will develop its own logics that, I feel certain, will also partake of important historical aspects of transnational relations. And, in the process, the fact that there is not a good parallel of nonmatching in egg donation with nonmatching in adoption will cease to be the dominant frame in which this question is considered.

In the cases discussed in this chapter, even when the individuals or couples were choosing an egg donor based on skin tone in relation to ethnic and racial classification, it was not the gamete but the donor who was classified. In some sense, this seems anodyne; it is a parallel for heterosexual courtship condoned throughout the world and assumed in many contemporary academic disciplines such as evolutionary psychology. One seeks certain characteristics in one's partner in part for one's own well-being and in part for what one is choosing for one's future offspring. It may be a dubious elision from donor to gamete, but it is nonetheless part of a deeply entrenched heterosexual calculative matrix. The central paradox of egg donation—that egg donation is organized according to psychological, social, and medical qualities by which donors are classified and by which price differentials between donors are justified, yet skepticism about biological heritability of these kinds of complex social and natural traits is advocated—should be understood in terms of its similarity to something that is so ingrained as to be taken for granted in "normal" reproduction.

In addition, in assisted reproduction with donor gametes, it is possible to indulge fantasy and to be even more selective than in "real life." I might balk at asking my partner if his or her grandparents had cancer, but I can get this information about many gamete donors. I might not be able to or wish to sustain a relationship with someone who would engage in reproductive sex with me who is also a doctor, or a concert pianist, or a beautiful person, but I can look for this in my donor. Furthermore, it is justifiable under another very familiar rubric: doing everything I can to give my child the best chance in life. In my fieldwork, egg donors, too, report the satisfaction and seduction of presenting themselves to a needy and well-off recipient who then chooses them for their superior or at least winning (in both senses of the word) characteristics. This state of affairs both supports the eugenics that naturalizes the market differentiation of donors and it also opens up a space for "mistakes," as in the by-now-familiar variants of the gendered joke about the child conceived with a model's egg and a Nobel Prize winner's sperm coming out with "his looks and her brains."

When considering egg donation, I have tried to show the salience of donor skin tone in donor selection and self-description, even where there is no skin in what is donated (eggs), let alone any definitive or relative skin tone, and even though popular ideas of heredity uphold the underdetermination of skin tone transmission. I have also tried to suggest the extraordinary amount of context that frames, disambiguates, obscures, and highlights our perceptions of skin tone. In sum, I have suggested that skin tone is not typically, or is only a perceptible physical property, arrayed on a continuum. Rather, as these cases show, skin tone is inextricably tied up in transnational historical and geopolitical and religious bases of identity and relations of power that manifest themselves in the minute disciplining and disciplined behaviors of patients, practitioners, and donors alike. Finally, a consideration of skin tone in egg donation illustrates active processes of the racialization of biology and the biologization of race.

9 Fair Enough?
Color and the Commodification of Self in Indian Matrimonials
Jyotsna Vaid

[A] Hindu is unsurpassed in his exaltation of colour and proneness to make a fetish of it. This comes out most blatantly in connexion with marriages, which . . . provide the most reliable test of the existence of color . . . prejudice among a people.[1]

MARRIAGE IS A CENTRAL ASPECT OF SOCIETAL FUNCTIONING in South Asia. For women, being married is considered to be "the ultimate fulfillment of their destiny, closely tied to the birth of children, . . . [because women in South Asia are] dependent on husbands and sons for economic security and well-being."[2] The vast majority of marriages in India are arranged marriages—that is, matches in which mate selection is initiated and often determined by an intermediary, usually a family member. The practice of arranged marriages was considered necessary to prevent alliances between individuals from differing classes, castes, or subcastes. Even today, a complex system of rules is in place that defines whom one can or cannot marry. Aside from birth, caste, and class considerations, other factors considered important in mate selection are the prospective partner's education, age, and appearance. A crucial aspect of physical appearance, and one that is highly prized as a marker of beauty for South Asians, is a light complexion. Complexion, then, acquires symbolic capital in marriage negotiations among South Asians.

Many South Asian languages have terms to refer to different shades of skin tone: In Hindi, for example, one finds *gora/gori* (fair/light skinned), *saanwala* (wheatish brown), and *kala/kali* (black). In Punjabi, a person's fair complexion is likened to the color of milk (*dudh waken*) or to the color of the moon; conversely, a dark person's complexion is compared with that of a crow or with the back of an iron skillet.

The origins of this color consciousness in the Indian subcontinent are obscure. There is apparently nothing in the ancient Vedic texts or religious scriptures to suggest a favoring of lighter over darker skin. In fact, popular paintings and idols depict Hindu gods (Krishna, in particular) as having dark, bluish skin. The British colonial presence in India may have reinforced an association between fair skin and social status, but the association likely predates the British rule. Color consciousness among South Asians has been suggested by some to originate from a belief that the upper castes/classes in the subcontinent descended from Aryan (and, thus, Caucasian) invaders from central Asia. However, although there are linguistic ties between Sanskrit and European languages, there is scant archaeological support for an Aryan invasion in north India. Indeed, the term *arya* may well have been used in the sense of "noble" rather than in the sense of an Aryan race.[3] Another speculation about the origins of color consciousness comes from the fact that the Sanskrit term for *caste* (*varna*) also means "color," and there are well-documented proscriptions against the mixing of upper and lower castes through marriage (*varna-sankara*). Thus, some ascribe the roots of color consciousness in the subcontinent to the belief in maintaining the purity of the bloodstream of the upper castes. Yet however important *varna-sankara* may have been as a driving force around which early Hindu society was organized, skin color, per se, is not likely to have been singled out as a marker of status given the variation in skin color within members of the same caste and even within members of the same family. Indeed, Philips suggests that the term for *light* in early Vedic texts may not have referred to skin color at all, but rather to the "light" associated with knowledge. Last, it is possible that rather than originating in proscriptions against intermarriage or in beliefs about the superiority of the upper castes, a preference for light-colored skin may simply have arisen from an association between a fair complexion and a life of leisure, and a dark complexion and a life spent in menial labor under a hot sun.

Whatever its origins, skin color as a legacy of the subcontinent's past has shaped and continues to shape South Asians' cultural perceptions of beauty, identity, and difference. Skin color assumes particular significance in the context of selecting a marriage partner. The association between fair skin, beauty, and marriage prospects usually starts at the time of birth of a female child when, after noting the gender of the infant, the next comment made by relatives is whether or not the baby is *gori,* or fair complexioned. Indeed, the pressure on families to have fair offspring in some cases begins even before the baby is born, as illustrated by such family practices as giving the expectant mother milk mixed with saffron to drink during her pregnancy as a way of enhancing the likelihood that the offspring will be fair. For young women entering marriageable age, traditional family remedies for lightening the skin (e.g., the application of turmeric paste) have now been supplanted by an array of beauty treatments aimed at giving them an edge in the marriage market.

Roksana Rahman describes a television ad in India for a popular skin-lightening cream called Fair & Lovely. In the ad, a mother proudly announces to her daughter that a prospective groom's family has selected the daughter's picture for a face-showing ceremony that is to happen in a month's time. (This is a ceremony during which the groom and his family see the prospective bride for the first time. If the family and groom find her acceptable, a formal proposal is sent to the bride's family.) The daughter is initially delighted at being selected until she remembers that she is not as fair as her pictures indicate. In despair, she calls her best friend who advises her that Fair & Lovely cream is what she needs. The prospective bride uses the cream for a month and is glowingly white on the day of the face-showing ceremony, making the groom's family choose her to marry their son. As if the connection were not obvious enough, the ad ends with the groom's mother proudly commenting on how fair her new daughter-in-law is.[4]

For diasporic South Asians, color consciousness survives and is promul-gated through transnational activities not the least of which has been the ex-plosion of Bollywood culture. A fair complexion continues to be perceived as a sign of beauty among South Asian immigrants as it does for their counterparts in the subcontinent. Vijay Prashad refers to this as color consciousness that is different from racism.[5] However, no matter how fair they may be within their own community, South Asian immigrants stand out as visible minorities in the context of a predominantly white-majority host culture. As such, they have been the subject of occasional acts of discrimination, either deliberate (as in the case of the "Dotbuster" attacks that targeted South Asian women in New Jersey in the 1980s) or inadvertent (as in the attacks on Sikhs who were mistaken for Arabs in post-9/11 America, or in border crossings when South Asians are taken to be Mexican.[6] The response of the South Asian community to these forms of racism has been twofold. The first has been somewhat biological and has taken the form of a kind of racism of its own. While reviewing the early history of racist legislation of the U.S. naturalization and immigration department, which restricted citizenship to those who were Caucasian or white, Sucheta Mazum-dar noted that "[i]nstead of challenging racism, the South Asian struggle be-came an individualized and personalized mission to prove that they were of 'pure-blood' Aryan stock."[7] The second response has been cultural. Rosemary

George noted that during the contemporary period, South Asian immigrants have sought to position themselves more in terms of their culture and class rather than in terms of phenotypic distinctness, as a way (perhaps) of providing an alternative to being considered in the same category as other visible minorities (e.g., African Americans, Mexicans) who are typically stigmatized in the United States.[8]

Current Research

In this chapter I examine, through the lens of matrimonial advertisements placed by and for members of the South Asian diasporic community in North America, how skin color functions in marriage negotiations in this community. Given the ambiguous and ambivalent positioning of South Asians in the racial hierarchy of the United States, I seek to problematize how color is used in the ads placed by or on behalf of different segments of this community: men versus women, previously married versus never married, and first- versus second-generation members.

What may we expect with respect to the significance of skin color for South Asian immigrants entering the marriage market? On the one hand, we may predict that a fair complexion (for women) will continue to exert an appeal for immigrants for the same reasons it does for their counterparts at home: as a marker of beauty. Indeed, its appeal may be enhanced in the diasporic context and may extend to men because of the symbolic value of lighter skin in settings where "not white" is equated with a lower social status. A fair skin color in a mate may also be desired by South Asian immigrants if they believe that it will make assimilation into the predominantly white-majority culture easier for their offspring. On the other hand, one could imagine that appearance or complexion may be less strongly weighted in a marriage partner in the diasporic context as a result of a perhaps waning influence of traditional values or because other attributes such as shared interests or cultural values may take on added importance. To determine which of these possibilities is the case, I will compare the incidence of mention of fair complexion in the ads placed by South Asian immigrants compared with those placed by their counterparts living in South Asia.

A second issue examined here is the strategic use of light skin in marriage negotiations. A lighter skin color has traditionally been associated with greater choice in a marriage partner: It can be used to compensate for status inconsistencies in cross-caste marriages, for an inadequate dowry, lack of education, or unemployment. By contrast, larger dowries may be demanded from women without education or employment, or from women considered dark or unattractive. Is skin color also used as a bargaining chip in marriage negotiations among diasporic South Asians? One may conjecture that dowry in this context is not as strong a compensation to offset a bride's lack of fair complexion since, as a Muslim Canadian mother of three daughters quoted by Zareena Grewal noted: ". . . here no one needs money. They all have money and so they can't compensate [for a] deficiency [in color] with money."[9] Might other kinds of compensation (e.g., U.S. citizenship) be offered by individuals who cannot lay claim to being fair in complexion? Conversely, will a fair complexion be among the compensatory inducements offered by those who are perceived to be disadvantaged in the marriage market—namely, divorced individuals—given the stigma in the South Asian community associated with being divorced?

For second-generation South Asians, as Raj points out, marriage negotiations are an important part of "the subtle processes through which assumptions about identity and cultural continuity are made explicit . . . [for it] is precisely at times like marriage when people are actively thinking about who they are and, in fact, who they will become."[10] Hints that color may figure prominently for this group are suggested by the findings of a study of South Asian Canadian adolescent women that being less fair was associated with less satisfaction with their bodies and with less self-esteem.[11] This suggests that skin color continues to matter to the second generation as it does to their immigrant parents. Alternatively, second-generation immigrants may be less bound to socialize within the community and may be more likely to react against what they perceive as the restrictive practices of their parents' generation, which may lead them to reject skin color as a basis for judging a person's worth or suitability for marriage. Second-generation women, in particular, may feel burdened by cultural expectations on them to serve as the bearers of tradition. This may lead more and more of them to seek relationships outside their ethnic community altogether.[12]

Matrimonial Advertisements

To examine these issues, I report an analysis of the prevalence and correlates of mention of skin color in matrimonial advertisements in the Indian immigrant community in the United States over three decades and compare the results with characteristics of ads placed by Indians residing in India.

The practice of placing matrimonial ads dates back to the early 1950s in the Indian subcontinent, emerging shortly after India and Pakistan gained independence. Such ads are now a staple of the South Asian press. With occupational mobility and the ensuing geographic dispersal of once-closely knit communities, there has been a weakening of traditional family and community networks and an increasing reliance on commercial modes of mate selection, through newspaper advertisements or online matrimonial sites. These modes are seen increasingly as a legitimate means of transcending the limitations of one's current location and of casting a wider net in the search for the best match. Rather than replacing the traditional arranged marriage system, the use of ads has become an extension of the traditional process of mate selection. Ads are typically placed by parents or other family members on behalf of the prospective brides or grooms, although, increasingly, particularly in web-based matrimonial sites, seekers themselves place the ad and often post rather personal narratives about themselves and the qualities they are looking for in a prospective mate.

Reliance on matrimonials has become an integral aspect of Indian immigrant life; ads are routinely consulted by those settled or seeking to settle abroad. Matrimonial ads are found in a variety of diasporic communities from the Indian subcontinent, Hindu and Muslim.[13] There is, in fact, extensive literature on personal ads and on matrimonial ads in particular.[14] Several studies have been conducted on various segments of the South Asian population and on Indians abroad.[15] Studies of immigrants have examined such aspects as green card marriages[16] and how members of special groups such as divorced individuals or second-generation immigrants portray themselves in the ads.[17] Findings from these studies show that compared with personal ads found in the press in Western countries, Indian matrimonials typically give more prominence to ascribed characteristics (e.g., family standing, caste, region of origin, and language) than to achieved characteristics (e.g., educational attainment, occupation, and personality traits). When personality attributes are mentioned, they tend to be restricted to such culturally valued qualities as "sincere" or "decent" for men and "home loving" or "smart" or "East–West values" for women. Physical attributes, when mentioned, refer to attractiveness, height, weight, and—of most relevance to the current analysis—complexion.

"Fair" in the Matrimonials

Although there is evidence for the use of the word *fair* in the earliest ads from the 1950s, and it has become commonplace to refer to and occasionally to caricature the use of *fair* in Indian matrimonials,[18] no previous scholarly investigation has focused on this variable. Before discussing my research, I provide a brief review of the few earlier studies of ads in which skin color was mentioned at all.

In one of the earliest studies of matrimonial ads in India, done in the 1950s, Noel Gist examined 400 ads from the *Hindustan Times.* One fifth of the ads by men and half of the ads by women referred to their physical appearance. Physical attractiveness was often associated with lightness of complexion. Although only seven of the ads by men (2.8%) mentioned their complexion (*fair*), twenty-three of the ads by women (13.5%) mentioned theirs; of the latter, three women said they were white, one used the term *milk-white,* sixteen used the term *fair,* and three said they were "wheatish." None of the women mentioned color in their specifications for a husband, but 11.1 percent of the men stipulated the color of their bride, asking for a fair or white bride in almost all cases; in no instance was darkness of skin mentioned, either as an asset or a liability.[19]

Another early study based in India that included mention of skin color was conducted by Arthur Niehoff in 1959. This study examined 213 ads in four English-language newspapers in India (*National Herald,* Lucknow; *Hindustan Times,* New Delhi; *Times of India,* New Delhi; and *Amrita Bazar Patrika,* Allahabad) from 1953 through 1954. The advertisers were all highly educated Hindus, of high income, and were urban dwellers. The vast majority of ads referring to women listed beauty in one way or another (89%), whereas beauty was mentioned by only 23 percent of the ads referring to men. Furthermore, 18 percent of the appearance stipulations for women were for fair-colored individuals, and no one asked for a dark-complexioned person. Women listed their lightness of skin twice as often as men actually stipulated it. In commenting on the desire for fair skin in women, Niehoff noted that in a 1954 editorial in the *National Herald* the then-Chief Minister of Madras exhorted Hindu men not to discriminate against dark-skinned girls, arguing that they were generally more intelligent and harder working than light-skinned girls; besides, he added, because the majority of Indian girls were dark, there were not enough light-skinned girls to go around.[20]

Two recent studies are of particular interest for their bearing on the issue of skin color in ads in a diasporic context. Siddiqi and Reeves compared 943 randomly selected ads in four daily regional English-language newspapers in India from 1974 to 1980 with 936 ads selected from the immigrant weekly, *India Abroad.* A ranking of relative mention of ad sender characteristics revealed that the most often-mentioned characteristic was region of origin in India, followed by language, and family background. Skin color was mentioned by 7 percent of the India-based group versus 3 percent of the immigrant sample. The relatively low mention of skin color in the India-based ads is at odds with the earlier estimates from India; more interesting is that color was mentioned even less often by immigrants. However, because these figures were not disaggregated by the gender of the seeker or by their marital or immigration status, it is difficult to know how to interpret them.[21]

In a more extensive analysis of ads from an immigrant outlet, Vaid examined a corpus of nearly 2000 ads from *India Abroad* compiled from 1976 to 1994. Skin color was mentioned in 11 percent of the ads in this corpus. By contrast, for ads featured in a randomly selected issue of the *Times of India* newspaper in India (the December 25, 1994, issue) there was a 26.6 percent mention of *fair* for Hindu women (n = 45) and a 44.4 percent mention of *fair* for Muslim women (n = 54); the corresponding percentages for men were 0 percent and 7 percent.[22]

Rationale and Research Questions

The current research extended the study by Vaid in 1998 and examined the prevalence and correlates of mention of skin tone in one print source and two online sources of matrimonial advertisements directed at the Indian immigrant population in the United States. Specific questions motivating this research were: What is the frequency of mention of skin color in the ads by gender compared with the frequency of mention of other attributes? Has mention of color remained stable over time? Is relative mention of skin color influenced by whether the ad is self-sponsored or family placed? Is it influenced by whether the seeker was previously married (is *fair* mentioned more often for divorced women than for unmarried women)? Last, is its mention influenced by the seeker's immigration status? By "mention," what I mean is whether *fair* is mentioned as an attribute of the seeker, rather than as a desired attribute in the prospective mate. The assumption here is that seekers will highlight those aspects of themselves that they perceive the prospective mate will find desirable.

Method

A corpus of matrimonial ads was compiled from three different sources (Table 9.1).

India Abroad

The first source was the New York City-based weekly *India Abroad*, the oldest, nationally circulated Indian immigrant newspaper in the United States. Ads were selected from this source from the time it first began publishing matrimonials in 1976 up to 2005. The ads comprising the *India Abroad* corpus contained

Table 9.1 Overview of Ads Sampled

Ads Placed In	Period Sampled	Current Residence of Sender	Total No. of Ads Sampled	Male Senders, n (%)	Female Senders, n (%)
India Abroad	1976–2005	United States	1663	821 (49.4)	842 (50.6)
1st Place Matrimonials, www.matrimonials-india.com/wedseekt.htm	2003–2005 (11/24/2005)	United States	1429	900 (63)	529 (37)
1st Place Matrimonials, www.matrimonials-India.com/wedseekt.htm	2003–2005 (11/24/2005)	India	4832	3085 (63.8)	1747 (36.2)
Vivaah.com, http://vivaah.com/	2003–2005 (11/26/2005)	India	1533	1015 (66.2)	518 (33.8)

all matrimonials featured in fifteen randomly selected issues from three time periods: 1976 to 1985, 1986 to 1995, and 1996 to 2005. There were a total of 1663 ads from *India Abroad,* divided fairly evenly by gender of seeker (49.4% ads were by men and 50.6% were by women). These ads are written as brief narratives of varying length and degree of detail. Thus, the ads vary widely in the range of characteristics mentioned for the seeker and the target. Two typical ads from this source are the following:

> [Matrimonial Groom] Affluent Punjabi Khatri family invite alliance for their handsome son, 25/5'11", US born and raised, fair, athletic, M.A. final year, well-settled and financially independent in his business (6 figure income); seeking beautiful, slim, tall, professional match, raised in US/Canada with strong cultural values. Respond with bio/photo.

> [Matrimonial Bride] N. Indian parents settled in the U.S. since 1965 invite correspondence from suitable match for their very fair & attractive daughter, who is charming, affectionate, 29, 5ft 2in., born & raised in the U.S. with Indian values. J.D., MBA currently working as Vice President, Legal & Finance for family-owned oil field equipment engineering & manufacturing business. Reply with photo.

In addition to *India Abroad,* two online sources were also consulted in this research: 1st Place Matrimonials and Vivaah.com.

1st Place Matrimonials

This online source allowed a screening of ads on the basis of country of current residence and citizenship. For the purposes of the current research, only ads from Indian or U.S. passport holders currently residing in India or the United

States, respectively, were selected. As of November 24, 2005, there were 1429 ads posted by individuals residing in the United States (63% male) and 4832 ads from individuals residing in India (63.8% male), with posting dates ranging from 2002 to 2005. Each ad on this website required information to be filled out on the seeker's age, height, marital status, name, city, date of ad, personal details (meaning, whether they drink, smoke, or eat meat), education level, country of residence, passport, culture (Indian or American), religion, and employment. In addition to this information, users could provide a free-form narrative as well. A typical ad from an unmarried female from this source is as follows:

Age: 24 **Height**: 5'8" **Marital Status**: Never Married

City: New Delhi

Date of Ad: 27/08/2002

Personal Details: Non-Vegetarian, Non-Smoker, Teetotaler

Education: MA/MSc/MBA **Country of Residence**: India

Passport: India **Culture:** North Indian **Religion:** Hindu

Employment: Management

Chetna is a healthy good looking, fair skinned girl. She is from a respected, educated family. Looking for a healthy, good-looking, educated, tall boy from a hindu family.

Here is an ad from a divorced male from this source:

Age: 33 **Height**: 5'7" **Marital Status**: Divorced

City: Bahadurgarh **Date of Ad**: 26/09/2004

Personal Details: Non-Vegetarian, Non-smoker, Teetotaler

Education: MA/MSc/MBA **Country of Residence**: India

Passport: India **Culture:** North Indian **Religion:** Hindu
Employment: Technology

I am down to earth, caring, loving, adjustable & sincere person; I get satisfaction to help others. I respect others feeling, emotions, & views & expect the same from other. I respect elders and believe in Indian traditions. . . . At present I am working as an Systems Manager. . . . Blood Group: B+. Height: 5 ft 7 inch. Weight: 67 Kg. Color: Whitish. Caste: Brahmin Gotra: Parashar. I am looking for a friend rather than relationship, who could make me smile at all the time, good as well as bad time. . . .

Vivaah.com

The other online source consulted, Vivaah.com, predominantly listed ads from India-based individuals. Like 1st Place Matrimonials, this source requires users to fill in required background information in a standard format. The categories in which information was solicited included body type (slim, average, athletic, a few extra kilos, heavy), marital status (never married, separated, divorced, widowed), country of current residence, residency status (work permit, citizen, permanent resident, student visa, temporary visa, refugee visa), cultural family values (traditional, moderate, liberal), and complexion (very fair, fair, wheatish, wheatish medium, wheatish brown, wheatish dark). As of November 26, 2005, there were 1533 such ads in total (66.2% from men), posted between 2002 and 2005.

Findings

What Were the Demographic Characteristics of Ad Placers?

Across the three sources, the predominant religion of the ad placers was Hindu (more than 60%), followed by Muslim (around 18%), Christian (around 10%), or some other religion (12%). In terms of age, the majority of seekers were between 25 and 35 years old. There was some regional variation across the corpora, but not enough to permit targeted analyses comparing characteristics of north versus south Indians, for example. In terms of gender composition, the majority of the online ads were from males, whereas the print ads (*India Abroad*) had an even distribution of males and females. With respect to marital status, as is typical for the South Asian community, the percent of ads from divorced individuals was fairly low; the *India Abroad* sample contained 8.4 percent divorced male and 6.9 percent divorced female ads. The 1st Place Matrimonials sample contained 8.1 percent divorced male and 10.3 percent divorced female ads, and Vivaah.com contained 7.9 percent divorced male and 8.4 percent female divorced ads.

For ease of presentation, the findings are summarized as they relate to specific research questions. Because of the way they were designed, some corpora are better suited than others in answering certain research questions. For example, comparisons of U.S.-based versus India-based seekers are best addressed in the 1st Place Matrimonials site, which contained a substantial number of ads from each group, whereas comparisons between first- and second-generation immigrants currently based in the United States are best addressed in the *India Abroad* source.

How Pervasive Is Mention of the Seeker's Skin Color in the Ads, Relative to Percent Mention of Other Attributes of Seekers?

The *India Abroad* sample (N = 1663) is the best suited to answer this question because the decision to mention skin color or any other seeker attributes was entirely at the discretion of the ad sender, rather than being required information, as in the online ad sources. Figure 9.1 illustrates percent mention by seeker gender of the most frequently mentioned nonphysical seeker attributes in the *India Abroad* ads; Figure 9.2 summarizes mention of physical seeker attributes, including skin color.

One can see that more than 60 percent of the ads by men and women seekers alike mentioned their occupation (men mentioning it slightly more often than women), immigration status, religion/caste, and region/language of origin, in roughly that order. By contrast, with the exception of height, which was mentioned by more than 60 percent of the sample, seeker physical attributes were mentioned in less than half the ads; for men, looks were mentioned by 40.4 percent, followed by complexion (6.7%) followed by build (2.4%). For women,

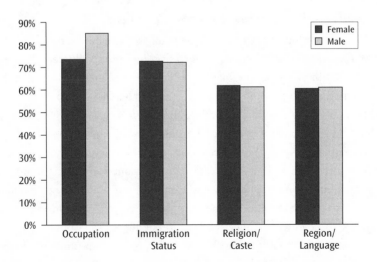

Figure 9.1 Percent Mention of Nonphysical Attributes of Seeker by Gender
SOURCE: *India Abroad*, 1976–2005; n = 1663.

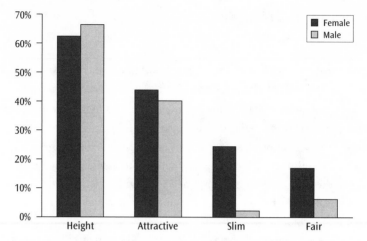

Figure 9.2 Percent Mention of Physical Attributes of Seeker by Gender
SOURCE: *India Abroad*, 1976–2005; n = 1663.

looks were mentioned in 44.1 percent of the ads, followed by build (slim, 24.7%) followed by fair complexion (17.2%). In summary, a fair complexion was mentioned in only a subset of the ads; nonetheless, it was mentioned more than twice as often by women to describe themselves than by men.

When Information About Skin Tone Was Required, How Do Male and Female Ad Senders Characterize Themselves?

The Vivaah.com source is the best suited to answer this question because it required seekers to specify their skin color, selecting from six different shades. As summarized in Table 9.2, the majority of India-based, never-married seekers referred to themselves as very fair or fair (63.8% of females and 59.7% of males). The next two shades—wheatish or medium—were selected by 32.3 percent of males and females, and 8 percent of the males versus 3.9 percent of the females described themselves as wheatish brown or dark in complexion. Thus, for never-married individuals, a fair color was mentioned somewhat more often by women than by men, whereas a dark complexion was mentioned much less often by women than by men. Interestingly, a divorced status in India-based ads was associated with an elevated mention of fair for the women (90%) and a much lower mention of wheatish complexion for women (only 3.9%). These results would suggest qualified support (given the small sample sizes of the divorced sample) for the notion that a fair complexion for women may serve to offset the stigmatizing effect of a divorced status.

Table 9.2 Distribution of Skin Tone of Seekers by Gender and Marital Status

	Male NM, % (N = 942)	Female NM, % (N = 480)	Male D, % (N = 70)	Female D, % (N = 40)
Very fair/fair	59.7	63.8	51.4	90.0
Wheatish/medium	32.3	32.3	8.0	3.9
Wheatish brown/dark	8.0	3.9	4.3	5.0

D, divorced; NM, never married.

SOURCE: Vivaah.com, India-based ads, 2003 to 2005.

How Does Mention of "Fair" Vary as a Function of Whether the Ad Is Placed by the Seekers Themselves or by Their Family Members?

The *India Abroad* sample is best suited to address this issue because the ad texts in this sample typically noted by whom the ad was placed. In this sample, 40 percent of the male ads and 60 percent of the female ads were stated as being placed by family or friends of the seeker. However, as shown in Figure 9.3, for female family-placed and self-placed ads alike, mention of the seeker's skin color is uniformly high (around 17%); for men, skin color is mentioned slightly more by ads placed by the seekers themselves (8.2%) relative to those placed on their behalf by family members (5%). Thus, the hypothesis that skin color mention will be elevated in family-placed ads was not supported.

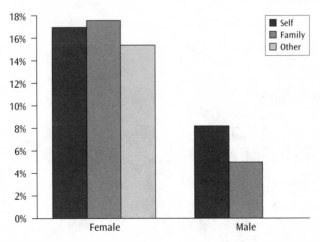

Figure 9.3 Percent Mention of Seeker's Fair Complexion by Gender and Adplacer

SOURCE: *India Abroad.*

Is Mention of Skin Color Influenced by the Immigrant Status of the Seeker?

This issue is best addressed with reference to the *India Abroad* sample. In this sample, 56 percent of respondents mentioned their immigration status. Of these, 32 percent stated they were visiting the United States, 45 percent said that they were permanent residents of the United States (green card holders), and 23 percent noted that they were born or raised in the United States.

Percent mention of fair skin color appears to be slightly higher among U.S.-born/raised seekers (13.7%, n = 212) relative to green card holders (10.9%, n = 422), and visitors to the United States (10.9%, n = 302). The U.S-born sample is discussed further later.

Has the Incidence of Mention of "Fair" Increased or Remained Stable in Matrimonial Ads Over Time?

The *India Abroad* sample is the only one that had a sufficient time span to permit comparisons across time periods. The overall distribution of ads and percent mention of fair over the three time periods (T1–T3) sampled is summarized in Table 9.3 and illustrated by gender in Figure 9.4.

Table 9.3 Change in Percent Mention of "Fair" Over Time

Time Period Sampled	No. of Ads Sampled	Mention of "Fair" in Seeker Description, %
T1: 1976–1985	260 (132 F)	11.5
T2: 1986–1995	916 (446 F)	10.0
T3: 1996–2005	487 (264 F)	15.9

F, female.
SOURCE: *India Abroad*.

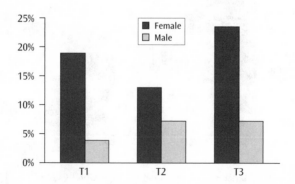

Figure 9.4 Percent Mention of Seeker's Fair Complexion by Gender over Time
SOURCE: *India Abroad*.

It appears that mention of fair was steady in time periods T2 and T3 (i.e., through 1995) and then increased in the most recent time period sampled (1996–2005), largely as a result of a sharp increase in the mention of fair among female seekers.

How Is "Fair" Mentioned by U.S.-Born/Raised Offspring of Indian Immigrants by Gender and Over Time?

Figure 9.5 shows the incidence of mention of fair by U.S.-born/raised offspring of immigrants in the *India Abroad* sample by gender and over T2 and T3. The pattern of results is striking in showing that although there was no appreciable difference in the mention of fair in the ads placed for men and women during T2, mention of fair for women has sharply increased in T3, found in nearly a quarter of these ads, whereas its mention in men has decreased. Thus, the data suggest that mention of fair color is on the rise among second-generation South Asian (Indian) American women.

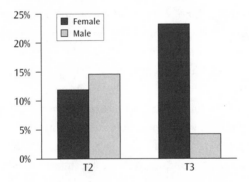

Figure 9.5 Change in Percent Mention of Fair by U.S. Born/Raised Seekers by Gender and Time
T2 = 1986–1995; T3 = 1996–2005
SOURCE: *India Abroad.*

Is There Any Evidence for a Resistance to or Critique of the Emphasis on Fairness as a Marker of Beauty?

To get at this issue I conducted a key word search of the ad narratives in the 1st Place Matrimonials database using the term *dark* and the phrase *color no bar.* Only three examples were uncovered. The first was from a 2002 posting by a woman living in Bombay:

> Though otherwise modest I must say I am very attractive, intelligent and caring person. I take pride in my family and upbringing and I am a very sincere, yet

fun-loving person with a very good sense of humour. I am honest, warm and af-
fectionate, and believe in good old Indian values. I am convent-educated with a
broad range of interests . . . I am well-respected and liked both at work and by my
friends. A very pleasing personality and good at domestic chores. . . . Please reply
only if you are very serious about marriage. I must tell upfront that although I am
beautiful, slim and tall, I am not fair (not black either, just "saanwali").

This was, in fact, the only ad (out of several thousand) in the database in which
the person's not being fair complexioned was explicitly mentioned; but, placed
as it is after the many positive attributes of the ad placer are described, one is
led to infer that the former are meant to offset the fact that the person is not fair.
However, by taking pains to note that she is not black either, the seeker shows
her refusal to see herself as overly dark and, by implication, her tacit acceptance
of the color hierarchy.

The second ad of note here is one that was posted by a never-married, forty-
three-year-old white American in 2004 seeking an Indian bride. It is included
here to illustrate that it contrasts markedly with ads by Indian seekers in specifically welcoming correspondence from dark-complexioned women: "Looking for a polite and easy-to-get-along-with girl of very dark black complexion.
Hindu. Broad-minded. Must be willing to settle in the U.S.A. and like music of
all types. Low caste, poor, or Dalit types very welcome."

The third ad, taken from a 2003 posting from a twenty-five-year-old Indian
male engineer who is a U.S. passport holder, is the only one uncovered in this
corpus that was placed by an Indian male who explicitly rejects the traditional
valuing of dowry, caste, virginity, and skin color in favor of other qualities:

Hardworking man, but realize the value of family and love. . . . Just bought new car
and house. Need a best friend to enjoy them with. Would like to find charming,
Indian woman . . . who has mind of her own and not confined to thinking of tradi-
tionals. . . . She must be strong, outspoken, and intelligent like American women,
yet should carry the grace of an Indian woman. . . . Would like girl to be Hindu, but
caste, widowhood, divorcee does not matter to me. Don't care about skin color or
body type! Very much against dowry. Parents of girls please do not reply.

The fact that this was the only ad that turned up in the search for ads that
rejected color as a condition indicates the pervasiveness of color as a valued
attribute in a marriage partner. The ad also illustrates that the process of seeking a mate through personal advertisements is an example of how members of

minority groups can be endogamous and yet disrupt and complicate cultural constructs. In this regard, Raj notes that marriage negotiations among immigrants are "one instance of the dynamism of cultural agency and structural constraint through which people can claim and uphold the necessary nostalgia for culture, and yet can live their lives in much more complex ways."[23]

Conclusions

What has this study of the role of skin color in Indian matrimonial advertisements in the immigrant context shown? First, it clearly shows that fair skin color is a distinctly gendered attribute, offered by women far more than by men. Second, the frequency of mention of color is not affected (for women) by whether the ad is placed by the seeker herself or by a family member.

Last, the findings paint a complex picture about the influence of fair skin in relation to immigrant status. Mention of fair skin color has increased sharply since the mid 1980s, and is currently close to 25 percent for second-generation Indian American women, based on the *India Abroad* ads sampled over the different time periods. Does this mean that traditional values continue to affect the lives of immigrants and their offspring? Is the persistence and possible increase in mention of fair skin color over time a signal that *fair* has taken on added value because of its racial significance for members of visible minorities? A racial analysis would lead one to expect an increase in mention of fair color for immigrants relative to nonimmigrants, both men and women, yet immigrants and in-immigrants in the *India Abroad* sample showed a comparable overall level of mention of this attribute. Perhaps skin color, at least in the arena of the matrimonials, is used more as a marker of (female) beauty than anything else. Based on the fact that there were hardly any ads that explicitly rejected the coupling of fair color and one's desirability as a prospective mate, there is no reason to expect that skin color has diminished in importance in the diasporic context. What the ads do not speak to, of course, is whether there is any sign of resistance to arranged marriages in general, or to the use of skin color as a negotiating chip in mate selection. The apparent increase in intermarriages, particularly among second-generation women relative to men of South Asian descent, suggests that color may be a variable of relevance to monitor. However, it is also clear that the ideology that fair is beautiful continues to exert a pernicious effect on the self-esteem of women who have been repeatedly reminded that if they are not the former, they cannot be the latter. The internalization of this ideology clearly needs to be challenged.[24]

10 Consuming Lightness

Segmented Markets and Global Capital in the Skin-Whitening Trade

Evelyn Nakano Glenn

DESPITE THE REIGNING IDEOLOGY OF *color blindness* that proclaims the irrelevance of race in the contemporary world, *colorism,* the preference for lighter skin and social hierarchy based on skin tone, has emerged as a pervasive and growing axis of inequality in many societies. Unlike *race,* which is based on the idea of mutually exclusive categories, skin color is arrayed along a continuum that crosscuts racial categories. For example, taken as a whole, African Americans have moved up the socioeconomic ladder during the past half century. However, aggregate data do not capture the within-group variation in mobility. When skin tone is taken into account, there are significant correlations among skin tone, socioeconomic status, and achievement, with lighter skinned members of racial minorities enjoying higher average levels of education, income, and occupational status than darker skinned members. Social psychologists have conducted experiments demonstrating that people's judgments about others are literally "colored" by skin tone, so that lighter skinned individuals are viewed as more intelligent, trustworthy, and attractive than darker skinned counterparts.[1] Thus, colorism is as much an issue for intragroup inequality as it is for intergroup inequality.

One way of conceptualizing light skin, then, is as a form of *symbolic capital,* an asset that furthers one's life chances. Given the correlation between skin color and perceived attractiveness, the symbolic value of light skin is especially critical for women. Men who are not physically prepossessing, but who have wealth, education, and other forms of human capital, may be considered "good catches," whereas women who are physically attractive may be considered desirable despite the lack of other forms of capital. Although skin tone is usually seen as a form of fixed or unchangeable capital, in fact, men and women may attempt to *acquire* light-skinned privilege. Sometimes this search takes the form of seeking light-skinned marital partners to raise one's status and to achieve intergenerational mobility by increasing the likelihood of having light-skinned children. Often, especially for women, this search takes the form of using cosmetics or other treatments to change the appearance of one's skin to make it look lighter.

This chapter focuses on the practice of skin lightening and the marketing of skin lighteners in various societies around the world, and on the multinational corporations that are involved in the global skin-lightening trade. An analysis of this complex topic calls for a multilevel approach. First, we need to place the production, marketing, and consumption of skin lighteners into a global political economic context. We ask: How is skin lightening interwoven into the world economic system and its transnational circuits of products, capital, culture, and people? Second, we need to examine the mediating entities and processes by which skin lighteners reach specific national/ethnic/racial/class consumers. We ask: What are the media and messages, cultural themes, and symbols used to create the desire for skin-lightening products among particular groups? Last, we need to examine the meaning and significance of skin color for consumers of skin lighteners. We ask: How do consumers learn about, test, and compare skin-lightening products and what do they seek to achieve through their use?

The issue of skin lightening may seem trivial at first glance. However, it is my contention that a close examination of the global circuits of skin lightening provides a unique lens through which to view the workings of the Western-dominated global system as it simultaneously promulgates a "white is right" ideology while also promoting the desire for and consumption of Western culture and products.

Skin Lightening and Global Capital

Skin lightening has long been practiced in many parts of the world. Women concocted their own treatments or purchased products from self-styled beauty experts offering special creams, soaps, or lotions, which were either ineffective sham products or else effective but contained highly toxic materials such as mercury or lead. From the perspective of the supposedly enlightened present, skin lightening might be viewed as a form of vanity or a misguided and dangerous relic of the past.

However, at the beginning of the twentieth-first century, the search for light skin, free of imperfections such as freckles and age spots, has actually accelerated, and the market for skin-lightening products has mushroomed in all parts of the world. The production and marketing of products that offer the prospect of lighter, brighter, whiter, skin has become a multibillion-dollar global industry. Skin lightening has been incorporated into transnational flows of capital, goods, people, and culture. It is implicated in both the formal global economy and various informal economies. It is integrated into both legal and extralegal transnational circuits of goods. Certain large multinational corporations have become major players, spending vast sums on research and development, and on advertising and marketing to reach both mass and specialized markets. Simultaneously, actors in informal or underground economies, including smugglers, transnational migrants, and petty traders, are finding unprecedented opportunities in producing, transporting, and selling unregulated lightening products.

One reason for this complex multifaceted structure is that the market for skin lighteners, although global in scope, is also highly decentralized and segmented along socioeconomic, age, national, ethnic, racial, and cultural lines. Whether the manufacturers are multibillion-dollar corporations or small entrepreneurs, they make separate product lines and use distinct marketing strategies to reach specific segments of consumers. Ethnic companies and entrepreneurs may be best positioned to draw on local cultural themes, but large multinational companies can draw on local experts to tailor advertising images and messages to appeal to particular audiences.

The Internet has become a major tool for the globalized segmented lightening market. It is the site where all the players in the global lightening market meet. Large multinational corporations, small local firms, individual entrepreneurs, skin doctors, direct-sales merchants, and even e-bay sellers use the Internet to disseminate the ideal of light skin and to advertise and sell their products. Consumers go on the Internet to do research on and shop for products. Some also participate in Internet message boards and forums to seek advice and to discuss, debate, and rate skin lighteners. There are many such forums, often as part of transnational ethnic websites. For example, IndiaParenting.com and sukhdukh.com, designed for South Asians in India and other parts of the world, have chat rooms on skin care and lightening, and Rexinteractive.com, a Filipino site, and Candymag.com, a site sponsored by a magazine for Filipina teens, have extensive forums on skin lightening. The discussions on these forums provide a window through which to view the meaning of skin color to consumers, their desires and anxieties, doubts and aspirations. The Internet is thus an important site from which one can gain a multilevel perspective on skin lightening.

Consumer Groups and Market Niches

Africa and African Diaspora

In southern Africa, colorism is just one of the negative inheritances of European colonialism. The ideology of white supremacy that European colonists brought included the association of blackness with primitiveness, lack of civilization, unrestrained sexuality, pollution, and dirt. The association of blackness with dirt can be seen in a 1930 French advertising poster for Dirtoff (Figure 10.1), which is a drawing of a dark African man washing his hands, which have

Figure 10.1 French Poster for Savon Dirtoff, Skin Cleanser for Auto Mechanics and Housewives c. 1930

SOURCE: www.charlesmichaelgallery.com/detailproduct26.php

become "white," as he declares *"Le Savon Dirtoff me blanchit!"* The soap was designed, not for use by Africans, but, as the poster notes, pour *mechanciens automobilises et menagers* [French auto mechanics and housewives]. Such images showing black people "dramatically losing their pigmentation as a result of the cleansing process," were common in late-nineteenth- and early-twentieth-century soap advertisements, according to art historian Jean Michel Massing.[2]

Some historians and anthropologists have argued that precolonial African conceptions of female beauty favored women with light-brown or yellow or reddish tints. If so, the racial hierarchies established in areas colonized by Europeans cemented and generalized the privilege attached to light skin.[3] In both South Africa and Rhodesia/Zimbabwe, those in an intermediate category considered to be racially mixed were classified as *colored* and were subjected to fewer legislative restrictions than those classified as *native*. Assignment to the colored category was based on ill-defined criteria, and, upon arrival in urban areas, people found themselves classified as native or coloured on the basis of skin tone and other phenotypic characteristics. Indians arriving in Rhodesia from Goa, for example, were variously classified as Portuguese mulatto or colored. The multiplication of discriminatory laws targeting natives led a growing number of blacks claiming to be colored in both societies.[4]

The use of skin lighteners has a long history in southern Africa, which is described by Lynn Thomas in her chapter in this volume and which I will not recount here. Rather, I will discuss the current picture, which shows both an increase in the consumption in skin-lightening products and concerted efforts to curtail the trade of such products. Despite bans on the importation of skin lighteners, the widespread use of these products currently constitutes a serious health issue in southern Africa because the products often contain mercury, corticosteroids, or high doses of hydroquinone. Mercury, of course, is highly toxic, and sustained exposure can lead to neurological damage and kidney disease. Hydroquinone (originally an industrial chemical) is effective in suppressing melanin production, but exposure to the sun—hard to avoid in Africa—damages skin that has been treated. Furthermore, in dark-skinned people, long-term hydroquinone use can lead to ochronosis, a disfiguring condition involving gray and blue–black discoloration of the skin.[5] The overuse of topical steroids can lead to contact eczema, bacterial and fungal infection, Cushing's syndrome, and skin atrophy.[6]

Perhaps the most disturbing fact is that mercury soaps used by Africans are manufactured in the European Union, with Ireland and Italy leading in the production of mercury soap. One company that has been the target of activists is Killarney Enterprises, Ltd. in County Wicklow, Ireland. Formerly known as W & E Products and located in Lancashire, England, the company was forced to close following out-of-court settlements of suits filed by two former employers who had given birth to stillborn or severely malformed infants as a result of exposure to mercury. However, W & E Products then secured a 750,000-pound grant from the Irish Industrial Development Authority to relocate to Ireland, where it changed its name to Killarney Enterprises, Ltd. The company remained in business until April 17, 2007, producing soaps under the popular names Tura, Arut, Swan, Sukisa Bango, Meriko, and Jeraboo (which contained up to 3% mercuric iodide). Distribution of mercury soap has been illegal in the European Union since 1989, but its manufacture has remained legal as long as the product is exported.[7] These soaps are labeled for use as antiseptics and to prevent body odor; however, they are understood to be and are used as skin bleaches. To complete the circuit, European Union-manufactured mercury soaps are smuggled back in to the European Union to sell in shops catering to African immigrant communities. An Irish journalist noted that the very same brands made by Killarney Enterprises, including Meriko and Tura (banned in both the European Union and South Africa) could easily be found in African shops in Dublin.[8]

As a result of the serious health effects, medical researchers have conducted interview studies to determine how prevalent the practice of skin lightening is among African women. They estimate that 25 percent of women in Bamaki, Mali; 35 percent in Pretoria, South Africa; and 52 percent in Dakar, Senegal; use skin lighteners, as did an astonishing 77 percent of female traders in Lagos, Nigeria.[9]

There have been local and transnational campaigns to stop the manufacture of products containing mercury in the European Union, and efforts to inform African consumers of the dangers of their use and to foster the idea of black pride. Governments in South Africa, Zimbabwe, Nigeria, and Kenya have banned the import and sale of mercury and hydroquinone products, but they continue to be smuggled in from other African nations.[10]

Despite these efforts, the use of skin lighteners has been increasing among modernized and cosmopolitan African women. A South African newspaper reported that whereas in the 1970s typical skin-lightening users in South Africa were rural and poor, currently it is upwardly mobile black women, those with technical diplomas or university degrees and well-paid jobs, who are driving the market in skin lighteners. A recent study by Mictert Marketing Research found that one in thirteen upwardly mobile black women aged twenty-five to thirty-five used skin lighteners. It is possible that this is an underestimation, since there is some shame attached to admitting to using skin lighteners.[11]

These upwardly mobile women turn to expensive imported products from India and Europe rather than cheaper, locally made products. They also go to doctors to get prescriptions for imported lighteners containing corticosteroids, which are intended for short-term use to treat blemishes. They continue using them for long periods, beyond the prescribed duration, thus risking damage.[12] This recent increase in the use of skin lighteners cannot be seen as simply a legacy of colonialism, but rather a consequence of the penetration of multinational capital and Western consumer culture. The practice, therefore, is likely to continue to increase as the influence of these forces grows.

African America

Color consciousness in the African American community has generally been viewed as legacy of slavery, under which mulattos, the offspring of white men and slave women, were accorded better treatment than "pure" Africans. Although dark-skinned Africans were considered suited to fieldwork, lighter skinned mulattos were thought to be more intelligent and better suited for indoor work as servants and artisans. Mulattos were also more likely to receive at least rudimentary education and to be manumitted. They went on to form the nucleus of many nineteenth-century free black communities. After the Civil War, light-skinned mulattos tried to distance themselves from their darker skinned brothers and sisters, forming exclusive civic and cultural organizations, fraternities, sororities, schools, and universities.[13] According to Audrey Elisa Kerr, common folklore in the African American community holds that elite African Americans used a "paper bag" test to screen guests at social events and to determine eligibility for membership in their organizations: Anyone whose skin was darker than the color of the bag was excluded. Although perhaps apocryphal, the widespread acceptance of the story as historical fact is significant. It has been credible to African Americans because it was consonant with their observations of the skin tone of elite African American society.[14]

The preference and desire for light skin can also be detected in the longtime practice of skin lightening. References to African American women using powders and skin bleaches appeared in the black press as early as the 1850s, according to historian Kathy Peiss. She noted that *American Magazine* criticized

African Americans who tried to emulate white beauty standards: "Beautiful black and brown faces by application of rouge and lily white are made to assume unnatural tints, like the vivid hue of painted corpses." How common such practices were is unknown. However, by the 1880s and 1890s, dealers in skin bleaches were widely advertising their wares in the African American press. A Crane and Company ad in *The Colored American Magazine* (1903) promised that use of their "wonderful Face Bleach" would result in a "peach-like complexion" and "turn the skin of a black or brown person five or six shades lighter and of a mulatto person perfectly white."[15]

Throughout the twentieth century, many African American leaders spoke out against skin bleaching, as well as hair straightening, and the African American press published articles decrying these practices. However, such articles were far outnumbered by advertisements for skin bleaches in prominent outlets such as the *Crusader, Negro World,* and the *Chicago Defender.* An estimated 30 percent to 40 percent of advertisements in these outlets were for cosmetics and toiletries, including skin bleaches. Many of the advertised lighteners were produced by white manufacturers; for example, Black and White Cream was made by Plough Chemicals (which later became Plough-Shearing), and Nadolina was made by the National Toilet Company. A chemical analysis of Nadolina Bleach conducted in 1930 found it contained 10 percent ammoniated mercury, a concentration high enough to pose a serious health risk. Both brands are still marketed in African American outlets, although with changed ingredients.[16]

The manufacture and marketing of black beauty products, including skin lighteners, provided opportunities for black entrepreneurs. Annie Turnbo Malone, who founded the Poro brand, and Sara Breedlove, later known as Madam C. J. Walker, who formulated and marketed the Wonder Hair Grower, were two of the most successful black entrepreneurs of the late-nineteenth and early-twentieth centuries. Malone and Walker championed African American causes and were benefactors of various institutions.[17] Significantly, both refused to sell skin bleaches or to describe their hair care products as hair straighteners. After Walker died in 1919, her successor, F. B. Ransom, introduced Tan-Off, which became one of the company's best sellers in the 1920s and 1930s. A third entrepreneur, Anthony Overton, founded Overton Hygienic in 1898 in Kansas City, moving it to Chicago in 1911. Starting first with High Brown Face Powder, he expanded his cosmetic line to some fifty-two products. By the late 1920s, Overton had built a multimillion-dollar empire that included a magazine, newspaper, bank, and an insurance company. The bank and insurance company failed

Figure 10.2 Cartoon Ad for Overton Bleach Ointment Attributed to African American Woman Cartoonist Jackie Ormes, 1945
SOURCE: www.clstoons.com/paoc/pioneerads/adwork.htm

in 1929, but the cosmetic company continued into the 1940s, as documented in an advertisement for High Brown Bleach Ointment (Figure 10.2) published in 1945, shortly before Overton's death. Unlike some white-produced products, black-manufactured lighteners such as High Brown Bleach Ointment did not contain mercury, but relied on such ingredients as borax and hydrogen peroxide.[18]

Currently, a plethora of brands are marketed especially to African Americans, including Black and White Cream, Nadolina (sans mercury), Ambi, Palmer's, DR Daggett and Remsdell (fade cream and facial brightening cream), Swiss Whitening Pills, Ultra Glow, Skin Success, Avre (which produces the Pallid Skin Lightening System and B-Lite Fade Cream), and Clear Essence (which targets women of color more generally). Some of these products contain hydroquinone whereas others claim to use "natural" ingredients, such as extract of licorice.[19] Transnational corporations such as the Mitchell Group, headquar-

The Mitchell Group believes that beauty is more than skin deep. Much more. Radiant skin is a birthright. We're all born wearing a beautiful, smooth, unblemished birthday suit that's baby soft to the touch. Time passes and we grow up, into a world that is not very friendly to our skin. Aging and the elements all conspire to damage skin, our first defense against the environment. Involved in creating advanced skin care treatments for over twenty years, the Mitchell Group's scientifically formulated products are created from only the best that nature has to offer.
Come discover the many new ways we have to give your skin that gorgeous glow all over again. Face it. Skin is in. Make yours even lovelier with the Mitchell Group beauty regimen that's just right for you. Beautiful skin begins here >

Figure 10.3 Contemporary Marketing of Skin Lightening Products to African American Women by the Mitchell Group, Distributor of Fair & White, 2007
SOURCE: www.mitchellgroupusa.com

tered in Switzerland, which produces Fair & White, advertises its products as formulated for "Black, Asian, mat, and cross skins" (Figure 10.3).

Discussions of skin lightening on African American Internet forums indicate that the participants seek, not white skin, but "light" skin like that of African American celebrities such as film actress Halle Berry and singer Beyoncé Knowles. Most women say they want to be two or three shades lighter, or want to get rid of dark spots and freckles to even out their skin tones, something that many skin lighteners claim to do. Some of the writers believe that Halle Barry and other African American celebrities have achieved their luminescent appearance through skin bleaching, skillful use of cosmetics, and artful lighting. Thus, some skin-lightening products, such as the Pallid Skin Lightening System, purport to offer the "secret" of the stars. A website for Swiss Lightening Pills claims that "[f]or many years Hollywood has been keeping the secret of whitening pills," and asks, rhetorically, "Have you wondered why early childhood photos of many top celebs show a much darker skin colour than they have now?"[20]

India and Indian Diaspora

As in the case of Africa, the origins of colorism in India are obscure and the issue of whether there was a privileging of light skin in precolonial Indian societies is far from settled. Colonial era and postcolonial Indian writings on the issue may themselves have been influenced by European notions of caste, culture, and race. Many of these writings expound on a racial distinction between lighter skinned Aryans, who migrated into India from the north, and darker skinned "indigenous" Dravidians of the south. The wide range of skin color from north to south and the variation in skin tone within castes makes it hard to correlate light skin with high caste. The most direct connection between skin color and social status could be found in the paler hue of those whose position and wealth enabled them to spend their lives sheltered indoors, compared with the darker hue of those who toiled outdoors in the sun.[21]

British racial concepts evolved throughout the course of its colonial history as colonial administrators and settlers attempted to make sense of the variety of cultural and language groups, and to justify British rule in India. British observers attributed group differences variously to culture, language, climate, or biological race. However, they viewed the English as representing the highest culture and embodying the optimum physical type; they made invidious comparisons between lighter skinned groups, whose men were viewed as more intelligent and martial and whose women were considered more attractive, and darker skinned groups, whose men were viewed as lacking intelligence and masculinity, and whose women were considered to be lacking in beauty.[22]

Regardless of the origins of color consciousness in India, the preference for light skin seems almost universal today, and, in terms of sheer numbers, India and Indian diasporic communities around the world constitute the largest market for skin lighteners. The major consumers of these products in South Asian communities are women between the ages of sixteen and thirty-five. On transnational South Asian blog sites, women describing themselves as "dark" or "wheatish" in color state a desire to be "fair." Somewhat older women seek to reclaim their youthful skin color, describing themselves as having gotten darker over time. Younger women tend to be concerned about looking light to make a good marital match or to appear lighter for a large family event, including their own weddings. These women recognize the reality that light skin constitutes valuable symbolic capital in the marriage market.[23]

Contemporary notions of feminine beauty are shaped by the Indian mass media. Since the 1970s, beauty pageants such as Miss World-India have been exceedingly popular viewer spectacles; they are a source of nationalist pride because India has been highly successful in international pageants such as Miss World (Figure 10.4). As might be expected, the competitors, although varying in skin tone, tend to be lighter than average. The other main avatars of feminine allure are Bollywood actresses, such as Isha Koopikari and Aiswarya Rai who also tend to be light skinned or, if slightly darker, green eyed.[24]

Many Indian women use traditional homemade preparations made of plant and fruit products. In various blog sites for Indians both in South Asia and in diasporic communities in North America, the Caribbean, and the United Kingdom, women seek advice about "natural" preparations and trade recipes. Many commercial products are made by Indian companies and are marketed to Indians around the globe under such names as "fairness" cream, herbal bleach cream, whitening cream, and fairness cold cream. Many of these products claim

Figure 10.4 Femina Miss India Beauty Pageant Winners, 2007
SOURCE: www.rediff.com/movies/2007/apr/11look.htm

to be based on ayurvedic medicine and contain herbal and fruit extracts such as saffron, papaya, almonds, and lentils.[25]

With economic liberalization starting in 1991, the number of products available on the Indian market, including cosmetics and skincare products, has mushroomed. Prior to 1991 Indian consumers had the choice of only two brands of cold cream and moisturizers, but today they have scores of products from which to select. With the deregulation of imports, the increased development of the Indian economy, and the growth of the urban middle class, multinational companies see India as a prime target for expansion, especially in the area of "personal care" products. Multinational corporations, through regional subsidiaries, have developed many different whitening product lines in various price ranges that target markets ranging from rural villagers to white-collar urban dwellers and affluent professionals and managers.[26]

Southeast Asia: The Philippines

Because of its history as a colonial dependency first of Spain and then the United States, the Philippines has been particularly affected by Western ideology and culture, which valorize whiteness. Moreover, frequent intermarriage among indigenous populations, Spanish colonists, and Chinese settlers has resulted in a substantially *mestizo* population that ranges widely on the skin color spectrum. The business and political elites have tended to be disproportionately light skinned with visible Hispanic and/or Chinese appearance. During the contemporary period, economic integration has led to the collapse of traditional means of livelihood, resulting in large-scale emigration by both working-class and middle-class Filipinos to seek better paying jobs in the Middle East, Asia, Europe, and North America. An estimated ten million Filipinos were working abroad as of 2004, with more than a million departing each year. Because of the demand for domestic workers, nannies, and care workers in the global North, women make up more than half of those working abroad.[27] Many, if not most, of these migrants remit money and send Western consumer goods to their families in the Philippines.[28] They also maintain transnational ties with their families at home and across the Diaspora through print media, phone, and the Internet. All these factors contribute to an interest in and fascination with Western consumer culture, including fashion and cosmetics in the Philippines and in Filipino diasporic communities.[29]

Perhaps not surprisingly, interest in skin lightening seems to be huge and growing in the Philippines, especially among younger urban women. Synovate, a market research firm reported that in 2004, 50 percent of respondents in the Philippines reported currently using skin lighteners.[30] Young Filipinas participate in several different Internet sites, seeking advice on lightening products. They seek not only to lighten their skin overall, but also to deal with dark underarms, elbows, and knees. Judging by their entries in Internet discussion sites, many teens are quite obsessed with finding "the secret" to lighter skin, and have purchased and tried scores of different brands of creams and pills. They are disappointed to find that these products may have some temporary effects but do not lead to permanent change. They discuss products made in the Philippines, but they are most interested in products made by large European and American multinational cosmetic firms, and Japanese and Korean companies. Clearly, these young Filipinas associate light skin with modernity and social mobility. Interestingly, the young Filipinas do not refer to Americans or Europeans as having the most desirable skin color. They are more apt to look to Japanese and Koreans or to Spanish or Chinese-appearing (and light-skinned) Filipina celebrities, such Michelle Reis, Sharon Kuneta, or Claudine Baretto, as their ideals.[31]

The notion that Japanese and Korean women represent ideal Asian beauty has fostered a brisk market in skin lighteners that are formulated by Korean and Japanese companies. Asian White Skin and its sister company Yumei Misei, headquartered in Korea, sell Japanese and Korean skincare products in the Philippines both in retail outlets and online. Products include Asianwhiteskin Underarm Whitening Kit, Japanese Whitening Cream Enzyme Q-10, Japan Whitening Fruit Cream, Kang Tian Sheep Placenta Whitening Capsules, and Kyusoku Bhaku Lightening Pills.[32]

East Asia: Japan, China, and Korea

East Asian societies have historically idealized light or even white skin for women. Intage, a market research firm in Japan, puts it: "Japan has long idolized ivory-like skin that is 'like a boiled egg'—soft, white and smooth on the surface." Indeed, prior to the Meiji Period (starting in the 1860s) men and women of the higher classes wore white-lead powder makeup (along with blackened teeth, and shaved eyebrows.) With modernization, according to Mikiko Ashikari, men completely abandoned makeup, but middle and upper class women continued to wear traditional white-lead powder when dressed in formal kimonos for ceremonial occasions, such as marriages, and adopted light-colored modern face powder to wear with Western clothes. Ashikari found through observations of 777 women at several sites in Osaka during 1996 to 1997 that 97.4 percent of women in public wore what she calls "white face"—that is, makeup that "makes their faces look whiter than they really are."[33]

Intage reports that skincare products, moisturizers, face masks, and skin lighteners account for 66 percent of the cosmetics market in Japan. Most cosmetic and skincare products, even those not explicitly stated to be whitening products, carry names that contain the word *white*—for example, facial masks labeled Clear Turn White or Pure White.[34] Additionally, numerous products are marketed specifically as whiteners. All the leading Japanese firms in the cosmetic fields—Shiseido, Kosa, Kanebo, and Pola—offer multiproduct skin-whitening lines, with names such as White Lucent and Whitissimo. Fytokem, a Canadian company that produces ingredients used in skin-whitening products, reports that Japan's market in skin lighteners topped five billion dollars in 1999.[35] With deregulation of imports, leading multinational firms such as L'Oreal have also made large inroads in the Japanese market. French products have a special cachet.[36]

Although the Japanese market has been the largest, its growth rate is much lower than that of Korea and China. Korea's cosmetic market has been growing at a 10 percent rate per year, and China has been growing by 20 percent. Fytokem estimated that the market for skin whiteners in China was worth one billion dollars in 2002, and was projected to grow tremendously. A 2007 Nielsen global survey found that 46 percent of Chinese, 47 percent of people in Hong Kong, 46 percent of Taiwanese, 29 percent of Koreans, and 24 percent of Japanese had used a skin lightener during the previous year. With regard to regular users, 30 percent of Chinese, 20 percent of Taiwanese, 18 percent of Japanese and people from Hong Kong, and 8 percent of Koreans used them weekly or daily. However, if money were no object, 52 percent of Koreans said they would spend more on skin lightening, compared with 26 percent of Chinese and 23 percent of people from Hong Kong and Taiwan, and 21 percent of Japanese.[37]

Latin America: Mexico and the Mexican Diaspora

Throughout Latin America, skin tone is a major marker of status and a form of symbolic capital, despite national ideologies of racial democracy. In some countries, such as Brazil, where there was African chattel slavery and extensive miscegenation, there is considerable color consciousness along with an elaborate vocabulary to refer to varying shades of skin. In other countries, such as Mexico, the main intermixture was between Spanish colonists and indigenous peoples, along with an unacknowledged admixture with African slaves. *Mestizaje* is the official national ideal. The Mexican concept of *mestizaje* was that, through racial and ethnic mixture, Mexico would gradually be peopled by a whiter "cosmic race" that surpassed its initial ingredients. Nonetheless, skin tone, along with other phenotypic traits, is a significant marker of social status, with lightness signifying purity and beauty, and darkness signifying contamination and ugliness.[38] The elite has remained overwhelmingly light skinned and European appearing whereas rural poor are predominantly dark skinned and indigenous appearing.

Ethnographic studies of Mexican communities in Mexico City and Michoacan found residents to be highly color conscious, with darker skinned family members likely to be ridiculed or teased. The first question that a relative often poses about a newborn is about his or her color.[39] Thus, it should not be a surprise that individuals pursue various strategies to attain light-skinned identity and privileges. Migration from rural areas to the city or to the United States has been one route to transformation from an Indian to a *mestizo* identity or from a *mestizo* to a more cosmopolitan urban identity; another strategy has been lightening one's family line through marriage with a lighter skinned partner. A third strategy has been to use lighteners to change the appearance of one's skin.[40]

In one of the few references to skin whitening in Mexico, Allan Knight claims that it was "an ancient practice . . . reinforced by film, television, and advertising stereotypes."[41] As in Africa, consumers seeking low-cost lighteners can easily purchase mercury-laden creams that are still manufactured and used in parts of Latin America (e.g., Recetas de la Farmacia—Crema Blanqueadora, manufactured in the Dominican Republic, contains 6000 ppm mercury).[42] The use of these products has come to public attention because of their use by Latino immigrants in the United States. Outbreaks of mercury poisoning have been reported in Texas, New Mexico, Arizona, and California among immigrants who used Mexican-manufactured creams such as Crema de Belleza—Manning. The cream is manufactured in Mexico by Laboratories Vide Natural SA de CV, Tampico, Tamaulipas, and is distributed primarily in Mexico. However, it has been found for sale in shops and flea markets in the United States in areas located along the U.S.–Mexican border in Arizona, California, New Mexico, and Texas. The label lists the ingredient calomel, which is mercurous chloride (a salt of mercury). Product samples have been found to contain 6 percent to 10 percent mercury by weight.[43]

For high-end products, hydroquinone is the chemical of choice. White Secret is one of the most visible products because it is advertised in a thirty-minute late-night television infomercial that is broadcast nationally almost nightly.[44] Jamie Winder and colleagues, who analyzed the commercial, note that the commercial continually stresses that White Secret is *"una formula Americana."* According to Winder et al., the American pedigree and English-language name endow White Secret with a cosmopolitan cachet and "a first worldliness." The infomercial follows the daily lives of several young urban women, one of whom narrates and explains how White Secret cream forms a barrier against the darkening rays of the sun whereas a sister product trans-forms the color of the skin itself. The infomercial conjures the power of sci-ence, showing cross-sections of skin cells. By showing women applying White Secret in modern, well-lit bathrooms, relaxing in well-appointed apartments, and protected from damaging effects of the sun while walking around the city, the program connects skin lightening with cleanliness, modernity, and mobility.[45]

Large multinational firms are expanding the marketing of skincare prod-ucts, including skin lighteners, in Mexico and other parts of Latin America. For example, Stiefel Laboratories, the world's largest privately held pharmaceutical company, which specializes in dermatology products, targets Latin America for skin-lightening products. Six of its twenty-eight wholly owned subsidiar-ies are located in Latin America. It offers Clariderm, an over-the-counter hy-droquinone cream and gel (2%) in Brazil; and Clasifel, a prescription-strength hydroquinone cream (4%), in Mexico, Peru, Bolivia, Venezuela, and other Latin American countries. It also sells Claripel, a 4 percent hydroquinone cream, in the United States.[46]

Middle-Age and Older White Women in North America and Europe

Historically, at least in the United States, the vast majority of skin-lightening users have been so-called white women. Throughout the nineteenth and early-twentieth centuries, European American women, especially those of south-ern and eastern European origins, sought to achieve whiter and brighter skin through the use of the many whitening powders and bleaches on the market. In 1930, J. Walter Thomson conducted a survey and found 232 different brands of skin lighteners and bleaches for sale. Advertisements for these products appealed to the association of white skin with gentility, social mobility, An-glo-Saxon superiority, and youth. In large cities, such as New York City and

Chicago, some Jewish women used skin lighteners and hair straighteners produced by black companies and frequented black beauty parlors.[47]

By the mid 1920s, tanning became acceptable for white women, and in the 1930s and 1940s, it became a craze. A year-round tan came to symbolize high social status, because it indicated that a person could afford to travel and spend time at tropical resorts and beaches. Additionally, there was a fad for "exotic" Mediterranean and Latin types, with cosmetics designed to enhance "olive" complexions and brunette hair.[48]

However, in the 1980s, as the damaging effects of overexposure to sun rays became known, skin lightening among whites reemerged as a major growth market. Part of this growth was fueled by the aging baby-boom generation determined to stave off signs of aging. Many sought not only toned bodies and uplifted faces, but also youthful skin—that is, smooth, unblemished, glowing skin without telltale age spots. Age spots are a form of hyperpigmentation that results from exposure to the sun over many years. The treatment is the same as that for overall dark skin: hydroquinone, along with skin peeling, exfoliants, and sunscreen.[49]

Multinational Cosmetic and Pharmaceutical Firms and Their Targeting Strategies

Although there are many small local manufacturers and merchants involved in the skin-lightening game, I want to focus on the giant multinational corporations, which are fueling the desire for light skin through their advertisement and marketing strategies. The accounts of the skin-lightening markets have shown that the desire for lighter skin and the use of skin bleaches is accelerating in places where modernization and the influence of Western capitalism and culture are most prominent. Multinational biotechnology, cosmetic, and pharmaceutical corporations have coalesced through mergers and acquisitions to create and market "personal care" products that blur the lines between cosmetics and pharmaceuticals. They have jumped into the field of skin lighteners and correctors, developing many different product lines to advertise and sell in Europe, North America, South Asia, East and Southeast Asia, and the Middle East.[50]

Three of the largest corporations involved in developing the skin-lightening market are L'Oreal, Shiseido, and Unilever. The French-based L'Oreal, with 15.8 billion Euros in sales in 2006, is the largest cosmetics company in the world. It consists of twenty-one major subsidiaries, including Lancôme; Vichy

Laboratories; La Roche-Posay Laboratoire Pharmaceutique; Biotherm; Garnier; Giorgio Armani Perfumes; Maybelline, New York; Ralph Lauren Fragrances; Skinceuticals, Shu Uemura; Matrix; Redken; and SoftSheen Carlson. L'Oreal is also a 20 percent shareholder of Sanofi-Synthelabo, a major French-based pharmaceutical firm. Three L'Oreal subsidiaries produce the best-known skin-lightening lines marketed around the world (which are especially big in Asia): Lancome Blanc Expert with Melo-No Complex, LaRoche-Posay Mela-D White skin-lightening daily lotion with a triple-action formula, and Vichy BiWhite (Figure 10.5), containing procysteine and vitamin C.[51]

A second major player in the skin-lightening market is Shiseido, the largest and best-known Japanese cosmetics firm, with net sales of $5.7 billion. Shiseido cosmetics are marketed in sixty-five countries and regions, and it operates factories in Europe, the Americas, and other Asian countries. The Shiseido Group, including affiliates, employs approximately 25,200 people around the globe. Its two main luxury lightening lines are White Lucent (for whitening) and White

Figure 10.5 Ad for Vichy BiWhite, Subsidiary of L'Oreal, Widely Marketed in Asia and the Middle East, c. 2004
SOURCE: www.fantom-xp.com/en_21__Vichy_Bi_-_White.html

Lucency (for spots/aging). Each product line consists of seven or eight different components, which the consumer is supposed to use as part of a complicated regimen involving applications of specific products several times a day.[52]

The third multinational corporation is Unilever, a diversified Anglo-Dutch company with an annual turnover of more than 40 billion Euros and net profits of five billion Euros in 2006.[53] It specializes in so-called Fast Moving Consumer Goods in three areas: food (many familiar brands, including Hellman's Mayonnaise and Lipton Tea), home care (e.g., laundry detergents), and "personal care," including deodorants, hair care, oral care, and skin care. Its most famous brand in the skincare line is Ponds, which sells cold creams in Europe and North America, and "whitening" creams in Asia, the Middle East, and Latin America.[54]

Through its Indian subsidiary, Hindustan Lever Limited (HLL), Unilever patented Fair & Lovely (Figure 10.6) in 1971, after the patenting of niacinamide, a melanin suppressor, which is its main active ingredient. Test marketed in South India in 1975, it became available throughout India in 1978. Fair & Lovely has become the largest selling skin cream in India, accounting for 80 percent of the fairness cream market. According to anthropologist Susan Runkle, "Fair

Figure 10.6 Hindustan Unilever's Fair & Lovely, the Most Widely Used Skin Lightening Product Line in the World, Unilever Website Image, 2008
SOURCE: www.unileverme.com/our-brands/personal-care/fairandlovely.asp

and Lovely has an estimated sixty million consumers throughout the Indian subcontinent and exports to thirty four countries in Southeast and Central Asia as well as the Middle East."[55]

Fair & Lovely ads claim that "with regular daily use, you will be able to unveil your natural radiant fairness in just 6 weeks!"[56] As with other successful brands, Fair & Lovely has periodically added new lines to appeal to special markets. In 2003, it introduced Fair & Lovely, Ayurvedic, which claims to be formulated according to a 4500-year-old Indian medical system. In 2004, it introduced Fair & Lovely Oil-Control Gel and Fair & Lovely Anti-Marks. In 2004, Fair & Lovely also announced the "unveiling" of a premium line, Perfect Radiance, a complete range of twelve premium skin care solutions containing "international formulations from Unilever's Global Skin Technology Center, combined with ingredients best suited for Indian skin types and climates." Its ads say: "Experience Perfect Radiance from Fair & Lovely. Unveil Perfect Skin." Intended to compete with expensive European brands, Perfect Radiance is sold only in select stores in major cities, including Delhi, Mumbai, Chennai, and Bangalore.[57]

Unilever is known for promoting its brands by being active and visible in the locales where they are marketed. In India, Ponds sponsors the Femina Miss India pageant, in which aspiring contestants are urged to "be as beautiful as you can be." Judging by photos of past winners, being as beautiful as you can be means being as light as you can be. In 2003, partly in response to criticism by the All India Democratic Women's Association of "racist" advertisement of fairness products, Hindustani Lever launched Fair & Lovely Foundation with a mission to "encourage economic empowerment of women across India" through educational and guidance programs, training courses, and scholarships.[58]

Unilever heavily promotes both Ponds and Fair & Lovely with television and print ads tailored to local cultures. In one commercial shown in India, a young dark-skinned woman's father laments that he has no son to provide for him, and his daughter's salary is not high enough. The suggestion is that she could neither get a better job nor marry because of her dark skin. The young woman then uses Fair & Lovely, becomes fairer, and lands a job as an airline hostess, making her father happy. A Malaysian television spot shows a college student who is dejected because she can't get the attention of a classmate at the next desk. After using Pond's lightening moisturizer she appears in class brightly lit and several shades lighter and the boy says, "Why didn't I notice her before?"[59]

Such advertisements can be seen as not simply responding to a preexisting need, but actually creating a need by depicting having dark skin as a painful and depressing experience. Before "unveiling" their fairness, dark-skinned women are shown as unhappy, suffering from low self esteem, ignored by young men, and denigrated by their parents. By using Fair & Lovely or Ponds, a woman undergoes not only a transformation of her complexion, but also her personality and her fate. In short, dark skin becomes a burden and handicap that can be overcome only by using the product being advertised.

Conclusion

The yearning for lightness evident in the widespread and growing use of skin bleaching around the globe can rightfully be seen as a legacy of colonialism, a manifestation of "false consciousness," and the internalization of "white is right" values by people of color, especially women. Thus, one often-proposed solution to the problem is reeducation that stresses the diversity of types of beauty and desirability, and that valorizes darker skin shades, so that lightness/whiteness is dislodged as the dominant standard.

Although such efforts are needed, focusing only on individual consciousness and motives diverts attention from the very powerful economic forces that help to create the yearning for lightness and that offer to fulfill the yearning at a steep price. The manufacturing, advertising, and selling of skin lightening is no longer a marginal, underground economic activity. It has become a major growth market for giant multinational corporations with their sophisticated means of creating and manipulating needs.

These corporations produce separate product lines that appeal to different target audiences. For some lines of products, the firms harness the prestige of "science" by showing cross-sectional diagrams of skin cells and by displaying images of doctors in white coats. Dark skin or dark spots become a disease for which skin lighteners offer a cure. For other lines, designed to appeal to those who respond to appeals to naturalness, corporations call up "nature" by emphasizing the use of plant extracts and by displaying images of light-skinned women against a background of blue skies and fields of flowers. Dark skin becomes a veil that hides one's natural luminescence, which natural skin lighteners will uncover. For all products, dark skin is associated with pain, rejection, and limited options; achieving light skin is seen as necessary to being youthful, attractive, modern, and affluent—in short, to being "all that you can be."

11 Skin Lighteners in South Africa

Transnational Entanglements and Technologies of the Self

Lynn M. Thomas

THIS CHAPTER EXAMINES THE USE OF AND OPPOSITION to skin lighteners in twentieth-century South Africa. First marketed to black South Africans in the early 1930s, the manufacture and sale of skin lighteners grew into a highly lucrative business totaling 70 million South African rand ($27 million) in annual retail sales by the late 1980s.[1] During the ensuing six decades, both the meanings attached to these cosmetics and the active ingredients used in them changed dramatically. Two distinct strands of opposition to skin lighteners emerged during the 1960s: one rooted in nationalist political ideologies and the other in medical concerns. As part of broader antiapartheid struggles, these critiques ultimately converged, compelling the South African government to ban most skin lighteners in 1991.

Historical scholarship on beauty culture offers little analysis of skin lighteners. This omission is most striking in the U.S. literature. Although acknowledging that skin lighteners were widely marketed to white and black Americans during the first half of the twentieth century, this scholarship often dismisses these cosmetics as ineffective and, hence, inconsequential.[2] This chapter takes the history of skin lighteners more seriously. By drawing on a range of sources, including advertisements, medical journal articles, business and regulatory correspondence, activist literature, and personnel memoirs, it seeks to understand the rise and decline of skin lighteners as a multimillion-dollar per-year enterprise in South Africa.

This history offers two interrelated insights to the study of skin color hierarchies. First, the proliferation of skin lighteners across much of the world in the twentieth century was the product of transnational entanglements. As we shall see, U.S. commodities and ideologies of race provided a crucial impetus to the marketing and manufacturing of skin lighteners in South Africa. Yet, these U.S. influences were not all determinative. Rather, they quickly became entangled with economic relations and racial hierarchies constructed through South Africa's particular history of slavery, segregation, and apartheid, as well as skin color preferences that likely predated European colonization. After South African companies began large-scale manufacturing of skin lighteners during the post-World War II period, they looked to create markets for their products elsewhere in the subcontinent. South Africa, thus, began an entrepot for the movement of skin lighteners across the Atlantic and into much of Africa.

Second, the appeal of skin lighteners emerged from the dense intersection of racial hierarchies, capitalist commerce, and individual desires for betterment. Skin lighteners and cosmetics, in general, are an intriguingly literal manifestation of what Michel Foucault termed a "technology of the self." Although Foucault elaborated this concept in relation to Greco-Roman philosophy and early Christian spirituality, his definition resonates with modern practices of bodily refinement and improvement. A "technology of the self," according to Foucault, is a technology that permits "individuals to effect by their own means or with the help of others a certain number of operations on their own bodies and souls, thoughts, conduct, and way of being, so as to transform themselves in order to attain a certain state of happiness, purity, wisdom, perfection, or immortality" (p. 18).[3] In a critique of Foucault's work, Thomas McCarthy explains that Foucault developed this notion when writing the second and third volumes of the *History of Sexuality,* as he sought to distinguish techniques "geared to normalization" from "ethical techniques aimed at living a beautiful life." McCarthy argues that the problem with this notion was that it ignored the insight of much of Foucault's earlier work that had elucidated the "interdependencies between structures and events at the personal and societal levels" (p. 458).[4] This chapter draws on McCarthy's critique of Foucault to examine skin lighteners as technologies of the self simultaneously constituted through personal fantasies and structural forces.

Importations and Entanglements

During the nineteenth and first half of the twentieth centuries, skin lighteners ranked among the most common cosmetics used by women of European descent living in the United States and various imperial outposts. Although white women used skin lighteners for a variety of reasons, ranging from concealing blemishes to evening out skin tone to bleaching their faces, these preparations became highly profitable commodities by playing on a bourgeois and racialized aesthetic that valued skin purged of evidence of outdoor labor and intimacy with dark-skinned "others." Such preparations whitened the skin by covering it with light-colored substances such as starch, rice, or chalk, and/or containing irritants (including ascorbic acid, hydrogen peroxide, or compounds of lead, mercury, bismuth, and zinc) that either stripped away the top layers of the epidermis, revealing lighter layers underneath, or interfered with the production of melanin within the skin cells.[5] Skin lightener advertisements targeting white South African women date back, at least, to the 1920s. Figure 11.1 demonstrates how such ads marketed bleaching creams as fixing damage from sun and wind.

In interwar South Africa, the elaboration of segregationist rule compounded the privileging of white skin. During the 1920s and 1930s, a series of Afrikaner/ English coalition governments whittled away at African men's limited voting rights, expropriated black land, and further restricted residence in urban areas according to "race." These policies heightened the consequences of being recognized as belonging to one of South Africa's four officially designated ra-

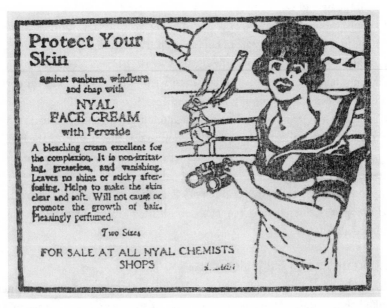

Figure 11.1 Ad Marketing a Bleaching Cream Containing Hydrogen Peroxide to White South African Women

SOURCE: *Rand Daily Mail* (Johannesburg), August 15, 1927, p. 9.

cial categories: European, Asiatic, Mixed and Other Coloured, and Native.[6] In segregationist South Africa, European included all whites, whether descended from Dutch (later known as Afrikaner) or British colonists, or more recent immigrants from eastern Europe, Australia, and the United States. Asiatic largely referred to indentured laborers and their descendants brought from South Asia and China from the midnineteenth century onward to work on sugar plantations and in gold mines. Coloured was a common racial designation for the descendants of mixed marriages and sexual liaisons between Europeans, African peoples indigenous to the Cape region (mainly speakers of Khoisan languages), and enslaved peoples brought from Southeast Asia, South Asia, Madagascar, East Africa, West Africa, and elsewhere during the Dutch colonial period (1652–1810). Native referred to the majority African population, most of whom spoke Bantu languages as their mother tongue.

Because segregationist rule in South Africa amplified the everyday consequences of race, markers of racial difference, including skin color, took on greater salience. Moreover, during this time, many daughters from impoverished Afrikaner and African families migrated from their rural homesteads to urban areas in search of waged employment to support themselves and their families. These young women especially may have used skin lighteners and other cosmetics as technologies of the self to don more urbane appearances as well as to ensure or obscure certain racial designations.

The earliest skin lightener ads targeting black women stemmed from a white Johannesburg businessman's marketing of African American-made beauty products. By the 1920s, some of the largest and most profitable black-owned businesses in the United States manufactured and sold cosmetics and hair products. Several of these companies, including Madame C. J. Walker, Poro, and Apex, were women owned and, in the United States, they marketed their products through female agents who sold door-to-door.[7] As Shane White and Graham White have argued, the success of these companies embodied a desire for "personal liberation" through self-improvement: "to an even greater extent than was true of the white beauty industry, black cosmetics were associated with modernity and, most importantly, with progress."[8] African American women's marketing of cosmetics created wealth and controversy. Although U.S. publications like the *Crisis,* the *Afro-American,* and *Negro World* received much of their revenue from advertising cosmetics, some black male leaders denounced certain products, notably skin lighteners and hair straighteners, as embodying racial self-loathing.[9]

Once imported into South Africa, these products generated similar debate. In 1933 and 1934, "Jolly" Jack Bernard ran ads for Apex products in the politically moderate and multilingual black newspaper *Bantu World*. Bernard probably learned of Apex from an American periodical or while traveling in the United States, and then imported their products to South Africa.[10] One 1933 *Bantu World* ad declared Apex to be the first "all-Negro Company" in South Africa. Although white American capital had been heavily invested in South Africa since the mineral revolution of the late nineteenth century, African American-manufactured goods were a novelty.[11] The Apex ads downplayed the involvement of a white capitalist by featuring drawings and photographs of black women. In the first Apex ad (Figure 11.2), a stylishly dressed woman

Figure 11.2 Ad Marketing Hair Products and a Skin Lightener Manufactured by the African American Company Apex to Black South African Consumers
SOURCE: *Bantu World* (Johannesburg), July 8, 1933, p. 11.

gazes into a handheld mirror. Other ads included photos of Mrs. E. Garson, a light-skinned black woman with relaxed hair, touting her as a "regular user of and firm believer in Apex products." By providing Garson's name, photo, and Johannesburg address, and sometimes providing product descriptions in the African language of Sotho, such ads cast these U.S.-made products as accessible to South Africans.

Several months into this ad campaign, *Bantu World* ran a feature about the founder and president of Apex, Sara Washington. This article positioned Washington as an African American success story and discussed how Apex had created "legitimate business" opportunities for many in the United States. It explained that the company's arrival in South Africa meant that the "Bantu race" could benefit from products "manufactured for them by their brothers and sisters in America."[12] Such logic situated cosmetics as technologies of the self that enabled racial uplift. In so doing, it discounted criticism of certain beauty products as embodying racial self-loathing and ignored that these particular black diasporic connections relied on a white middleman.

It is difficult to know how *Bantu World* readers interpreted the Apex campaign. At the time that the ads appeared, a debate raged in the paper about black women's use of white face powder. A number of male writers criticized black women who wore face powder for being ashamed of their black skin and looking like the disreputable urban figures of the prostitute and beer brewer.[13] Such criticism of white face powder often appeared on the same page as the Apex ads. Yet, no one ever commented on the ads. Although these critics of white face powder may have welcomed the arrival of Apex's face powder in "all shades," it is difficult to imagine that they felt anything but contempt toward Apex's skin bleach. As was the case with much of the African American press, the revenue to be gained from cosmetics advertising presumably placed these products beyond reproach. U.S. influences in the marketing of skin lighteners to black South Africans continued when, in 1936, ads for Valmor Products, another African American cosmetics company, began appearing in *Bantu World*.

By the late 1930s, at least one white South African company had begun marketing skin lighteners and other cosmetics to black consumers. In 1939, the Keppels Company ran an ad (Figure 11.3) in *Bantu World*, promoting a freckle wax (another term for skin lighteners) and an olive-tint face powder among other products. This ad, with before-and-after illustrations and a dancing couple, boasted that Keppels's cosmetics could "brighten" dark faces and

Figure 11.3 Ad for Acne Cream, Freckle Wax (Skin Lightener), and Olive Tint Face Powder Manufactured by White-Owned South African Company and Marketed to Black Men and Women

SOURCE: *Bantu World* (Johannesburg), April 1, 1939, p. 17.

futures, notably of both men and women. Six years later, Keppels ran an ad in the *Cape Times,* promising that their products could combat the harmful effects of South Africa's "cruel" climate by restoring "pristine skin-texture and colour." Although the *Cape Times* primarily targeted whites, blacks literate in English would have also read it. With its avocado-tinted powder and image of a woman with dark-gray skin, this Keppels ad may have aimed to appeal to the paper's coloured readers. In comparison with the Apex ads, these Keppels ads touted local, rather than foreign, affiliations and marketed their products through pharmacists rather than sales agents. They mark the beginning of a trend, much more apparent in the 1950s, whereby white South African cosmetic companies aggressively targeted blacks as consumers of skin lighteners.

The Apex, Valmor, and Keppels advertisements made no mention of the ingredients contained in their products. Other sources, however, indicate that by the 1930s, ammoniated mercury was the most common active ingredient found in over-the-counter skin lighteners manufactured in the United States. Medical textbooks routinely prescribed ammoniated mercury as an effective treatment for skin infections, particularly acne, and for fading freckles. For many users, creams containing ammoniated mercury lightened their skin, but usually only temporarily. Dermatologists agreed that although ammoniated mercury might lighten skin in the short term, prolonged use at higher concentrations could result in patches of darker pigmentation as the mercury oxidized and deposited in the skin.[14] Since at least the 1870s, some medical doctors warned of the health risks of over-the-counter cosmetics that contained mercury or lead.[15] In 1939, the U.S. Food and Drug Administration (FDA) began requiring manufacturers to limit ammoniated mercury concentrations in cosmetics to 5 percent or less.[16] As we shall see, in later decades, South African manufacturers of skin lighteners would consult such FDA regulations as part of efforts to claim compliance with international standards.

Skin lighteners quickly became situated within the particularities of South African racial hierarchies. Fragmentary evidence suggests that by the late 1930s, some black consumers were not just viewing ads for skin lighteners but buying and using these products. In 1939, James R. Korombi wrote a letter to *Bantu World* chiding "African youth" who "attempted to change their colour with expensive cosmetics." In contrast to earlier writers who criticized black women's use of face powder as a vain attempt to become white, Korombi identified other objects of racial mimicry: "African youth could be taught to be proud of their race and colour and should not be encouraged to pretend to be Indians or

Coloureds."[17] According to Korombi, the use of skin lighteners was not about looking white, but passing for a lighter shade of black.

In 1941, Zilpah Skota wrote to her husband in Johannesburg, requesting a jar of skin lightener. Skota sent the letter from her family home in Klerksdorp, where her husband's economic misfortunes had compelled her to return. She wrote: "[S]end me one jar of Karroo [as] I am already dark through the sun."[18] After World War II, Karroo became one of the most widely marketed South African-made skin lighteners. Skota's request suggests how skin lighteners had become a desired commodity for some school-educated women, even one living in financial hardship. It also reveals how some women linked their need for such products to increased exposure to the sun. In Belinda Bozzoli's history of labor migrancy, *Women of Phokeng*, interviewee Mrs. Mokale recalled that being out of the sun was one of the few positive aspects among the many hardships of being a domestic worker in white households during the 1920s and 1930s. She explained, "What we liked about being indoors was . . . our complexion lightened and turned very beautiful." [19] Similarly, in her recent book on black beauty in South Africa, Nakedi Ribane explains how in former times African brides-to-be would remain indoors for several days so that they could avoid "the harsh rays of the sun" and "look radiant" at their wedding ceremonies. Ribane also recounts a popular wedding song performed in the Pedi, Tswana, and Sotho languages that proclaimed, "Come out and behold, the bride is so pretty she looks Coloured!"[20] Such evidence demonstrates that during the twentieth century some black South African women preferred their skin not to be darkened or made rough and dry by the sun, but it says little about the longer history of such preferences.

It is difficult to discern whether such valuing of lighter colored skin was rooted in precolonial conceptions of beauty, a product of racial hierarchies introduced through colonialism and segregation, or, most likely, some entanglement of the two. In their accounts of Tswana and Xhosa conceptions of beauty from the 1930s, largely based on research in rural areas, South African anthropologists Isaac Schapera and Monica Hunter described a preference for "light-skinned girl[s]" and those with "thin lips, an aquiline nose, and light brown skin."[21] Timothy Burke, in his pioneering study of toiletry consumption in twentieth-century Zimbabwe, emphasizes how colonial racial hierarchies supported the privileging of light-colored skin. Burke notes, however, that some black businessmen involved in the skin lightener trade insisted that light-colored skin was a "traditional" preference, and that people used skin lighteners to improve the "'glow' of their skin" rather than to look white.[22] For *Bantu World*'s largely urban readership, any precolonial preferences for lighter skin would have, by the interwar period, run headlong into the privileging of whiteness amid segregation's hardening racial hierarchies. The marketing and use of skin lighteners in interwar South Africa reveals the dense entanglement of personal fantasies and structural forces in South African considerations of skin color. As the outgrowth of African American beauty culture, the Apex and Valmor ads promised self-improvement and racial uplift through cosmetics use and capitalist enterprise. In turn, the Keppels ads, the product of white South African entrepreneurship, linked black cosmetics consumption to romance and leisure. Skota's and Korombi's letters suggest that interwar African motivations for using skin lighteners ranged from countering the darkening effects of outdoor labor to claiming bourgeois refinements to passing for Indian or coloured. Although racial hierarchies and color preferences in the United States and South Africa resonated enough for entrepreneurs to recognize a potential market for Apex and Valmor products in South Africa, they were not identical.

Mass Manufacturing and Marketing

South African particularities played an even greater role in the expansion of skin lightener manufacturing and consumption after World War II. Skin lightener sales took off in southern Africa with the postwar economic boom and growth of secondary industry. In his analysis of this phenomena in Zimbabwe, Timothy Burke demonstrates how marketing campaigns of the 1950s and 1960s built on colonial ideologies and institutions that had long promoted soap and other manufactured toiletries, and conflated "whiteness, purity, and social power" (p. 159).[23] Such ideologies received an infusion of new energy in 1948 when the conservative National Party gained state power in South Africa. Under apartheid, white manufacturing capital of the sort that produced consumer goods, including skin lighteners, received increased support from the state.[24] At the same time, nuances in skin color took on greater significance. Even more so than under interwar segregation, under apartheid, skin color informed where one lived, one's school and work opportunities, whether one could vote, and whether one needed a government pass to move in and out of urban areas. Within this economic and political context, the manufacturing and marketing of skin lighteners flourished.

One of the most important venues for advertising skin lighteners was popular black magazines. In 1949, *Zonk!*—"The African People's Pictorial"—became the first mass-produced photo magazine to target a black South African audience. Financed and edited by white South Africans with black South African World War II veterans serving as writers and photographers, this English-language magazine highlighted African Americans as role models and downplayed South African politics. With a circulation of more than 35,000 copies in the early 1950s, *Zonk!* sought to increase its profitability by courting advertisers.[25] It carried ads for skin lighteners from, at least, January 1951.[26] By 1954, an issue of *Zonk!* could carry up to five ads for skin lighteners, with some occupying the prominent position of a full page on the inside front cover. Figure 11.4 demonstrates how such ads often featured local music or film stars. During the 1950s,

Figure 11.4 Cosmetics Ad That Appeared in a Popular Black Photo-Magazine and Featured a Local Music Star with Light-Colored Face

SOURCE: *Zonk!* (Johannesburg), July 1954, p. 1.

skin lightener ads became a much less prominent feature in African American periodicals as the political and cultural influences of the Civil Rights Movement gained momentum.[27] In South Africa, by contrast, an enhanced effort by white manufacturers to tap black consumer markets amid the elaboration of apartheid rule fueled the proliferation of skin lightener ads.

Skin lighteners quickly became part of *Zonk!*'s promotion of photography and beauty competitions. In April 1951, an ad for Sweet Sue skin lighteners encouraged those entering the *Zonk!* beauty competition to use their products: "They will certainly help your chances and enhance your beauty." The next month, another ad (Figure 11.5) featured Mary Kel, the winner of the previous

Figure 11.5 In This Ad, Beauty Contest Winner (Center) Attributes Her Success to Using "Sweet Sue" Freckle Cream (Skin Lightener)

SOURCE: *Zonk!* (Johannesburg), May 1951, p. 1.

Zonk! competition, proclaiming that Sweet Sue freckle cream had helped her to win the contest.[28] In the midst of this competition, *Zonk!* published a letter to the editor insisting that the competition was not restricted to light-colored girls: "I should like to advise those who think that they are dark and can't win, that they are mistaken. There may be a marvelous face hidden behind that mask!" The editor appended a note affirming that the reader was "quite right."[29]

Raising similar concerns about skin color, Selina Khumalo wrote to *Zonk!*'s "Aunt Thandi," complaining that her complexion was "very dark" and stating that she had used "face creams since 1949 without success." "Aunt Thandi" offered frank advice and proposed a dark-skinned African American role model: "Look my dear, if you were born dark, no cream in the world can make you light. All you can do is try to develop a smooth and clear skin. Hazel Scott the American pianist is dark, and is regarded as one of the most beautiful women in America."[30] Despite these assurances that dark skin could be beautiful, the women who won *Zonk!*'s contests had light-colored skin and, when they featured as cover girls, their faces looked whitish, seemingly altered by skin lighteners, face powder, or a combination of the two.

By the mid 1950s, a number of other periodicals targeting black southern Africans, including *Drum, The African Weekly, The African Parade, Bantu Mirror, Bantu Opinion, Golden City Post, Hi-Note,* and *Ilanga lase Natal,* also carried skin lightener ads.[31] *Drum* probably did more than any other single publication to promote skin lighteners. Begun in 1951 in Johannesburg, *Drum* grew to feature the glamour and grittiness of black urban life, and became one of the most influential publications in sub-Saharan Africa, with regional editions published in Nairobi, Lagos, and Accra. It reported selling 250,000 copies per month by the late 1950s, and claimed to reach 3.5 million readers in South, Central, East, and West Africa.[32] A 1958 Bu-Tone skin lighteners ad proclaimed that their products were currently available in thirteen African countries or colonies, suggesting how the marketing of these cosmetics went hand-in-hand with the expansion of *Drum.*[33] Through ad campaigns such as this one, *Drum* helped create an "African" market for skin lighteners that extended beyond South Africa.

Like interwar skin lightener ads, most ads from the 1950s do not mention the products' ingredients. A 1959 ad for Artra, a product manufactured in Johannesburg, is an instructive exception. Suggesting the continued U.S. influence on South African developments, the ad announced hydroquinone (referred to as "H.Q.") as a new "miracle ingredient" that, unlike ammoniated mercury, would not cause skin "to burn, peel or break out." According to the ad's copy, hydro-quinone had been developed in "America's most modern laboratories."[34] U.S. manufacturers began using hydroquinone in skin lighteners after a series of industrial accidents in the late 1930s and early 1940s revealed the compound's ability to cause temporary depigmentation.[35] South African manufacturers of skin lighteners picked up this innovation and, in this ad, highlighted its U.S. origins as a sales point. As Irwin Manoim has demonstrated in his history of black media in postwar South Africa, advertisers deployed American—and, specifically, African American references—to signal a black consumer culture outside of South Africa's political and racial hierarchies.[36]

By the 1970s, skin lighteners were common commodities in most of south-ern Africa. And young women ranked among their most prolific users. One 1972 marketing survey found that more than half of the young African women (sixteen to thirty-four years) living in Salisbury (today, Harare) reported "regular use" of skin lighteners.[37] A 1969 presentation by white businessman L. M. Guthrie on "Bantu Marketing" explained some of the strategies used by manufacturers to reach these consumers. Speaking at a conference in Durban, Guthrie lauded Twins Products as a company that had succeeded against much larger competitors through "direct promotions" at retail outlets, by sharing a greater portion of their profits with wholesalers, and by ensuring that "their product . . . [was] peddled far and wide by illicit hawkers."[38] Through advertising campaigns, Twins recruited sales agents with the promise of "big money" and popularity in their distribution areas.[39] This strategy was similar to the door-to-door marketing used so successfully by U.S. cosmetics companies earlier dur-ing the twentieth century, suggesting how, in poor communities, sales agent systems both encouraged consumers to devote some of their meager resources to cosmetics and provided much-needed employment opportunities.

Guthrie concluded his 1969 presentation with his own marketing triumph: the development of Ambi into "the most successful skin lightening cream in Africa." He explained that a few years earlier, he had encouraged a pharma-cist from Salisbury to manufacture a hair straightener or bleach cream. The pharmacist obtained a license to manufacture the U.S. skin lightener Ambi. Initially, the venture struggled as the market was so dominated by Artra, Bu-Tone, and Karroo that retailers and wholesalers would not purchase the new product. In a last-ditch effort, according to Guthrie, they decided to give away Ambi in a "massive sampling campaign." They soon discovered that the press ads run by other companies were only "assimilated" by "the more sophisticated

Bantu" whereas their samples and the "whispering campaign" that ensued was far more effective at reaching the "masses."[40] From Guthrie's perspective, Ambi ultimately succeeded, because people's first- or second-hand experiences convinced them that it worked.

As in earlier decades, motivations for buying products that might even or lighten skin color varied. In economic contexts, where one's racial designation opened or closed opportunities, some people sought to look lighter. Phyllis Ntantala, in her autobiography *A Life's Mosaic*, describes how in 1940s Cape Town "many Africans . . . crossed over the colour line and were living as Coloureds." To secure better jobs and housing, they spoke Afrikaans and changed their last names from the likes of Ndlovu and Siphondo to Oliphant and Spawn.[41] Skin lighteners were another tool deployed by some seeking to alter their racial designation. This was, in fact, what James Korombi had argued in his 1939 letter to *Bantu World*. Similarly, in her autobiography *Strikes Have Followed Me All My Life*, Emma Mashinini explains how, during the late 1960s, she and other black women around Cape Town "started using skin lighteners, mainly to compete with the fair-skinned, so-called 'coloured,' women who have better status socially and at work."[42]

Yet, when assessing why people purchased skin lighteners, any instrumental use of skin lighteners for passing is outweighed by a more diffuse belief that skin lighteners helped to improve one's appearance. This, of course, was the persistent message of the skin lightener ads: People—particularly young women—who used these products would become more appealing, especially to the opposite sex, and more successful. Marketing studies done among urban black South Africans in the mid 1970s concluded that those who were swayed by skin lightener ads tended to view the ads' models as attractive and/or highly educated.[43] Beauty expert Nakedi Ribane, who today opposes skin lightener use, recalls why some used these products in the 1960s and 1970s: "The danger of these creams and lotions was that, initially, they seemed to work. They did a good job of 'taking away the Blackness' and making you look good. On first application, the skin would become smooth and yellowish, giving a lovely complexion, all pimples and blemishes vanishing like magic." With greater use, Ribane explains, the lightening and clarifying effects of ammoniated mercury or hydroquinone turned to darkening as people developed *chubabas* ("purpled patches of skin on their cheeks and below the eyes"). Such results did not deter all from using skin lighteners. As one woman told Ribane, "'Anybody who knew anything used those creams. If you don't have *chubabas*, then you were not an "it" girl of the moment!'"[44] For such consumers, evidence of skin lightener use signaled someone who was up-to-date and modern.

The persistent association of skin lighteners with beautification and modernity suggests that they became technologies of the self deployed by individuals to improve their appearances and future prospects. Yet, the appeal and prevalence of these technologies of the self depended upon expansive political and economic structures that privileged light-colored skin, made manufactured cosmetics widely available, and promoted their use through glossy magazines and local sales agents.

Political and Medical Opposition

From the 1960s, the growth in sales of skin lighteners was accompanied by increasing criticism of them by African political leaders and primarily white medical professionals. Until the late 1970s, these two lines of critique remained relatively distinct. African political leaders, usually male nationalists, denounced skin lightener use as racial betrayal, a vain attempt to turn white. Medical professionals, by contrast, opposed skin lighteners on health grounds. They argued that the active ingredients in skin lighteners—could damage skin if used in high concentrations and for prolonged periods. They insisted that such ingredients should be carefully regulated or prohibited altogether from over-the-counter cosmetics.

A number of newly independent East African governments took action against skin lighteners, many of which would have been manufactured in South Africa. In 1968, Tanzania banned them along with wigs, miniskirts, short shorts, and tight trousers as part of African socialism's efforts to safeguard youth against the "moral decadence" of Western culture.[45] Under Idi Amin's leadership, Uganda followed suit in 1972.[46] The Kenyan National Assembly debated but never passed a ban on skin lighteners. It did, however, censor Ambi ads deemed as insinuating that "new Africans" were "light-skinned Africans who had used Ambi."[47] Health arguments rarely surfaced during these debates; rather, they condemned the women who used them as "ashamed of the colour of their skins" and not "proud of being Africans."[48] According to these critics, skin lighteners were an affront to African nationalism.

Such moral condemnation of skin lighteners reduced the varied motivations behind skin lightener use to a black desire to be white. They also largely disassociated men from skin lighteners, ignoring how some men used them whereas others encouraged their use by preferring women with "brown" skin.[49]

In 1972, Audrey Wipper, a Canadian sociologist living in East Africa, offered an analysis of the bans. Although Wipper agreed that skin lighteners should be criticized because they were "physically . . . [and] psychologically danger-ous," she argued that prohibitions on Western fashions and beauty aids were a piece of broader efforts by postcolonial male politicians to use urban women as scapegoats for the nation's problems and to situate themselves as the nation's puritanical and authoritarian fathers.[50] Her analysis suggests how the gender politics of anticolonial and postcolonial nationalism could inform opposition to skin lighteners.

In 1960s and 1970s South Africa, where white-minority rule held sway and major antiapartheid political organizations (including the African National Congress) had been banned, it was Black Consciousness activists who led the moral condemnation of skin lighteners. Influenced by African nationalism and the Black Power Movement in the United States, Black Consciousness advo-cated black pride and political self-reliance. Black Consciousness activists, in-cluding most famously Steve Biko, urged Africans, Indians, and coloureds to reject the racial categories and oppression of apartheid and together unite as blacks. These advocates attributed the desire for lighter skin to racism and they reduced salient color distinctions to black and white. From their perspective, the appeal of skin lighteners stemmed from structural racism. In 1972, James Matthews, a writer aligned with the Black Consciousness Movement, published a poem denouncing "my sister" whose face is "smeared with astra cream" as a "schemer and a scene-stealer"; for her, "'black is beautiful' has become as artifi-cial as the wig she wears."[51] When interviewed in the 1980s, Black Consciousness activists Malusi Mpumlwana, Thoko Mbanjwa, and Mamphela Ramphele cited the continued use of skin lighteners by some in the predominately coloured western Cape as evidence of the need for further "conscientization" in that area. Mpumlwana, in a subsequent interview, portrayed the rejection of skin light-eners as a common first step in becoming politically aware.[52] Attesting to the power of a political ideology to rework everyday practices, Emma Mashinini attributed her and other African women's abandonment of skin lighteners to Black Consciousness: "[It] saved us from hating the colour of our skin."[53]

A marketing survey done in 1975 found that many black South African con-sumers agreed with the Black Consciousness perspective on skin lighteners. Roughly the same portion of interviewees said that blacks would not buy a par-ticular skin lightener because they were "proud of their skin colour" as said that they would buy it because they wanted "to be lighter." Noting health concerns, a significant minority also stated that blacks would not buy the product because it caused "skin disease" or was "bad for skin."[54]

South African doctors first reported medical complications from over-the-counter skin lighteners in the mid 1970s. The government banned mercury from cosmetics in 1975 after recognizing that it could cause kidney damage. This ban followed a similar U.S. prohibition by two years.[55] However, a year after the South African ban, doctors at Baragwanath Hospital in Soweto reported still seeing female patients with chronic mercury intoxication from prolonged skin lightener use.[56] An epidemic of approximately 1000 cases of leukomelanoderma (confettilike depigmentation) occurred in Johannesburg when one manufacturer replaced ammoniated mercury with monobenzyl ether of hydroquinone (MBH) rather than hydroquinone as the active ingredient in its skin lightener.[57] In the wake of this epidemic, the South African Health Department also prohibited the use of MBH in skin lighteners.[58]

Subsequent medical debates over skin lighteners in South Africa focused on hydroquinone itself. In 1974, Twins Products inquired about U.S. guidelines regarding hydroquinone in skin lighteners. A U.S. Department of Health official responded that hydroquinone was considered a drug, thus the FDA required approval for both its prescription and nonprescription use.[59] In general, FDA officials advised that hydroquinone concentrations be kept to 1 to 2 percent and that warning labels be provided.[60] The Twins query demonstrates how, in the emerging debate over hydroquinone, some South African manufacturers turned to U.S. FDA guidelines to bolster arguments about their own products' safety. By the mid-1970s, dermatologists and pathologists in Pretoria (G. H. Findlay, J. G. L. Morrison, and I. W. Simson) had concluded that prolonged use of skin lighteners with hydroquinone (usually three years or longer), particularly at higher concentrations (more than 3%), combined with intense sun exposure often resulted in hyperpigmentation rather than depigmentation. This darkened and disfigured skin most commonly manifested as colloid milium (cavierlike clusters of papules on the skin that are darker than surrounding areas) and exogenous ochronosis (patches of bluish black pigmentation)—what Ribane and her informant called *chubabas*. A remarkable 30 percent of all the black patients seen at the dermatology outpatient clinic at Kalafong Hospital in Pretoria sought treatment for hydroquinone-induced ochronosis. Findlay and his colleagues believed that the disfigurement was long term, if not permanent. They also surmised that the roots of this epidemic dated back to 1966, when a number of manufacturers increased the concentrations of hydroquinone in their skin lighteners from 3 percent to 6 to 8 percent.[61] A follow-up study published in 1980 analyzed thirteen brands of skin lighteners and found that they contained anywhere between 2.5 to 7.5 percent concentrations. That study recommended that, although short-term use of these products could be helpful in removing blemishes, they should not be used as overall lighteners.[62]

In contrast to Black Consciousness condemnation of skin lighteners that stressed the influence of structural racism, medical researchers articulated multiple motivations behind skin lightener use and suggested that skin preferences could not be reduced to a black-and-white binary. For instance, dermatologists from the University of Natal explained that Africans used these products to improve their facial appearance, achieve a "smoothening effect," and to elevate their social status. Pursuit of these goals together with a belief that painful medicines were powerful medicines, they argued, led to aggressive usage:

> "[S]moothening," as the Africans term it, is highly prized by both male and female purchasers. Although in our opinion more lightening exists in the mind than in the skin, our patients feel that if a preparation "stings or burns" on application it must be better than one that does not. Consequently, higher and higher strengths are used, applied frequently and vigorously until a good contact dermatitis has appeared. Hypermelanosis [hyperpigmentation] follows the erythema [irritation] and patients then attend the clinic demanding yet another and more powerful "lightener."[63]

These dermatologists further reported that although coloureds also often used skin lighteners, Indians and whites did not. Suggesting how much white attitudes toward their own skin color had changed since the 1920s, they reported having seen only one white patient for skin lightener-induced leukomelanoderma: "an eighty-two-year-old English woman who had preserved her lily-white complexion for over fifty years with a mercurial preparation without ill effect until, without her knowledge, the formula was altered and MBH substituted for the mercury." Whites in mid 1970s South Africa, they wrote, "generally prefer bronzed to pale faces."[64] Findlay and his co-authors insisted that for Africans, too, preferred skin color was not a matter of white and black; rather, Africans sought to achieve a "light brown as against a dark brown skin" and a skin that was not "dull, drab, dusty, or scaly," but defined by "brightness."[65] Such observations highlighted the complex and varied meanings of skin color and tone.

Within the context of rising antiapartheid activism, however, white medical professionals also increasingly recognized the political meanings of skin lightening. In one 1980 publication, Findlay and a collaborator provided an extended quote from a cosmetics marketer explaining how the "post-riot [Soweto uprising of 1976] political situation" had combined with publicity about ill-health consequences to decrease the appeal of skin lighteners.[66] Political and health critiques of skin lighteners had begun to converge. When interviewed in 2004, Dr. Hilary Carmen, one of the main dermatologists who campaigned against skin lighteners during the 1980s, explained that she became involved out of desire to put the medical research of Findlay and others toward "activist" ends.[67]

During the 1980s, antiskin lightener activists focused on hydroquinone. The South African Health Department in 1981 limited the maximum concentration of hydroquinone in over-the-counter cosmetics to 2 percent, bringing South African regulations in line with those of the U.S. FDA.[68] A number of groups, including the progressive adult literacy magazines *Learn and Teach* and *Upbeat,* continued to push for a complete ban on hydroquinone. Together with articles and letters emphasizing the dangers of skin lighteners and affirming the Black Consciousness motto that "black is beautiful," *Learn and Teach* featured photographs of black consumers whose faces had been disfigured from skin lighteners. Figure 11.6 demonstrates how such campaigns linked skin damage to specific products. Such photos were an implicit retort to the countless images of skin lightener users with light and smooth faces that had appeared in magazines like *Drum.* In a more direct challenge, *Learn and Teach* requested all newspapers and magazines to stop advertising skin lighteners. In 1982, after nearly three decades of promoting these products across the subcontinent, *Drum* complied with the request.[69]

For the remainder of the 1980s, a coalition of consumer, medical, and women's organizations campaigned for a complete ban on hydroquinone-based skin lighteners. Activist doctors argued that although preparations with 2 percent hydroquinone continued to be deemed safe for over-the-counter use in the United States, in South Africa, where black consumers generally experienced more intense exposure to sunlight and seemed to apply skin lighteners more heavily, more frequently, and for longer durations, they were often disfiguring.[70] Twice during the late 1980s, the Ministry of Health promised a ban. Pressure from skin lightener manufacturers apparently kept those promises unfulfilled.[71] Finally, in 1991, while the white South African government and the African National Congress negotiated the country's democratic transition, the Ministry of Health banned hydroquinone from all cosmetics and deemed

Skin lightening creams: a big new problem

LEARN AND TEACH 1982

Figure 11.6 Photo That Appeared in a Progressive Adult Literacy Magazine as Part of a Campaign to Educate Black Consumers About the Harmful Effects of Skin Lighteners and to Urge the South African Government to Ban Them
SOURCE: *Learn and Teach* (Johannesburg), v. 2, n. 5, 1982, p. 1.

it exclusively a prescription drug.[72] Today, dermatologists in South Africa describe seeing fewer skin lightener-caused disfigurements than they did in the late 1980s. But, as elsewhere in the world, skin lighteners containing mercury, hydroquinone, steroids, and other active ingredients remain widely—if often illegally—available.[73]

Conclusion

This chapter explains the rise and decline of skin lighteners as a multimillion-dollarper-year enterprise in South Africa. As we have seen, transnational entanglements—both ideological and commercial—between the United States, South Africa, and much of the subcontinent fueled the trade in skin lighteners. Beginning with "Jolly" Jack Bernard and extending through the men behind Ambi and Twins Products, white southern African entrepreneurs turned to U.S. companies and agencies for inspiration and guidance in the marketing and manufacturing of skin lighteners for black consumers. Following on aggressive advertising and sales campaigns, many consumers in apartheid South Africa and elsewhere in the subcontinent, especially young women, purchased and used skin lighteners. Their motivations ranged from lightening sun-darkened skin to eliminating blemishes to "brightening" to looking "modern" to passing for another racial designation. Such varied motivations reveal how skin lighteners emerged as commonplace technologies of the self resulting from the convergence of racial hierarchies, capitalist commerce, and individual desires for betterment. As McCarthy insisted in his critique of Foucault's later writings, technologies of the self emerged from the intertwining of personal fantasies and structural forces.[74]

By making opposition to skin lighteners a corollary of antiapartheid struggles, activists necessarily occluded the varied motivations and complex convergences that animated skin lightener use and sales. Although medical critiques revealed the health dangers posed by these cosmetics, it was Black Nationalist critiques that powerfully cast skin lighteners as harmful and immoral technologies of the self. Black Consciousness leaders interpreted the continued use of skin lighteners in an area as evidence of low political awareness whereas progressive publications like *Learn and Teach* countered skin lightener marketing campaigns with the motto "black is beautiful." Such campaigns framed and fixed skin lightener use as evidence of racial self-loathing, sidelining alternative motivations and interpretations.

Most, if not all, readers of this volume probably also view skin lightener use as a repugnant practice born of structural racism. This similarity of perspective stems, in part, from the fact that South African opposition to skin lighteners emerged through transnational ideologies of antiracism. Yet, as this chapter and others in this volume make poignantly and, at times, painfully clear, it is not a perspective that all have shared during the past or the present.

IV

Countering Colorism

Legal Approaches

COLORISM CLAIMS IN U.S. COURTS LAW RELY on two statutes: an 1866 post-Civil War law that guarantees all male persons the same rights as "white citizens," "without distinction of race or color, or previous condition of slavery or involuntary servitude," and the Civil Rights Act of 1964, which prohibits discrimination in accommodation, public facilities, education, federal assistance programs, and employment on account of color, race, religion, or national origin. The discussion of how courts have treated colorism claims under these statutes echoes the questions raised in the chapters at the beginning of this book, namely: What is the relationship between race and color, and between racism and colorism?

The inclusion of both *color* and *race* in these laws would seem to indicate that their framers saw these as separate forms of discrimination. However, courts have often been confused about whether a color claim is really a race claim. The three authors of Part IV, all distinguished law professors, offer different perspectives on this issue. Trina Jones argues that racism and colorism are separate forms of discrimination, and that for civil rights law to be used to address color-based discrimination, legal actors need to understand the history and contemporary manifestations of colorism as a serious and distinct form of discrimination. Taunya Lovell Banks argues that color discrimination is actually a form of race discrimination (what she calls "race-related" discrimination) in that it is discrimination based on negative reactions to phenotypically black characteristics. As such, color-based bias is unintentional, an unconscious and automatic response. Colorism claims confront difficulties in being recognized because courts increasingly require that plaintiffs establish that the alleged discrimination was intentional. Both Banks and Tanya Katerí Hernández make the case that courts have had difficulty dealing with colorism claims that diverge from the dichotomous black–white racial model. When analyzing colorism claims involving Latino/a plaintiffs, Hernández notes that the dominant racial model of the United States in which color and race are more or less equivalent—that is, black–white corresponds to both color and racial categories—does not take into account the dynamics of a tricolor system in which there are degrees of whiteness and blackness.

All three authors agree that one reason U.S. courts have failed to recognize many colorism claims is because they do not fit the template that has been established for racial discrimination claims, which involves a member of one racial category discriminating against a member of another racial category. However, colorism may take the form of a member of one racial category discriminating against only some members of another category, or it may involve intragroup discrimination.

These chapters also hark back to the question of convergences and divergences between societies with respect to race and color. Just as Telles identifies problems in Brazil's adoption of American–style affirmative action that uses racial rather than color categories, Banks and Hernández point to the likelihood that antidiscrimination law based on fixed racial categories may also become less relevant as the United States becomes more Latin American in its racial dynamics. As this occurs, those concerned with developing legal recourses to harmful discrimination will have to formulate language and frameworks that address the new realities.

E.N.G.

12 Multilayered Racism
Courts' Continued Resistance to Colorism Claims
Taunya Lovell Banks

IN 1993, LAW PROFESSOR CHERYL HARRIS RECOUNTED how her light-skinned grandmother used her "white" skin to secure a better paying job to support her family.[1] Harris acknowledged that her grandmother would not have gotten a job reserved for white women had her black racial ancestry been known. Thus, her grandmother's light skin tone served as a surrogate for whiteness.

Today, antidiscrimination laws make it illegal for Harris' grandmother to be denied a job for which she was qualified based only on her race. The law is less clear about whether the hiring of Harris' grandmother over another similarly qualified black person because of her light skin tone—colorism—is illegal. Courts have been reluctant to acknowledge the increasing complexity of race because legal race theories do not provide sufficient guidelines for courts to apply. Additionally, proof of intent to discrimination is required to prevail even though empirical studies suggest that increasingly race-based discrimination in America is unintentional—that is, unconscious and automatic, but nonetheless harmful.

Empirical Evidence of Skin Tone Bias

Literature on colorism tends to treat skin tone bias as an internal phenomenon within nonwhite communities, but skin tone discrimination can be either interracial or intraracial. There is a body of literature dating from the late nineteenth century about the American "mulatto" that reflected and fostered color bias within the white community.[2] Many early-twentieth-century eugenicists argued that possession of partial white ancestry accounted for the success of some black people.[3]

213

Colorphobia also infected nonwhite communities, especially black communities in America. Bias against dark-skinned people created a color hierarchy within the group labeled as *black*. In other words, colorphobia, colorism, or skin tone bias creates different levels of status and power within a racial group. Thus, scholars recognize that members of the same racial group can be differentially racialized.[4]

The famous Swedish economist Gunnar Myrdal wrote in the 1944 that "without a doubt a Negro with light skin and other European features has in the North an advantage with white people when competing for jobs available to Negroes."[5] In the 1950s, E. Franklin Frazier, a controversial black social scientist, agreed, cautioning that although light skin tone conferred an advantage, it did not overcome the stigma of being black.[6] Several later empirical studies support Myrdal's and Frazier's claims. These studies found that light-skinned blacks were more likely to be better educated, better employed, and have better (socioeconomic) marital outcomes than dark-skinned blacks.[7]

One scholar qualifies these findings, arguing that although skin tone-based differences exist among black Americans, they are less pronounced for blacks born after World War II; and employment differences between light- and dark-skinned persons has decreased significantly since the 1980s.[8] This study, however, has been questioned by other researchers who conclude that during the late twentieth century, skin tone still had a significant impact on the wages of black males. Black male workers with medium and dark skin lost at least 10 percent in wages compared with white male workers. Whereas the wage differences between light-skinned black male and white male workers was insignificant. These researchers conclude that there is "a line of separation in labor market experiences for light-complexioned black males and all others" (p. 245).[9]

Skin tone bias is not limited to black Americans. Empirical studies also suggest a correlation between skin tone and education or income for Mexican Americans. Mexican Americans with dark skin tones and indigenous features fair poorly compared with Mexican Americans with light skin tones and more European features.[10] Another study using the New Immigrant Survey 2003 found that light-skinned legal immigrants earned between 8 to 15 percent more than comparable immigrants with darker skin tones.[11] The researcher notes that the study only looked at immigrants currently employed; thus, if skin tone influences hiring decisions, the effect on wages could be even greater.[12]

More recent studies suggest that the public associates dark skin tones with criminality and untrustworthiness. After the controversy surrounding *Time*

Magazine's darkening of O. J. Simpson's mug shot on the cover of its June 27, 1994, issue, social scientist Dwayne Proctor conducted a study in which the skin tone in a photograph accompanying a news article about the arrest of an accused murderer was manipulated. Proctor found that study respondents, when shown the two photographs of the same black man, were more likely to find the black man with dark skin tone guilty than the same man with light skin tone. Proctor concludes that there is a learned association between the word *black* and guilt, and that the accused black "man with light colored skin . . . was judged as less guilty because he was not seen as 'black.'"[13]

Proctor's reasoning might explain the outcome of another study. Since 1865, a disproportionate percent of black elected officials in Congress have been light-skinned, causing social scientists to speculate about whether skin tone differences among black political candidates has any effect on black voters' attitudes, and whether skin tone may be a factor, in addition to race, considered by white voters when evaluating black political candidates.[14] Another researcher concluded that white voters would evaluate dark-skinned black political candidates more negatively than light-skinned black candidates.[15]

The preference for light skin tones may not be a result of conscious bias, but of what Jerry Kang calls "racial mechanics—the ways in which race alters intrapersonal, interpersonal, and inter-group interactions."[16] There are explicit and implicit racial meanings assigned to the racial categories created by law and cultural practices, and the racial meanings associated with that category are triggered when we interact with others.[17] As a result, implicit racial biases— negative stereotypes and prejudices—influenced these interactions. These reactions are automatic in the sense that they are unintentional and outside the actor's awareness.

Individual members of the same race may be treated differently based on whether they have what social psychologist Irene Blair characterizes as "Afrocentric features"—dark skin, wide nose and full lips.[18] Individuals with these features are likely to be judged more harshly than members of the same race with less Afrocentric features as a result of automatic or implicit racial attitudes.[19] The consequences of implicit skin tone and phenotypic biases may be significant.

Using a Florida Department of Corrections photographic database of convicted offenders, and controlling for crime charged and criminal history, Blair compared the length of sentences, looking at race and physical features. Although there was no significant disparity between the sentences of blacks and whites, Blair found that criminal defendants with Afrocentric features received longer sentences than offenders of the same race with less pronounced Afrocentric features. Unconscious or automatic stereotyping may even transcend race. Blair found that white offenders "with high levels of Afrocentric features (relative to their racial group)" received slightly longer sentences than whites with low levels of Afrocentric features.[20]

Based on the findings of this and earlier research, Blair posits that the sentencing differences within racialized groups may be a consequence of sentencing judges who subconsciously associate criminality more with dark-skinned blacks than with light skinned blacks. Blair and her co-authors speculate "judges were unaware . . . that Afrocentric features might be influencing their decisions and were not effectively controlling the impact of such features." The researchers conclude that "[r]acial stereotyping in sentencing decisions is . . . not a function of the racial category of the individual. Instead, there is perhaps an equally pernicious and less controllable process at work."[21] I characterize the phenomena Blair describes as race-related discrimination.

The implications of Blair's studies about automatic stereotyping are significant. As a general rule, legal relief under antidiscrimination law is based on a showing of some explicit or conscious intent to discriminate. If, as the growing body of social science data suggests, race-related discrimination, especially feature-based stereotyping like colorism, is not only unintentional, but automatic, then current laws provide ineffective remedies.

Confusion in the Court: Title VII and Other Colorism Cases

Courts and some academic scholars express confusion about the legal basis for color-based discrimination claims. In an earlier article I argued that the courts should treat adverse employment decisions based skin tone as a form of race-based discrimination.[22] Employment discrimination cases based on colorism claims usually rely on two federal antidiscrimination statutes: 42 U.S.C. § 1981, a post-Civil War reconstruction statute that guarantees all persons the same rights as "white citizens," but makes no reference to the words *race* or *color*[23]; and Title VII of the Civil Rights Act of 1964, which prohibits employment discrimination based on color as well as race, but defines neither term. Title VII also prohibits discrimination on the basis of ethnicity, gender, religion, and national origin.[24]

Most courts refused to acknowledge race-related discrimination when the employment decision involves two people "raced" the same. Thus, when one black litigant claims color-based discrimination in hiring by an employer, courts usually dismissed the claim if the employer proves that another black person was hired for the position. However, during the early 1990s, two federal court decisions, *Walker v. Internal Revenue Service,* an employment discrimination case, and *Franceschi v. Hyatt Corp.,* a public accommodations case, recognized intraracial or intraethnic discrimination claims but use different reasoning. The federal judge in the *Walker* case treated the colorism claim like a race discrimination claim, concluding that the light-skinned black plaintiff was alleging discrimination by her dark-skinned black supervisor based on the plaintiff's remote white ancestry.[25] In contrast, the federal district judge in *Franceschi* avoided determining whether Puerto Ricans are white or a separate race, ruling instead that intraracial discrimination claims are actionable if the complaining party was treated like a minority.[26] Although both courts recognized colorism as a legal claim, neither plaintiff recovered.

Colorism cases are hard to prove because, as the *Walker* and *Franceschi* cases suggest, courts are confused about what constitutes a valid colorism claim. In some cases, courts analyze the race and color discrimination claims separately. If there is no evidence that the employer failed to hire applicants based on their race, then the court looks at whether there is evidence that the employer only hired applicants from that racial group with a particular skin tone.[27]

In other cases in which the litigant asserted a race and color claim, the court acknowledged that, in reality, the litigant was setting out a race claim and treated it as such, using the terms *color* and *race* interchangeably. For example, the plaintiff in *Maingi v. IBP, Inc.* sued, alleging employment discrimination based on national origin (Kenyan/East African) and color.[28] However, it seems his color claim was really a race claim, that he had been discriminated because he was black, and the court treated his case as a race discrimination claim. Similarly, the plaintiff in *Vester v. Henderson* filed a race and color discrimination claim based on her race (Caucasian) and her color (white)[29]; the federal district court treated the case as a race claim. Of course, it is possible that the litigants in these cases were not alleging colorism claims, but were using the terms *race* and *color* interchangeably.

A few courts seem willing to acknowledge colorism claims between Latina/o litigants, demonstrating that courts can handle colorism claims, although not always well or uniformly—a point explored more fully by Tanya Katerí Hernández in Chapter 14. Most of these judicial discussions about colorism claims come from the federal district court in Puerto Rico and involve Puerto Rican parties. Puerto Rico is governed by the same antidiscrimination laws as the United States.

In *Santiago v. Stryker Corp.,* for example, the plaintiff complained of discrimination based on national origin and color. The district judge observed that although both parties were Puerto Rican: "Falero describes himself as a darker skinned, or mulatto, Puerto Rican. . . . Cabrera's skin color, on the other hand, is admittedly white," thus recognizing a colorism claim.[30] The judge continued: "The fact that Cabrera's skin is of a different color places him outside Falero's protected class, and is enough to satisfy a key element of plaintiff's case. Although the plaintiff's pleadings established a colorism claim, the court dismissed the case for other reasons.

Cases like *Santiago* and *Johnson v. Wegman's* raise an interesting question— namely, who determines skin tone? The plaintiff, defendant, or judge? In *Johnson,* the court accepted the defendant employer's affidavit describing the skin tone of its black employees. In *Santiago,* the trial judge relied on the plaintiff's self-description and the judge's visual observation of the defendant in making this determination. Each method is problematic. Naturally an employer will describe the skin tone of employees in the manner most favorable to its case, whereas reasonable judges and plaintiffs may disagree on a party's skin tone.

In another Puerto Rican colorism case *Felix v. Marquez,* the plaintiff, Carmen Felix, described herself as dark olive whereas the judge described her as of a medium shade.[31] The terms *medium brown* and *brown,* as they relate to skin tone, have a distinct racial connotation in the United States. These terms describe nonwhites. However, the term *olive,* used in *Felix* is often used to describe southern Europeans like Italians, ethnic groups considered white in the United States. Descriptions of skin tone in this country invariably convey racial meaning.[32]

One of the few successful colorism cases also involved Latino plaintiffs. In *Rodriguez v. Gattuso,* a 1992 federal district court in Illinois recognized interracial discrimination in the leasing of property based on skin tone.[33] The plaintiffs, a dark-skinned Afro-Latino and his light-skinned Latina wife, attempted to lease an apartment from a white landlord. Carole Rodriquez met with the landlord, who agreed to rent the apartment but wanted to meet Carol's husband before finalizing the deal. When Roberto, her Afro-Latino husband, appeared, the landlord claimed that two other couples were ahead of them on the list for the apartment, adding that he doubted whether Roberto and Carol Rodriguez could pay the rent.

The trial judge found that the landlord only had one Latino tenant in each of his buildings and those tenants were of "white Latino ancestry." The judge based this determination on his visual observations. He wrote: "[t]his Court's physical observation of [the Latino tenants in the apartment] light-skinned Latino Mitchell Gonzalez (whose wife Laura was described as 'white') and . . . light-skinned Latino Carol, as contrasted with Roberto's characterization as a 'black Latino,' demonstrates graphically that persons such as Gattuso's [the landlord] could be (and in this case was) biased against Roberto because of his color and that Gattusos discriminated against him for that reason and that reason alone."[34] The judge, although treating the case as a colorism claim, was nonetheless relying on conventional racial references: white and black.

Is Colorism a Form of Race Discrimination?

Arguably, the judge in the *Rodriguez* case, like the judge in the *Walker* case, treated the colorism claim like a racial discrimination claim in which a landlord prefers white tenants over black tenants. What remains unclear is whether colorism practices constitute race-based or race-related discrimination, or some entirely new form of discrimination. Law professor Trina Jones argues that colorism is a form of discrimination independent of race.[35]

According to Jones, colorism evokes different stigmas and stereotypes that are not based on race, but on skin tone. "[I]t is the social meaning afforded skin color itself that results in differential treatment. . . . [A]ny difference in treatment results not from racial categorization per se, but from values associated with skin color itself." She concedes that race and colorism claims may overlap, but argues that colorism claims are "analytically different" from race discrimination claims.[36] Professor Jones' more recent discussion of colorism practices also appears in this volume (Chapter 13).

Increased recognition by social scientists of skin tone's impact on important life decisions like employment and criminal punishment confirms racism's persistence in the twenty-first century, and its ability to reinvent itself in ways that both disguise and deny its continued existence. From a remedial legal perspective, it also matters whether colorism claims are race or nonrace claims. Race-based claims have the benefit of a long, although tortured, jurisprudence grounded in constitutional, federal, and state laws. Judges and legislators understand the underlying reasons for race-based laws. Creating a new cause of action independent of race raises questions about the legal basis for the action and the appropriate analytical framework courts would use when assessing colorism claims.

Jones' approach to colorism claims ignores the ability of racism to meta-morphose into new forms and assumes a willingness of increasingly hostile courts to consider new legal actions expanding the basis for discrimination claims. In the short term, this country's race discrimination jurisprudence, however flawed, may be a more promising avenue for securing some legal redress. Nevertheless, legal scholars need to explore the possibility for developing new and effective theories to remedy harmful colorism practices outside of race discrimination law.

Moving Beyond the Intent Requirement

Although intentional race-based or race-related discrimination may have become less common during the twenty-first century, automatic and unconscious discrimination has not disappeared. Thus, the biggest obstacle to colorism claims remains the requirement that the plaintiff prove the discrimination was intentional. This country's current race jurisprudence resists acknowledging that most race-based discrimination today is unintentional. Arguments by several legal writers for expanding antidiscrimination laws to cover unintentional acts of discrimination have fallen on deaf ears.[37]

As mentioned previously, numerous empirical social science studies establish the existence of unconscious or automatic negative stereotype bias toward groups on the basis of race, age, or gender and demonstrate that these unintentional biases influence decision making.[38] A few studies found that the automatic stereotyping process can be controlled or minimized using a variety of methods and strategies, including sensitizing decision makers to control their unconscious racial stereotyping.[39] Thus, sensitivity training might be appropriate for some decision makers like employers, and special instructions or cautions might be warranted for legal decision makers like judges and juries.[40] These changes might be instituted as safeguards without abandoning the intent-to-discriminate requirement.

However, sensitizing methodologies do not address one disturbing finding from a Blair study. The same individuals who, if sensitized, can control their racial stereotypical attitudes are unable to control stereotypes based on skin tone and Afrocentric features even when sensitized to the existence of these stereotypes.[41] Thus, the thorny question is whether a predictable and fair legal standard can be developed that addresses automatic stereotyping based on skin tone or phenotype, because automatic skin tone stereotyping is as damaging as intentional race-based or race-related discrimination.

Broader Implications of Colorism and Phenotypic Bias

United States v. White illustrates how unconscious skin tone and phenotypic bias may impact in other areas like jury selection and relief for the discriminatory exclusion of blacks from juries.[42] John Terrence A. Rosenthal recounts how the judge in *White*, when quizzing potential jurors, asked whether "they could be fair and impartial given that the defendant was a black male."[43] The trial judge observed that only one potential juror "appeared to be African-American. . . . At that point, [another] juror, . . . stated that she wanted the judge to know that she was African-American. The judge thanked her for her candor, and stated that he would not have recognized her as African-American and he believed that not many others would have recognized her as being African-American."[44]

Both the prosecution and the defense may dismiss, with the judge's permission, any potential juror for "cause" (obvious bias in favor or against one of the parties, lawyers or witnesses). Each side also has a number of preemptory challenges that may be used against potential jurors without stating a reason. The prosecutor exercised his preemptory challenge dismissing only the "visibly black" juror.[45] The exclusion of one of two black jurors, the visibly black but not the racially ambiguous-looking juror, raises interesting legal questions about what constitutes impermissible race-based exclusion of jurors.

In 1986, the United States Supreme Court in *Batson v. Kentucky* revised the process for establishing racial discrimination in jury selection.[46] To prevail, the defendant must establish that (1) the prosecution used its preemptory challenges to exclude a member of the juror panel from the same racial group as the defendant and (2) the circumstances surrounding the exclusion of the juror raises an inference of racial motivation—intentional conduct.

If racially motivated, the use of a preemptory challenge against the visibly black juror in *White* might be the basis of a *Batson* challenge. However, in cases like *White*, a successful challenge may be problematic because only one of the two identified black potential jurors was struck. Because one known black person was left on the jury, a *Batson* challenge may be inappropriate under the current legal regime because the rule is grounded on a view of race as monolithic.

Should it matter for race discrimination purposes whether the light-skinned black person is not regarded as black by the lawyers? Furthermore, it may be difficult or impossible to determine whether the prosecutor's actions in *White* were intentional or the product of automatic stereotyping. Both reasons are equally harmful for criminal defendants, but the law as currently constructed does not prohibit unconscious or automatic racially biased decision making.

Conclusion

The faces of the people left behind at the Convention Center and Superdome in New Orleans during Hurricane Katrina in 2005 remind us of the continuing connection between race, skin tone, and socioeconomic class in America. *CNN News* commentator Wolf Blitzer's unselfconscious comments reflect the reaction of the nation. Blitzer, in obvious distress, reported to the television viewing audience that the New Orleans residents left behind were "so poor and . . . so *black*."[47] His "so black" comment highlighted the reality of the post-Katrina tragedy. A disproportionate number of people the media identified as left behind and most in need of help were not simply black, poor, aged, and infirm, they were dark-skinned black people. The empirical studies suggest that this circumstance was not a mere accident of fate. Legal institutions, like courts, facilitate colorism practices in the United States by failing to provide effective legal remedies for this form of race-related discrimination. This failure reinforces existing dominant social, economic, and cultural norms that operate against black people with the darkest skin tones.

The continuing importance of skin tone in how race is experienced in the United States, and the persistence of courts and legal scholars in viewing race as a monolithic phenomenon actionable only if intentional, highlights the need to rethink progressive race jurisprudence in America. The studies on implicit automatic stereotyping are new weapons to use in attacking the intent-based requirement in antidiscrimination law. Social science research may be an effective means to persuade courts to remedy more subtle and pernicious forms of race-based discrimination like colorism. New legal theories must be flexible enough to address the varied faces of racism in the twenty-first century.

As more empirical studies help us better understand how race-related discrimination is manifested, how automatic stereotyping perpetuates race-related decision-making, and how to measure and thwart implicit stereotyping, legal scholars will be better able to craft effective theories to combat this and other more subtle forms of discrimination like colorism. Unless courts can be persuaded to acknowledge how automatic race-related stereotyping, like colorism, results in economic discrimination and possible loss of liberty, discriminatory racialized decision making will not be eliminated. The failure to develop more complex definitions of actionable race-based or race-related discrimination and to expand recovery to include instances of unintentional conduct means that racial injustices will persist well into the twenty-first century.

13 The Case for Legal Recognition of Colorism Claims

Trina Jones

In December 2000, Dwight Burch began working as a server at an Applebee's restaurant in Atlanta, Georgia. Less than ninety days later, the store manager fired him. Mr. Burch subsequently filed a charge with the EEOC alleging that the store manager, a light-skinned African American, had consistently made derogatory remarks about Mr. Burch's dark skin color. In August of 2003, the EEOC settled the lawsuit for $40,000 and certain injunctive relief.[1]

In recent years, the Equal Employment Opportunity Commission (EEOC) has witnessed a sharp increase in skin color discrimination charges.[2] Although colorism charges are rising, their overall number is still relatively small, constituting about 3 percent of the 85,000 charges received annually by the EEOC.[3] In addition, there have been relatively few litigated cases and judicial opinions to date.[4] Because colorism claims comprise such a small percentage of all discrimination cases, questions remain concerning their theoretical legitimacy and practical feasibility.

This chapter responds to some of these questions by setting forth an argument for legal recognition of colorism.[5] Importantly, for courts and legal actors to recognize and to accept the legitimacy of skin color discrimination claims, they must appreciate the difference between race and skin color. This chapter thus begins by distinguishing skin color from race before proceeding to examine doctrinal and other practical challenges to colorism claims. My analysis focuses on colorism as it relates to the African American community in the United States. Similar issues exist in other communities throughout the world. The absence of analysis of these larger communities in this chapter should not be read as an attempt to minimize the significance of colorism to South Asians, Latinos, and other groups.

In addition, it is important to note that persons of any race can engage in colorism. For purposes of this chapter, the phrase *intraracial colorism* refers to cases in which the discriminator and the person discriminated against are of the same racial group (e.g., a light-skinned black person discriminating against a darker skinned black person). *Interracial colorism* refers to those situations in which members of one race distinguish between two or more members of a different race on the basis of skin color (e.g., a white person differentiating among two black individuals).

Distinguishing Race from Skin Color

The terms *race* and *color* have been used interchangeably throughout U.S. history. More precisely, the word *color* or *colored* has been used frequently to reference race and racial groups (e.g., nonwhite or biracial persons). Historical and contemporary examples are plentiful, including common phrases like "colored people" and "colored folk," institutional names like the National Association for the Advancement of Colored People, W. E. B. Dubois' use of "the color line" and similar references to the "color barrier," and literary titles like Ntozake Shange's powerful work "for colored girls who have considered suicide when the rainbow is enuf." When read in context, even Dr. Martin Luther King's exhortation that his children be judged not by the "color of their skin but by the content of their character" can be seen as a call for the elimination of racial discrimination.

The law has not escaped the tendency to conflate race and color. For example, the Louisiana statute at issue in *Plessy v. Ferguson,* the famous case validating the "separate but equal" doctrine, provided "that all railway companies carrying passengers in their coaches in this State, shall provide equal but separate accommodations for the white, and colored races."[6] States used similar terminology in other Jim Crow legislation, including pre-*Brown*[7] statutes mandating segregation in public education and pre-*Loving*[8] statutes outlawing miscegenation.[9] Significantly, the word *color* appears in both the Fifteenth Amendment to the U.S. Constitution, which prohibits infringements on the right to vote "on account of race, color, or previous condition of servitude," and the Civil Rights Act of 1964,[10] which prohibits discrimination on the basis of a variety of factors, including race and color, in public accommodations, employment, and programs receiving federal financial assistance, among other things. Although these critically important legal provisions use the words *race* and *color,* color has generally been read to mean race. Indeed, one can find hundreds of cases in which plaintiffs alleged discrimination on the basis of race or color, but which were treated automatically and solely as race claims.[11]

Although they are related concepts, race and skin color are not synonymous. Skin color, like ethnicity, ancestry, hair texture, facial features, and body type, among other things, is one indicator of race. That is, like these other variables, skin color is used to assign persons to racial classifications. It is important, however, not to confuse the indicator with the thing that it is indicating. Skin color is a device used in assigning persons to a racial category. Race is the social meaning attributed to that category—namely, it is a set of socially constructed beliefs or assumptions about individuals falling within that category.[12] These beliefs vary across time and space and may be wide ranging, comprising assumptions about a group's intellect, physical attractiveness, work ethic, socioeconomic class, morality, criminality, and so forth. For example, if one were to see Oprah Winfrey and Diane Sawyer on the street, Winfrey's brown skin tone would likely cause the viewer to conclude that she is a member of the black race. However, her skin color would not be the determinant of her status. Rather, the conclusion that she falls within the black race and societal views about blacks versus whites would lead to differential treatment.

With colorism, skin color does not serve as an indicator of race. Rather, it is the social meaning afforded skin color itself that results in the differential treatment. For example, instead of Winfrey and Sawyer, imagine that one sees two black women on the street. Assume that one woman is light chocolate brown, like say Beyoncé Knowles, and the other is dark chocolate brown, like India Arie. Despite the fact that both women are of the same race, one may receive superior treatment based upon her skin color. When encountering these two individuals, the viewer does not use skin color to assign the women to a particular racial category. Rather, any difference in treatment results not from racial categorization per se, but from values associated with skin color itself. Because views about color trigger the differential treatment in this circumstance, this form of discrimination is most accurately called *colorism*. Thus, with racism, it is the social meaning afforded one's race that determines one's status. With colorism, it is the social meaning afforded one's color that determines one's status.

Arguments for Legal Recognition of Color Discrimination

Colorism can occur in a variety of different contexts. An employer may prefer lighter skinned black people (or darker toned blacks depending upon the circumstances) as workers. A realtor may show a preference for black people who look a certain way—in this context, people with lighter (or darker) skin. A police officer may be more suspicious of darker skinned black men. Television viewers may prefer news anchors and female romantic leads with lighter skin tones. To state a legal claim, however, an aggrieved person must establish a legal right to relief. This can be done by invoking a state or federal constitutional or statutory provision that renders the conduct in question illegal. In federal anti-discrimination law, the equal protection clause of the Fourteenth Amendment provides perhaps the most common source of relief for discriminatory acts engaged in by state actors. That clause states that "[n]o State shall . . . deny to any person within its jurisdiction the equal protection of the law." A number of federal statutes also provide a basis for relief. For example, the Fair Housing Act prohibits discrimination in the sale and rental of housing,[13] and Title VII of the Civil Rights Act of 1964 prohibits discrimination in the workplace.[14] More generalized statutes also exist. Section 1981 of the Civil Rights Act of 1966 prohibits state and private entities from discriminating in the making and enforcement of contracts, among other things,[15] and Section 1983 of the Civil Rights Act of 1871 prohibits state actors (or persons acting under color of state law) from interfering with the exercise of a person's federally protected rights.[16]

Although the U.S. Supreme Court is still frequently called upon to delineate the parameters of constitutional and statutory protections, U.S. antidiscrimination law is fairly developed. Over time, a number of classifications receiving special protection have emerged, including race, religion, sex, national origin, age, and disability. Broadly speaking, to make a claim based upon one of these factors, aggrieved persons must show that they were treated adversely because of a particular trait. This is usually done by showing that they were treated worse than someone outside their group. Thus, a woman would need to establish that she was treated differently from a man, an African American differently from a white person, a Muslim differently from a Christian, and so on. Claims can be made using direct evidence (e.g., smoking gun evidence establishing action motivated by unlawful intent) or inferential proof (e.g., circumstantial evidence from which the foregoing can be inferred). When a plaintiff establishes animus and action, a defendant may generally defend by denying the action occurred, denying that the action was improperly motivated, or by coming forth with a suitable, nondiscriminatory reason for the action. With both constitutional and statutory claims, much judicial time is spent assessing the adequacy of a defendant's justification, and the degree of scrutiny and review given to these assertions varies based on the nature of the claim (e.g., under the equal protection clause, race claims are scrutinized more carefully than gender claims,[17] and under statutory regimes a defendant's burden may vary depending upon the plaintiff's chosen method of proof[18]). Importantly, when considering the scope of protection afforded to individuals falling within any protected classification, courts look to precedent (i.e., decisions rendered in previous cases raising similar factual and legal questions), the intent of the enacting legislature, and the language of the statute or constitutional provision at issue, among other things.

As noted earlier in the chapter, although colorism charges are increasing, there have been relatively few litigated cases. Although the trend appears to be in favor of recognizing these claims, it is too early to conclude that these claims are (or will continue to be) an uncontested part of U.S. antidiscrimination law. Notably, even when plaintiffs successfully establish a legal basis for colorism claims, they tend to lose when it comes to proving the underlying merits of their cases.[19] Thus, it is important to consider some of the reservations that courts and defendants have raised about these claims. Objections usually relate to one of the following concerns: (1) a lack of clarity regarding the statutory basis of colorism claims, (2) the fact that colorism does not neatly fit historical understandings of discrimination in the United States and the legal frameworks built thereon, (3) judicial reluctance to expand the legal bases upon which plaintiffs may seek redress for discrimination, and (4) judicial hesitancy to get into the "unsavory business" of differentiating between skin tones. This section addresses each of these matters in turn.

Statutory Basis for Colorism Claims

Because courts have examined the question of color discrimination most extensively in the area of employment, this analysis will focus on claims brought under Title VII of the Civil Rights Act of 1964 (Title VII) and 42 U.S.C. § 1981 of the Civil Rights Act of 1866 (Section 1981). Title VII prohibits discrimination in employment on the basis of race, color, religion, sex, and national origin.[20] Section 1981 provides, in part, that "[a]ll persons shall have the same right . . . to make and enforce contracts . . . as is enjoyed by white citizens."[21] Importantly, Section 1981 contains neither the word *race* nor the word *color*. The U.S. Supreme Court, however, has held that Section 1981 affords a remedy against racial discrimination in private as well as public employment.[22]

Title VII   As noted earlier, there are hundreds of cases in which plaintiffs have alleged both race and color discrimination, but which courts have treated solely as race claims. Because of this treatment, it is hard to know exactly what was at issue in these cases (e.g., whether color was an aspect of the alleged discrimination as well as race). It could be that the plaintiffs were without the necessary analytical tools to differentiate color and race and to argue effectively on the basis of colorism. It could be that the plaintiffs acquiesced in the racial characterization of their claims because it was simply more efficacious to argue within existing, established legal frameworks as opposed to charting new territory and laying the groundwork for a new theory. Or, it could be that the plaintiffs viewed their claims solely as race claims and their inclusion of the word *color* was redundant.

Although we do not know exactly what was happening in all of these cases, the fact that these claims were treated as race claims caused some defendants, when initially faced with skin color claims, to conflate race and color and to argue that color had no independent significance.[23] This argument should not, however, preclude the bringing of color claims (and, fortunately, most courts to consider the argument have rejected it). Title VII readily supports this conclusion given that the statute expressly includes color as a protected category. Although Title VII does not define "color," the plain meaning of the term should prevail. In other words, absent strong evidence to negate the ordinary meaning of the statutory language, a textual approach to statutory interpretation favors recognition of color claims. Moreover, to exclude colorism claims from Title VII would render the statutory language superfluous. As noted by the federal district court in *Walker v. Internal Revenue Service,* a landmark colorism case:

> [because] the statutes and case law repeatedly and distinctly refer to race and color [t]his court is left with no choice but to conclude, when Congress and the Supreme Court refer to race and color in the same phrase, that "race" is to mean "race," and "color" is to mean "color." To hold otherwise would mean that Congress and the Supreme Court have either mistakenly or purposefully overlooked an obvious redundancy.[24]

The conclusion that color is a distinct claim under Title VII is buttressed by the historical record establishing that color has meaning independent of race and by evidence in Title VII's legislative history suggesting that Congress intended to provide protection against "shade" discrimination.[25] The EEOC has also stated, unfortunately without detailed explanation, that color and race are distinct claims.[26]

Section 1981   More extensive analysis is required under Section 1981, because that statutory provision does not use the word *color* and therefore does not expressly proscribe discrimination on that basis. This fact, however, should not prevent the inclusion of color claims under Section 1981. Although the U.S. Supreme Court has stated that the phrase "as enjoyed by white citizens" clarifies Congress' concern with the racial character of the rights protected under Section 1981, the U.S. Supreme Court has never directly addressed the issue of color, nor has the Court been forced to distinguish race from color. Thus, nothing on the face of the statute or in its interpretive history prohibits its application to color claims. To the contrary, use of the term *white* in Section 1981 supports recognition of such claims. The U.S. Supreme Court has noted, "[w]hen terms used in a statute are undefined, we give them their ordinary meaning."[27] Today, as in 1866, white can refer to both a racial category and to skin color. Just as the omission of the word *race* from Section 1981 does not preclude the bringing of race claims, the omission of the word *color* should not preclude the bringing of color claims.[28]

In sum, Title VII should continue to be read to cover claims of discrimination based on skin color given that the statute explicitly includes color as a protected category. Although Section 1981 uses neither the word *race* nor the word *color,* that statute also should be interpreted to embrace color claims.

Fitting Colorism Claims into Existing Analytical Frameworks

As noted at the beginning of the chapter, persons of all races engage in colorism. Whether colorism is practiced intraracially by members of the same racial group (e.g., a light-skinned black person discriminating against a darker skinned black person) or interracially by members of different racial groups (e.g., a white person differentiating among two black individuals), these claims present challenges to existing legal frameworks.

Intraracial Colorism Claims   Assuming that Title VII and Section 1981 provide a legal basis upon which complainants can seek relief, the question becomes: How does one go about stating a claim? In the typical employment discrimination case, if there is no direct evidence of discrimination (e.g., something akin to a smoking gun), a plaintiff sets forth a prima facie case by showing (1) she is a member of a protected classification, (2) that she applied and was qualified for the position in question, (3) that notwithstanding her qualifications she was rejected, and (4) her rejection was under circumstances that give rise to an inference of discrimination. The typical race case involves a white employer who refuses to hire a black applicant, instead hiring a lesser qualified white applicant.

If this is the typical profile for discrimination cases, then the first conceptual difficulty with intraracial colorism arises from the fact that the employer and employee are of the same race. The leading colorism case to date, *Walker v. Internal Revenue Service,* involved precisely this scenario. In that case, a light-skinned black female employee alleged that her supervisor, a dark-skinned black woman, discriminated against her because of her lighter skin tone. The defendant argued that, as a legal matter, there can be no claim if the discriminator and the person discriminated against are of the same race, because presumably people do not harbor negative animus against members of their own race. This argument is flawed. Indeed, two years before *Walker,* in *Saint Francis College v. Al-Khazraji,*[29] the U.S. Supreme Court rejected it. In *Saint Francis,* the defendant argued that Section 1981 does not cover claims of discrimination by one Caucasian against another. Although the Court noted that Section 1981, "reaches discrimination against an individual because he or she is genetically part of an ethnically and physiognomically distinctive sub-grouping of *homo sapiens,*" the Court also made clear that "a distinctive physiognomy is not essential to qualify for Section 1981 protection."[30] The Court determined that even if a plaintiff and defendant are of the same race, a plaintiff can bring a race claim if she can show that the defendant acted on the basis of her ancestry or ethnicity, because both ancestry and ethnicity were bases for claims under Section 1981 at the time the statute was adopted.

Although both *Saint Francis* and *Walker* support that there is no legal bar to bringing intraracial color claims, the harder question is whether there should be a *factual* presumption that a black defendant did not discriminate because the plaintiff is also black. In other words, even if courts recognize color claims, should they, as at least one court has done,[31] impose higher evidentiary requirements on plaintiffs based on the assumption that intraracial discrimination is rare or against the norm (i.e., less believable and more suspect).

Such a presumption of nondiscrimination in the intraracial context ought to be insupportable. It is well documented that individuals within protected classifications are not immune from the forces of socialization at work in the larger society. These persons may incorporate the dominant society's views and may unconsciously act upon those views in ways that are harmful to members of their own groups. Thus, women discriminate against women (e.g., on the basis of race or gender). Men also discriminate against men (e.g., on the basis of gender or gender nonconformity). And, black individuals discriminate against other blacks (e.g., on the basis of skin color). Although this type of analysis can be used in intraracial colorism cases to destroy any factual presumption that discrimination does not occur between individuals of the same race, an understanding of colorism helps in this effort by identifying a causal variable (skin color) that may lead to the differential treatment. In short, knowledge of colorism enables courts to look beyond the broader category of race and to investigate the ways in which more subtle forms of discrimination happen.

Arguments for Interracial Colorism Claims   Although most colorism cases have involved intraracial discrimination, interracial color discrimination also exists (i.e., when a member of one race uses skin color to distinguish among two or more persons of a different race). Note that like intraracial colorism claims, interracial claims also do not fit neatly within traditional legal frameworks. Historically, race discrimination cases involved a discriminator who favored one race over another (e.g., a white applicant over a black applicant). In contrast, interracial colorism claims involve a discriminator who distinguishes among individuals of the same race. Instead of the wholesale exclusion of members of a particular race, the discriminator engages in a sophisticated and nuanced form of intragroup "preferencing" or screening. The question thus arises: Should the fact that a white person awards benefits to a light-skinned black individual create a factual presumption that she has not discriminated against a darker skinned black person?

If one understands the essence of a color claim, the answer is clear. Fundamentally, interracial claims are no different from intraracial claims. As with intraracial claims, the key is that courts not overlook the fact that interracial discrimination exists by assuming that a white person cannot be discriminatory if she awards benefits to someone within the same race as the plaintiff (i.e., if she likes some black people). The fallacy of this assumption becomes readily apparent when we acknowledge that a white person might draw a distinction between a black immigrant from Haiti (who has a French accent) and an African American who was born in the United States. In that situation, national origin and accent supply the basis for the intragroup comparison. Recent work by Devon Carbado and Mitu Gulati demonstrates how people make other intragroup distinctions based upon how individuals perform their identity (i.e., distinguishing between two African American women based upon one woman's decision to wear braids or locks as opposed to chemically straightened or permed hair, or her decision to wear attire associated with a particular ethnic group as opposed to adopting a Western European style of dress).[32] The point here is that color operates like these other variables—indeed, in an arguably more pernicious fashion than dress and grooming differences because color is not something that a person can choose, readily change, or hide. Again, the central point is that one cannot allow a focus on broad racial categories to obscure the fact that individuals within racial groups are not monolithic and that nuanced forms of intragroup discrimination, like colorism, exist.

The Slippery Slope and Differentiating Among Shades of Brown

Two other challenges to legal recognition of color claims bear mention. First, some observers may question whether skin color is different from any number of other legally permissible factors upon which people make distinctions (e.g., eye color, hair color, height) and may assert that recognition of discrimination on the basis of skin color will, in effect, spark downward movement on the proverbial slippery slope. The most compelling difference between skin color and these other factors is the pervasive and well-documented history of oppression on the basis of skin color in this country. This historical practice was of sufficient magnitude and consistency that the word *color* was explicitly included in the Fifteenth Amendment to the Constitution, in early versions of the Civil Rights Act of 1866, and in Title VII of the Civil Rights Act of 1964. In addition, skin color (like race) has been and continues to be used as a basis for identifying underrepresented discrete and insular minorities. For these reasons, discrimination on the basis of skin color is more like discrimination on the basis of race than discrimination on the basis of hair color, height, or eye color.

Second, in an early colorism case, a federal district court alluded to the difficulty of delineating among skin tones in examining colorism claims.[33] Because there are many shades of brown, the court suggested that it would be hard to know where to draw the line in terms of the meaning attached to an individual's skin color (e.g., when is a person too light or too dark). This is an admittedly complicated issue (and is made even more so when one considers the myriad factors in addition to color that defendants may use to differentiate individuals). Although racial categorization is becoming increasingly complicated in this country, historically we have assumed that persons could be placed into racial classifications readily and reliably (in part because of the one-drop rule). Although there have always been difficulties on the margins, and litigants have challenged racial designations,[34] we have (for the most part) assumed that race, national origin, gender, and even religious distinctions can be made with some degree of accuracy. Despite the inherent fallacy in drawing hard lines, a person was either black, Latino, Asian, or white; a woman or a man; Christian, Jewish, Muslim, or of some other specified faith. This either-or characterization is not possible with skin color claims because there are many gradations of skin tone. Thus, establishing that a plaintiff was too light or too dark presents challenging evidentiary questions. (This problem is heightened when plaintiffs attempt to establish a pattern of color discrimination in workplaces where there are few employees of color or where the skin color of applicants is unknown.[35])

To this concern, two preliminary responses are appropriate. First, the federal court referenced in the preceding paragraph stated that "it" did not want to be placed in the "unsavory business of measuring skin color." The issue, however, is not necessarily what a court thinks about a plaintiff's skin tone. The key question is whether there is evidence to suggest that the defendant believed the plaintiff was too light or too dark. It is only when the plaintiff is unable to marshal direct proof of the defendant's colorism (e.g., comments and remarks showing that the defendant was motivated by skin color differences) that the court or the fact finder will be forced to consider whether there is a meaningful distinction between the plaintiff's color and that of other individuals the defendant may have preferred (e.g., the person who was ultimately hired for the position the plaintiff sought). Even if courts are called upon to consider differences in skin color, this task does not differ significantly from what courts do in other contexts when considering factual questions. For example, sexual harassment claims often turn on subtle nuances like the tone and context in which certain words are expressed or actions taken. Yet, courts render judgments on these issues daily. In addition, the task of determining whether behavior constitutes negligence and ruling out competing causal factors of a plaintiff's harm is often difficult and murky. Again, courts do not reject these claims simply because of the difficulty of the task before them. The same should hold true with color claims. I do not mean to suggest that these evidentiary issues are not substantial. Indeed, my current research probes more closely the complex problems of proof presented by intragroup discrimination. My point here is merely that these obstacles are not necessarily insurmountable and should not be used to withhold recognition of colorism claims.

Conclusion

This chapter has addressed some of the conceptual and practical barriers to legal recognition of color claims. One of the biggest obstacles to date has been the failure of the courts and the EEOC to articulate a clear statement of what a color claim is and how it differs from a race claim. The key point that needs to be understood is that colorism and racism are distinct phenomena that sometimes overlap. At times, racism will occur regardless of a person's color. Thus, a person whose skin is white, but whose ancestors are known to be black, may be classified as black and subject to racist acts on that basis. At times, colorism will operate independently of race. Thus, two individuals within the same racial classification may be subject to different treatment because of their varying skin tones. In this situation, the basis for distinction is not their placement in a particular racial category, but rather their color within that category. Of course, the meaning afforded color may result from racist beliefs—that is to say, being light or dark may have meaning because being light or dark is associated with being closer to or farther from a certain racial ideal. However, the meaning afforded color merits additional study, for color bias may result from factors unrelated to racist beliefs. Colorism may stem from historically based assumptions about the correlation between color and socioeconomic class, color and beauty, color and intellect, or color and criminality, among other things. And finally, at times, colorism and racism will overlap—that is, a person will be treated differently because of assumptions about both her race and her color. Thus, a black woman with chocolate-brown skin may be subject to both racism and colorism simultaneously.

In sum, although they are closely related, colorism claims are analytically different from racism claims. The separation of individuals into racial categories and subsequent discrimination against them on that basis is, in essence, racism. The negative treatment of individuals on the basis of skin color is colorism. This distinction is important because if courts focus solely on race, they may overlook colorism because it may be difficult to believe that a white person who hires some black people may engage in discrimination against other black people, or that a person who is black would discriminate against someone falling within her own racial category. If, however, courts understand the history of colorism and the important role it has played in this country, then they are more likely to see the intricate ways in which discrimination is practiced. Such insight is particularly important as (1) the United States becomes more diverse with the growing presence of immigrants from countries where color plays a vital role in the formation of hierarchy and (2) as racial categorization becomes increasingly complicated as a result, not only of immigration patterns, but of rising rates of interracial sex and marriage. In this more fluid context, color (rather than race) may become the more frequently used basis for distinction.

14 Latinos at Work

When Color Discrimination Involves More Than Color

Tanya Katerí Hernández

DESPITE BEING AN ACTIONABLE CLAIM UNDER TITLE VII of the Civil Rights Act of 1964 for more than forty years, employers continue to be confused by what constitutes color discrimination in the workplace, and how to address it when it is not filed jointly with the separate claim of racial discrimination.[1] Indeed, the Civil Rights Act of 1964 does not provide definitions of what race or color discrimination is, nor how they differ. This confusion is only magnified by the fact that, currently, a large share of interracial color-based employment discrimination claims are filed by Latinos, followed by Asians, and Middle Easterners.[2] Furthermore, there has been a substantial increase during the past fifteen years in the number of color discrimination charges filed with the EEOC, from 374 in 1992, to 1241 in 2006.[3] Accordingly, the importation of Latino color paradigms into the U.S. workplace and courts is a dynamic that needs attention and explication for decision makers to navigate appropriately. This chapter will delineate the ways in which judges misapprehend the permutations of color discrimination when it is alleged to occur in multiracial Latino workplace settings that do not strictly conform to a white Anglo–African American binary understanding of racial stratification. The chapter concludes by suggesting that the use of a "functional whiteness and blackness" concept for assessing color discrimination cases will assist courts in better understanding color discrimination in Latino multiracial workplaces.

In a fascinating article about color discrimination jurisprudence, legal scholar Taunya Lovell Banks asserts that judges have difficulty understanding the nature of color discrimination as a form of racism when it occurs among African American parties because of the view that one drop of black blood makes you black and that there are no degrees of blackness in the cultural mind-set.[4] She then notes that these same judges have an easier time of understanding the connections between skin tone, race, and ethnicity bias in Latino plaintiff cases. From my assessment of the Latino cases, I agree with her conclusion, but have detected that, despite the greater judicial receptivity or willingness to consider colorism claims of Latinos, there are still jurisprudential problems with the evaluation of the claims. This chapter seeks to explicate the emerging judicial difficulties with assessing Latino color discrimination claims.

In many of the Latino colorism cases for which there are published court opinions available on the electronic databases of Westlaw and Lexis, Latino plaintiffs were only successful at having their colorism claim recognized by the court when their experience of discrimination was at the hands of a white Anglo employer or supervisor. This premise is borne out by my analysis of successful and unsuccessful color discrimination lawsuits filed by Latino plaintiffs. For instance, in *Cubas v. Rapid American Corp.*, a self-described "Cuban-born naturalized American citizen" named Rose Mary Cubas alleged she was discharged based on her "nonwhite" status as a Cuban American.[5] Yet, the court did not address the question of whether, as a Cuban American, Cubas can be considered nonwhite for purposes of alleging racial discrimination. Instead, the court focused on the fact that Cubas was discharged in retaliation for her labor-organizing activities on behalf of "nonwhite minority" workers. It was a context the court could readily understand as a white versus nonwhite racially charged workplace. It was thus not problematic to the court that Cubas' skin color was not mentioned as relevant to her experience of discrimination. In fact, even though she characterized her experience as discrimination against Cuban Americans as a "nonwhite racial group," the court failed to reach the question of whether that is indeed the case. Instead, the court concluded that even if one presumed that Cubas was white, there would still be an actionable claim for being discharged because of her defense of nonwhite minority workers. In other words, Cubas was able to have her claim for discrimination recognized as actionable, not because the court completely appreciated the nuances of color discrimination against Latinos as a group, but because the direct parallel between Cubas' white versus nonwhite workplace, and the white versus black discrimination paradigm, enabled her lawsuit to survive the motion to dismiss brought by the employer.

Similarly, in *Manzanares v. Safeway*, Anthony Manzanares asserted that he was an employee of "Mexican American descent" who experienced racially discriminatory treatment that was different from the "Anglo employees" of the company.[6] As a result, the court concluded that he had raised a viable claim of racial discrimination even though it was unclear to the court whether persons of Mexican descent are a legally cognizable racial group. The court reached this result because "the prejudice is asserted to be directed against the plaintiff in contrast to Anglos. This in our view is sufficient. It is equivalent to the 'all persons' compared to 'white citizens' discrimination contemplated by § 1981" of the civil rights law. Accordingly, Manzanares' claim survived the motion to dismiss filed by the employer. As in *Cubas,* the *Manzanares* court had the comfort of assessing the discrimination claim within the white versus nonwhite framework that directly resonates with the white versus black judicial understanding of civil rights.

A corresponding comfort with the white Anglo versus nonwhite employment backdrop to discrimination claims also informs those cases in which Latino plaintiffs not only survived the procedural motions to have their claims dismissed, but also succeeded in having their claims litigated before a jury.[7] This was the case in the color discrimination lawsuit of *Galdamez v. Potter,*[8] in which a Honduran-born U.S. postal service postmaster in Oregon, who spoke English with a "discernible accent," was treated differently than a white postmaster in another Oregon town. Plaintiff Arlene Galdamez was immediately greeted with racial hostility by customers and employees alike when she assumed the position of postmaster in Willamina, Oregon. Local media even covered the disputes that arose when Galdamez instituted policy changes that customers disliked. Like the customers who disliked Galdamez, the media coverage always mentioned her foreign birth and accent. This culminated in discriminatory treatment at the hands of her employer when Galdamez's supervisors refused to support her in the face of community resistance to her operational changes, despite having provided such support in the past for a white postmaster with a similar situation of community resistance. More important, Galdamez alleged that the employer's decision to discipline her formally was based upon her color, race, and national origin, rather than their stated reasons. Their stated reasons included her being "rude" to customers, and her insistence on regulatory compliance that undermined good customer service. Thus, in the face of Galdamez's stark allegations of a white versus nonwhite adversarial work context, it is no surprise that the plaintiff was allowed to bring her case before a jury.

Another Latino plaintiff who also managed to have his color discrimination claim litigated all the way through a jury trial was in the case of *Torres v. White.*[9]

Although that court opinion did not mention what the racial composition of the workplace was, it did note that the plaintiff, Miguel Torres, was a Puerto Rican former employee of the City of Cleveland who was "the only Hispanic manager, of the Human Resources Division of the City's Department of Personnel in 1992." Being racially isolated in the workplace is also a context that resonates with the judicial historic exposure to black claims of discrimination in a white workplace that thereby facilitate judicial recognition of Latino plaintiff color claims. Accordingly, even though no racially charged incidents were presented as having precipitated Mr. Torres' discharge, his claims of color, race, and national origin discrimination were permitted to go forward to trial.

The dynamic of racial isolation evoking the recognition of color discrimination because of its resonance with the black–white paradigm of discrimination is also evident in the color discrimination case of *Metzger v. Martinez*.[10] Racial isolation was noted in the fact that the plaintiff, Rafael Metzger, "the only Hispanic Senior Community Builder in the Northwest HUD region from the time he arrived," was treated differently than "non-Hispanic" coworkers and failed to receive supervisory support in his efforts to serve the Hispanic community of Spokane, Washington. In the court opinion, the court stated that "a reasonable jury could infer racial animus toward Hispanics motivated" the supervisor's failure to support the plaintiff's outreach efforts to the Hispanic community.

In short, because many of the Latino colorism employment cases have been brought in the context of discrimination at the hands of white Anglo parties, or scenarios that resonate with such white versus nonwhite binaries, courts have easily been able to recognize colorism as a cognizable claim.[11] However, when Latinos bring claims of color discrimination that draw from a more ethnically diverse workforce composition, judges are more puzzled about how to assess the claims because they do not understand Latino conceptions of functional whiteness and blackness that are foundational to their color discrimination experiences. The color discrimination case of *Felix v. Marquez*,[12] provides a helpful example.

In this case, Carmen Felix, a Puerto Rican of "partial African ancestry" was terminated from employment as a secretary with the Office Commonwealth of Puerto Rico in Washington (OCPRW), DC, at the behest of both the Puerto Rican administrator of the office, Jose Cabranes, and the Puerto Rican supervisor, Providencia Haggerty. Although the *Felix* case is noteworthy for its recognition of how "the plaintiff's skin tone and phenotype used in tandem with genealogy operated as racial markers,"[13] the court opinion still presented a confused assessment of Latino colorism experiences. To prove her claim of color discrimination, Felix introduced the personnel cards of 28 fellow employees to demonstrate that only two others were as dark or darker than she, and argued that there was thus a prevailing bias against dark-skinned employees in the office in the allocation of promotions that privileged what she termed "white" employees with higher ranked positions. The court purported to dispute Felix's premise of dark-skin bias by enumerating the employees she had presumably misclassified as white when in the court's view they were some shade of brown.

The court then went on to say, "[t]hese observations tend to contradict the placement of a rigid line between white and nonwhite employees of the OCPRW drawn by Felix in her testimony and reflect the fact that a substantial number of Puerto Ricans have mixed ancestry." And therein the court misperceived the actualization of colorism within Latino communities and workplaces such as the OCPRW; the persons the judge viewed as brown skinned were perceived by Felix, and perhaps her coworkers, as white by virtue of their phenotype, hair texture, and socioeconomic class, and not simply because of their skin shade.

There exists a vast literature that documents the ways in which Latinos often manifest white skin preferences in their mode of self-identification and in choice of associations in ways that recall/mirror Latin American racial ideology.[14] What this literature demonstrates, in particular, is how Latino expressions of color bias are intimately connected with assessments of phenotype, hair texture, size and shape of noses and lips, and socioeconomic class standing. Latino race labeling thus factors in considerations of bodily features other than color that are considered to be racial signifiers of denigrated African ancestry.[15] Accordingly, when a plaintiff like Felix in a predominantly Latino workplace enumerates the coworkers deemed to be white, she is referring to coworkers who have achieved that racial characterization not simply because of their skin color.

For example, two individuals can be of the same light skin shade, but if one has African facial features and hair texture, a Latino would not likely categorize such an individual as white absent indicators that the person was wealthy or of high social status.[16] In turn, the nonwhiteness attributed to that light-skinned person with African features would better position another light-skinned person with less prominent African features to be perceived as white in that context. In essence, Latinos treat racial categorization in a functional manner. In any given context, there are functional whites and blacks, regardless of their degree of pigment. However, although this Latino categorization scheme is fluid and context specific, it still forms the foundation for racially exclusionary conduct.[17] In other words, the absence of scientific precision in Latino racial categorization methods does not mitigate the allocation of social benefits based on the approximation to whiteness.

The complexity of a Latino racial hierarchy cannot be captured by a simplistic assessment of employee skin shades. Thus, what the judge in *Felix v. Marquez* failed to appreciate is how nuanced and perverse Latino/Latin American assessments of color and status are. Instead the judge fell prey to the Latino/Latin American romanticization of racial mixture (*mestizaje*) as being an indicator of racial ambiguity and harmony.[18] Thus, despite the fact that the court recognizes colorism as a cognizable claim that is a particularly "appropriate claim for a Puerto Rican to present" given the mixture of races that presumably make rigid racial categories harder to apply for purposes of a racial discrimination claim, the court then uses that very recognition of racial mixture to undermine the ability to mount a successful colorism claim. There is a direct clash between the judicial focus on color as a unique dimension of chromatic differences, and the Latino conceptualization of color as a taxonomy informed by hair texture, phenotypic features, class, place, and space. The situational deployment of Latino colorism is overlooked by the judges.

In short, there is a judicial inclination to act as a spectrometer rather than examining how the full scope of colorism racial preoccupations are deployed in the workplace. Even the color discrimination cases filed within the federal district court of Puerto Rico (in which the body of U.S. federal civil rights laws are applied) before Puerto Rican judges are not immune from judicial misperceptions that color discrimination only involves skin color. For instance in the case of *Falero v. Santiago*,[19] plaintiff Milton Falero Santiago alleged that he was terminated from his position as a sales director because of his color. In his court papers, Falero Santiago described himself as a "darker-skinned, or mulatto, Puerto Rican" and then juxtaposed his color with the white skin color of the Puerto Rican employee who took over some of his duties when Falero Santiago was terminated. Although the court did recognize Falero Santiago's allegation as a cognizable claim for color discrimination, the plaintiff's case did not survive the motion for summary judgment.

The dismissal of Falero Santiago's case is in part justified by the court based on its view that the disrespect Falero Santiago experienced on the job lacked a racial or color bias connotation. Specifically, Falero Santiago alleged that his white Latino supervisor called him "boy" on several occasions. And, indeed, there is a long racial history of black men being called boys as a method to subordinate them by imbuing persons of their racial status as incapable of full human personhood.[20] The U.S. Supreme Court has even acknowledged that such references can be presented as evidence of racial animus.[21] Yet, the trial court in *Falero* simply stated that "[w]hile the attributed remark is somewhat disrespectful, it seems obvious that the term 'boy' refers to a person's age and lacks racial and/or color connotations."[22] Thus, even a Puerto Rican judge in Puerto Rico privy to the dynamics of Latino/Latin American racialization methods is just as susceptible to misconstruing colorism when the legal cause of action is equated as solely a skin shade matter. In short, when the legal claim of color discrimination is judicially limited to the issue of skin color gradations in a workplace rather than encompassing all the ways in which biased notions about color status are intertwined with a racialized notion of hierarchy, the legal enforcement against discrimination in the workplace is undermined.

In conclusion, this chapter's review of the existing Latino colorism cases reveals a disturbing trend. To date, judges have been unable to discern a cognizable colorism claim unless the Latino plaintiff is able to deploy a white Anglo versus nonwhite narrative of racial discrimination. In the absence of a stark white Anglo versus a nonwhite workplace, judges are seemingly confused by the dynamics of Latino colorism concepts of functional whiteness and blackness, because they are still searching for their "pure" white versus nonwhite paradigm of racism rather than its equivalents. In effect, what judges lose sight of when colorism cases appear in Latino multiracial contexts is the connection between color and race discrimination. Although the Civil Rights Act of 1964 does not provide definitions for either race or color discrimination, the EEOC as the governmental entity charged with enforcing the Civil Rights Act of 1964 treats race and color discrimination as closely intertwined. The EEOC *Compliance Manual*[23] specifically states that although race and color are not synonymous, they do overlap such that race discrimination includes discrimination based upon a person's color. Yet, as Banks argues, color discrimination should similarly be viewed as encompassing concerns with race and not solely skin shade.[24] This chapter's concept of functional whiteness and blackness is one proposed mechanism for doing so.

To be precise, the inclusion of considerations of whether an employer's employment decisions in hiring and promoting inappropriately favored employees who were treated as the functional whites of that workplace while disadvantaging the functional blacks would greatly enhance the efficacy of the color discrimination legal claim when filed by a Latino plaintiff in a multiracial work setting. With the demographic growth of the Latino population, it will become increasingly important to improve the legal assessment of Latino colorism claims.[25] Demographers predict that one in four job seekers will be the child of a Latino immigrant by the year 2020, and that Latino workers will increase their representation in the workforce from the current rate of 12 percent to 25 percent by the year 2050.[26] Latino-owned businesses increased 232 percent from 1987 and 1997, and, in 1997 alone, employed 1,492,773 people (many of whom were Latino).[27] Furthermore, some of the Latino employment discrimination cases that are now emerging demonstrate a growth in the number of allegations involving Latino color bias.[28]

In addition, the functional whiteness and blackness approach might come to be applied more broadly beyond Latino cases if the system of U.S. race relations is transformed into what Bonilla-Silva describes as the "Latin Americanization" of racial stratification (see Chapter 3). The Latin American version of racial stratification uses a triracial hierarchy of whites, honorary whites, and collective blacks to maintain white privilege in the midst of a racial demography where actual whites are the numerical minority. Those whites who wish to maintain their socioeconomically privileged status while disavowing the existence of racism use a buffer class of honorary whites to defuse any binary notions of racial distinctions, while simultaneously ranking whites as privileged. Within the Latin American triracial system, a great emphasis is placed on color gradations, phenotype, and class status when bestowing racial status, according to whether such factors closely approximate a notion of whiteness. With the presumed flexibility of bestowing racial status according to appearance rather than ancestry (as has been traditionally done in the United States in a binary fashion), all members of a triracial system can become invested in pursuing their own individual claims to whiteness, rather than focusing on the existence of a color-based hierarchy. Concerns with race and racism are thus defused and the triracial system views itself as emblematic of racial harmony. In such a system there is little incentive to file a charge of racial discrimination.[29] When individuals are discouraged from viewing themselves as aligned by race while striving for the prestige of whiteness, it is considered illogical to raise the issue of race. Such has been the case in Latin America until very recently.

As the proportion of Caucasians decrease in the United States, the U.S. racial system is being transformed into a triracial system.[30] Indeed, there are indications that many U.S. elites favor a form of color-blind rhetoric that permits racial inequality to persist nonetheless.[31] Should the triracial system of racial stratification become the U.S. norm, the suggestions proposed in this chapter for Latino cases will have a broader application.

This will be the case not only because the triracial system emphasizes color distinctions as part of a multifaceted and complex social ordering, but also because individuals in that system are more inclined to recognize color rather than race as a mode of social differentiation. To be specific, with a transformation into a triracial system, we will likely see a decrease of racial discrimination claims filed with a simultaneous increase of color discriminations cases. Although this chapter maintains that color and race are profoundly connected, preserving a separate color discrimination cause of action may prove particularly useful in the advent of a U.S. triracial system. Aggrieved employees who are disassociated from notions of race and a racial identification may be more inclined instead to file a color discrimination claim. With the color-blind rhetorical disdain for the language of race and racism, developing a nuanced concept of color discrimination more fully may prove to be the key to retaining the efficacy of civil rights laws. Beginning to do so with Latino colorism cases could be the first step.

Reference Matter

Acknowledgments

THE IMPETUS FOR THIS VOLUME came from the Colorism Project at the Center for Race and Gender at the University of California, Berkeley. The project and this volume owe a huge debt of gratitude to Professor Percy Hintzen of the African American Studies Department at Berkeley. Percy's interest in and expertise on such issues as the significance of skin color in the Caribbean and Latin America, and medical dangers posed by the use of skin-lightening products in Africa and diasporic African communities were critical in the formation of the Colorism Project. The Project's purpose has been to further the scholarly study of social hierarchy based on skin color. The Project launched a working group made up of faculty and graduate students that met regularly to hear presentations and to discuss readings. Its most ambitious activity was to organize a national conference, "Hierarchies of Color: Historical and Transnational Perspectives on the Significance of Skin Tone," that was held in Berkeley, California, in December 2005. The presentations at the conference constitute the bulk of the chapters in this volume, with some additional chapters that were subsequently solicited to round out the coverage.

The staff of the Center for Race and Gender, Donna Hiraga-Stephens, Janet Duong, and Glenn Robertson, as well as undergraduate assistant Daniel Paredes, and graduate assistants Johnny George and Michael Barnes provided crucial logistical and administrative support for the conference. Michael Barnes took a very active role in helping to organize the conference and assumed major responsibility for maintaining communication with presenters in the initial stages of transforming talks into formal papers.

The volume that has resulted would not have been possible without the editorial assistance of Amy Fujiwara-Shen. Our weekly discussions of papers ranged far and wide, and pointed in interesting and fruitful directions. She distilled our discussions of each paper into memos that guided authors' revisions. Her keen eye and good judgment made this volume much better than it otherwise would have been.

I am, as always, grateful to Gary Glenn, who was engaged in the project from its inception and whose ideas were critical to the intellectual development of the volume. He also read and provided discerning suggestions for my chapter.

Last, I wish to honor the memory of Lynnea Stephens, who worked for a year as a graduate research assistant at the Center for Race and Gender to help launch the Colorism Project. She collected and catalogued material on colorism and did the logistical work of organizing the Colorism Working Group meetings. Tragically, Lynnea passed away a few months before the conference was held. She had been valiantly battling cancer for several years, but remained fully engaged with life and committed to completing her degree. Her enthusiasm and engagement with the issue of colorism—the topic of her doctoral dissertation in sociology—were truly inspiring.

E.N.G.

Notes

Chapter 1

Acknowledgments. The majority of the information contained in this chapter is drawn from the author's other works. See, specifically, Edward Telles, "The Social Consequences of Skin Color in Brazil" (paper presented at the Colorism: Global Perspectives on How Skin Color Still Matters conference, Pennsylvania State University, University Park, PA, April 23, 2006); Edward Telles, "The Social Consequences of Skin Color in Brazil" (paper presented at the Colorism Conference, University of California, Berkeley, CA, December 20, 2005); Edward Telles, *Race in Another America: The Significance of Skin Color in Brazil* (Princeton: Princeton University Press, 2004).

1. Roberto Da Matta, "Notas sobre o racismo a brasileira," in *Multiculturalismo e Racismo:* Uma comparação Brasil-Estados Unidos, ed. Jessé Souza (Brasília: Paralelo 15, 1997), 69–74. [*O papel da ação afirmativa nos Estados Democráticos Contemporâneos* (Brasília: Ministério da Justiça, 1996).]

2. From Stuart Hall, "Is Race a Floating Signifier?" The Sage Anniversary Lecture and the Hayard Lecture Goldsmiths College/Lewisham Council, 1996.

3. Marvin Harris and Conrad Kottack, "The Structural Significance of Brazilian Categories," *Sociologia* 25 (1963), 203–208; Oracy Nogueira, *Tanto Preto Quanto Branco: Estudos de Relações Racias* (São Paulo: T.A. Queoroz, [1955] 1995).

4. James F. Davis, *Who Is Black? One Nation's Definition* (University Park, PA: Pennsylvania State University Press, 1991).

5. Ibid.; Anthony Marx, *Making Race and Nation: A Comparison of the United States, South Africa and Brazil* (Cambridge: Cambridge University Press, 1998).

6. The Brazilian conception of race is thus similar to the situational or relational conception of ethnicity used by Frederick Barth. See Frederick Barth, ed., *Ethnic Groups and Boundaries: The Social Organization of Culture Difference* (Boston: Little,

Brown, 1968). Also see Livio Sansone, "The New Politics of Black Culture in Bahia, Brazil," in *The Politics of Ethnic Consciousness,* ed. Cora Govers and Hans Vermuellen (New York: St. Martin's Press, 1997), 227–309; Peter Wade, *Blackness and Race Mixture: The Dynamics of Racial Identity in Colombia* (Baltimore: Johns Hopkins University Press, 1997).

7. The small number of Asians and indigenous peoples are generally classified outside the color continuum.

8. Nelson Silva, "Distância Social e Casamento Inter-Racial no Brasil," *Estudos Afro-Asiaticos* 14 (1987), 54–84.

9. For a list of all these terms see "A Cor do Brasilero," *Folha de Sao Paulo,* June 25, 1995, Caderno Especial, 5.

10. Harris and Kottack, 203–208; Rosa Pacheco, "A questão da cor nas relações raciais de um grupo de baixa renda," *Estudos Afro-Asiaticos* 14 (1987), 85–97; Oracy Nogueira, *Tanto Preto Quanto Branco: Estudos de Relações Racias* (São Paulo: T.A. Queoroz, [1955] 1995); Livio Sansone, "Pai Preto, Filho Negro: Trabalho, Cor e Diferenças de Geração," *Estudos Afro-Asiáticos* 25 (1993), 73–98; Thomas Stephens, *Dictionary of Latin American Racial and Ethnic Terminology* (Gainesville: University of Florida Press, 1989).

11. For more information on these definitions, see Stephens.

12. Pacheco, 85–97; Sansone, "Pai Preto, Filho Negro," 73–98.

13. Although never incorporated as an official category, *negro* has a long history of use by civil societal organizations since the 1930s, with the *Frente Negra Brasileira.* Also, the *Teatro Experimental do Negro* was founded in 1940 "to raise black [*negro*] consciousness," the first *Congresso do Negro Brasileiro* was held in 1950, the *Associação Cultural do Negro* was founded in 1954, and the *Movimento Negro Unificado Contra Discriminação Racial* (MNUCDR, later shortened to MNU) was organized in 1978.

14. Michael George Hanchard, *Orpheus and Power: The* Movimento Negro *in Rio de Janeiro and Sao Paulo, Brazil, 1945–1988* (Princeton: Princeton University, 1994).

15. Despite the recommendations of the ministry of justice, census planners, in consultation with various experts and interested parties, and after survey testing various formats of the race question, decided to keep the same categories used in previous censuses.

16. Marvin Harris, "Racial Identity in Brazil," *Luzo-Brazilian Review* 1 (1963), 21–28.

17. The survey did not ask respondents how many ancestors of each background they had, but merely whether they had any at all. Thus, although many white Brazilians claim to have African or indigenous ancestors, they are likely to have a relatively higher proportion of European ancestry than browns and blacks, confirming that race or color is defined mostly by appearance.

18. In a separate analysis, I found little difference by income in the proportion of whites claiming African ancestry.

19. Sergio P. J. Pena, "Retrato Molecular do Brasil," *Ciencia Hoje* (April 2000), 17–25; Denise R. Carvalho-Silva et al., "The Phygeography of Brazilian Y-Chromosome Lineages," *American Journal of Human Genetics* 68 (2001), 281–286.

20. Dark African Americans (medium brown, dark brown, and very dark) earn about 80 percent of what their brown counterparts (very light and light brown) earn. This compares with a black-to-brown earnings ratio of 90 percent in Brazil. A large difference in skin tone prevails in human capital studies that seek to measure discrimination. See Verna Keith and Cedric Herring, "Skin Tone Stratification in the Black Community," *American Journal of Sociology* 97 (1991), 760–778; Walter Allen, Edward Telles, and Margaret Hunter, "Skin Color, Income and Education: A Comparison of African Americans and Mexican Americans," *National Journal of Sociology* 12 (2000), 129–180.

21. Nelson do Valle Silva, "White-Non-White Income Differentials: Brazil" (Ph.D. dissertation, University of Michigan, 1978); Nelson do Valle Silva, "Updating the Cost of Not Being White in Brazil," in *Race, Class, and Power in Brazil*, ed. P.-M. Fontain (Los Angeles: UCLA Center for Afro-American Studies, 1985), 42–55.

22. Edward E. Telles and Nelson Lim, "Does It Matter Who Answers the Race Question? Racial Classification and Income Inequality in Brazil," *Demography* 35 (1998), 465–474.

23. For a review of these studies, see William A. Darity, Jr., and Patrick L. Mason, "Evidence on Discrimination in Employment: Codes of Color, Codes of Gender," *Journal of Economic Perspectives, American Economic Association* 12 (1998), 63–90.

24. Keith and Herring, 760–780.

25. Carlos H. Arce, *Mexican Origin People in the United States: The 1979 Chicano Survey* [Computer file] (Ann Arbor, MI: University of Michigan, Survey Research Center, ICPSR08436-v1, 1997); James S. Jackson and Gerald Gurin, *National Survey of Black Americans, 1979–1980* [Computer file] (Ann Arbor, MI: University of Michigan, Survey Research Center, ICPSR, 1999).

26. Aaron Gullickson, "The Significance of Color Declines: A Re-Analysis of Skin Tone Differentials in Post-Civil Rights America," *Social Forces* 84, 1 (2005), 157–180.

27. The ICERD also requires race to be based on self-classification, maintaining that this is an individual's right.

28. Fernando Henrique Cardoso, Presidential Speech (December 20, 2001), translated by author.

29. Amy Harmon, "Seeking Ancestry in DNA Ties Uncovered by Tests," *New York Times,* April 6, 2006. Available on: www.nytimes.com/2006/04/12/us/12genes.html (accessed on August 18, 2008).

Chapter 2

1. Marita Golden, *Don't Play in the Sun: One Woman's Journey Through the Color Complex* (New York: Doubleday, 2004), 9.

2. Ibid., 10.

3. E. Franklin Frazier, *The Negro in the United States* (New York: Macmillan, 1957), 67–68; M. Hunter, *Race, Gender, and the Politics of Skin Tone* (New York: Routledge-Taylor Francis, 2005), 67–68; H. E. Ransford, "Skin Color, Life Chances, and Anti-White Attitudes," *Social Problems* 18 (1970), 164–179.

4. C. Anderson and R. Cromwell, "'Black Is Beautiful' and the Color Preferences of Afro-American Youth," *Journal of Negro Education* 46 (1977), 76–88; M. Cunningham, A. Roberts, A. Barbee, P. Druen, and C. Wu, "Their Ideas of Beauty Are, on the Whole, the Same as Ours: Consistency and Variability in the Cross-Cultural Perception of Female Physical Attractiveness," *Journal of Personality and Social Psychology* 68, 2 (1995), 261–279; E. Marks, "Skin Color Judgments of Negro College Students," *Journal of Abnormal and Social Psychology* 38 (1943), 370–376; C. Parrish, "Color Names and Color Notions," *Journal of Negro Education* 15 (1946), 13–20; M. Seeman, "Skin Color Values in Three All-Negro School Classes," *American Sociological Review* 11 (1946), 315–321.

5. K. A. Rocquemore and D. L. Brunsma, "Beyond Black?: The Reflexivity of Appearances in Racial Identification Among Black/White Biracials," in *Skin Deep: How Race and Complexion Matter in the "Color-Blind" Era*, ed. C. Herring, V. M. Keith, and H. Horton (Chicago: University of Illinois Press, 2004), 99–127.

6. A. Davis and J. Dollard, *Children of Bondage: The Personality Development of Negro Youth in the Urban South* (Washington, DC: American Council on Education, 1940), 235; J. Dollard, *Caste and Class in a Southern Town* (New York: Harper, 1949), 62–97; S. C. Drake and H. Cayton, *Black Metropolis* (New York: Harcourt Brace, 1945), 543; M. E. Hill, "Color Differences in the Socioeconomic Status of African American Men: Results of a Longitudinal Study," *Social Forces* 78 (2000), 1437–1460; M. Hughes and B. R. Hertel, "The Significance of Color Remains: A Study of Life Chances, Mate Selection, and Ethnic Consciousness Among Black Americans," *Social Forces* 68, 4 (1990), 1105–1120; J. H. Johnson, E. J. Bienenstock, and J. A. Stoloff, "An Empirical Test of the Cultural Capital Hypothesis," *The Review of Black Political Economy* 23 (1995), 7–27; S. Bond and T. F. Cash, "Black Beauty: Skin Color and Body Images Among African-American College Women," *Journal of Applied Social Psychology* 22 (1992), 874–888; N. Boyd-Franklin, "Recurrent Themes in the Treatment of African-American Women in Group Psychotherapy," *Women and Therapy* 11, 2 (1991), 25–40; T. F. Cash and N. C. Duncan, "Physical Attractiveness Stereotyping Among Black American College Students," *Journal of Social Psychology* 1 (1984), 71–77; J. W. Chambers, T. Clark, L. Dantzler, and J. A. Baldwin, "Perceived Attractiveness, Facial Features, and African

Self-Consciousness," *Journal of Black Psychology* 20, 3 (1994), 305–324; W. Grier and P. Cobb, *Black Rage* (New York: Basic Books, 1968); A. Neal and M. Wilson, "The Role of Skin Color and Features in the Black Community: Implications for Black Women in Therapy," *Clinical Psychology Review* 9, 3 (1989), 323–333; M. Okazawa-Rey, T. Robinson, and J. V. Ward, "Black Women and the Politics of Skin Color and Hair," *Women and Therapy* 6 (1987), 89–102.

7. E. Klonoff and H. Landrine, "Is Skin Color a Marker for Racial Discrimination? Explaining the Skin Color–Hypertension Relationship," *Journal of Behavioral Medicine* 23 (2000), 329–338; I. Blair, C. M. Judd, and K. Chapleau, "The Influence of Afrocentric Facial Features in Criminal Sentencing," *Psychological Science* 15, 10 (2004), 674–679; K. B. Maddox and S. A. Gray, "Cognitive Representations of Black Americans: Reexploring the Role of Skin Tone," *Personality and Social Psychology Bulletin* 28 (2002), 250–259.

8. Grier and Cobb, 40–41; M. E. Hill, "Skin Color and the Perception of Attractiveness Among African Americans: Does Gender Make a Difference?" *Social Psychology Quarterly* 65, 1 (2002), 77–91; Neal and Wilson, 323–333; T. J. Wade, "The Relationship Between Skin Color and Self-Perceived Global, Physical, and Sexual Attractiveness, and Self-Esteem for African Americans," *Journal of Black Psychology* 22, 3 (1996), 358–373; W. L. Warner, B. H. Junker, and W. A. Adams, *Color and Human Nature* (Washington, DC: American Council on Education, 1941).

9. K. Dion, E. Berscheid, and E. Walster, "What Is Beautiful Is Good," *Journal of Personality and Social Psychology* 24 (1972), 285–290; S. Hesse-Biber, *The Cult of Thinness* (Oxford: Oxford University Press, 2007), 110–111.

10. Boyd-Franklin, 25–40; Okazawa-Rey et al., 89–102.

11. Hunter, *Race, Gender,* 69–71; Grier and Cobb, 40–48, Drake and Cayton, 498; I. Jawahar and J. Mattson, "Sexism and Beautyism Effects in Selection as a Function of Self-Monitoring Level of Decision Maker," *Journal of Applied Psychology* 90, 3 (2005), 563–573.

12. Hunter, *Race, Gender,* 7.

13. M. Omi and H. Winant, *Racial Formation in the United States* (New York: Routledge, 1994), 48–76.

14. Hunter, *Race, Gender,* 17–21.

15. G. Myrdal, *An America Dilemma: The Negro Problem and Modern Democracy* (New York: Harper & Row, 1944), 696.

16. Frazier, *Negro in the United States,* 274–275; Myrdal, 696; D. G. White, "Female Slaves: Sex Roles and Status in the Antebellum Plantation South," *Journal of Family History* 8 (1983), 248–261.

17. Frazier, *Negro in the United States,* 68; L. Wirth and H. Goldhamer, "The Hybrid and the Problem of Miscegenation," in *Characteristics of the American Negro,* ed. Otto Klineberg (New York: Harper, 1944), 240–369.

18. H. Bodenhorn, "The Mulatto Advantage: The Biological Consequences of Complexion in Rural Antebellum Virginia," *Journal of Interdisciplinary History* XXXIII, I (2002), 21–46.

19. B. Landry, *The New Black Middle Class* (Berkeley: University of California Press, 1987), 30–36.

20. Davis et al., 245–256; E. F. Frazier, *The Black Bourgeoisie* (New York: Free Press, 1957), 200; E. Mullins and P. Sites, "The Origins of Contemporary Eminent Black Americans: A Three-Generation Analysis of Social Origin," *American Sociological Review* 49 (1984), 672–685.

21. Drake and Cayton, 543–544; Landry, 36–39.

22. E. F. Frazier, *The Black Family in the United States* (New York: The Dryden Press, 1951), 320–321; Landry, 40.

23. M. Hunter, "'If You're Light, You're Alright': Light Skin Color as Social Capital for Women of Color," *Gender and Society* 16, 2 (2002), 175–193; W. W. Dressler, "Social Class, Skin Color, and Arterial Blood Pressure in Two Societies," *Ethnicity and Disease* 1 (1991), 60–77.

24. The 1982 General Social Survey also collected information on complexion. However, even with oversampling, only 510 African Americans are included. The Multi-City Survey of Urban Inequality is limited to four metropolitan areas. Thus, the NSBA, with a sample size of 2,107, affords more flexibility in exploring the influence of skin tone while exploring simultaneously the effects of other variables. Other phenotypic features such as facial features, and hair and eye color were not measured in either survey. A new data set, the National Survey of American Lives conducted by the University of Michigan, is not yet widely available.

25. Hunter, *Race, Gender,* 37–51; Hughes and Hertel, 1105–1120; V. M. Keith and C. Herring, "Skin Tone and Stratification in the Black Community," *American Journal of Sociology* 97, 3 (1991), 760–778.

26. A. Davis and J. Dollard, *Children of Bondage: The Personality Development of Negro Youth in the Urban South* (Washington, DC: American Council on Education, 1940), 280–281.

27. Hunter, "'If You're Light, You're Alright,'" 22–44.

28. C. Herring, "Skin Deep: Race and Complexion in the 'Color-Blind Era,'" in *Skin Deep: How Race and Complexion Matter in the "Color-Blind" Era,* ed. C. Herring, V. M. Keith, and H. Horton (Chicago: University of Illinois Press, 2004), 1–21.

29. A. Gullickson, "The Significance of Color Declines: A Re-Analysis of Skin Tone Differentials in Post-Civil Rights America," *Social Forces* 84, 1 (2005), 157–180.

30. Gullickson was not completely able to rule out the effects of sample attrition, although his analysis is perhaps as sophisticated as possible given the data with which he worked. However, given the relationship between skin tone, SES, and health, it is reasonable to assume that the most disadvantaged and thus the darkest would have

higher attrition rates. If so, the remaining dark-skinned blacks would have been more advantaged, thus reducing the differences by complexion.

31. Multivariate analyses of education controlled for age, parent's education, marital status, southern residence, interviewer-assessed attractiveness measured on a 7-point scale ranging from unattractive to attractive, and interviewer-assessed weight measured on a 7-point scale ranging from underweight to overweight.

32. Multivariate analyses of occupational status controlled for age, parent's education, marital status, southern residence, employment status, interviewer-assessed attractiveness measured on a 7-point scale ranging from unattractive to attractive, and interviewer-assessed weight measured on a 7-point scale ranging from underweight to overweight.

33. Multivariate analyses of personal and family income controlled for age, parent's education, marital status, southern residence, employment status, interviewer-assessed attractiveness measured on a 7-point scale ranging from unattractive to attractive, and interviewer-assessed weight measured on a 7-point scale ranging from underweight to overweight.

34. It is noteworthy that the NSBA data indicate a color gradation in family income but not in personal income for women, suggesting that women continued to "marry up." However, data from the Multi-City Survey of four metropolitan areas revealed no complexion variations in the probability of African American women being married, and only a modest relationship between complexion and spousal earnings. See K. Edwards, K. Carter-Tellison, and C. Herring, "For Richer, for Poorer, Whether Dark or Light: Skin Tone, Marital Status, and Spouse's Earnings," in *Skin Deep: How Race and Complexion Matter in the "Color-Blind" Era,* ed. C. Herring, V. M. Keith, and H. Horton (Chicago: University of Illinois Press, 2004), 65–81.

35. Gullickson, 257–280; K. Keenan, "Skin Tones and Physical Features of Blacks in Magazine Advertisements," *Journalism and Mass Communication Quarterly* 73, 4 (1996), 905–912.

36. E. Goffman, *Stigma: Notes on the Management of Spoiled Identity* (Englewood Cliffs, NJ: Prentice-Hall, 1963); R. D. Harvey, N. LaBeach, E. Pridgen, and T. M. Gocial, "The Intragroup Stigmatization of Skin Tone Among Black Americans," *Journal of Black Psychology* 31, 3 (2005), 237–253.

37. Hunter, *Race, Gender,* 53–67.

38. J. R. Porter and R. E. Washington, "Black Identity and Self-Esteem: A Review of Studies of Black Self-Concept: 1968–1978," *Annual Review of Sociology* 5 (1979), 53–74.

39. M. Rosenberg, *Conceiving the Self* (New York: Basic Books, 1986), 62–70.

40. J. Twenge and W. K. Campbell, "Self-Esteem and Socioeconomic Status: A Meta-Analysis," *Personality and Social Psychology Review* 6, 1 (2002), 59–71.

41. Rosenberg, 153–156. R. Robins, K. Trzesniewski, S. Gosling, and J. Potter, "Global Self-Esteem Across the Life Span," *Psychology and Aging* 17, 3 (2002), 423–434;

B. Gray-Little and A. R. Hafdahl, "Factors Influencing Racial Comparisons of Self-Esteem: A Quantitative Review," *Psychological Bulletin* 126, 1 (2000), 26–54; J. Twenge and J. Crocker, "Race and Self-Esteem: Meta-Analyses Comparing Whites, Blacks, Hispanics, Asians, and American Indians and Comments on Gray-Little and Hafdahl (2000)," *Psychological Bulletin* 128 (2002), 371–408.

42. Gray-Little and Hafdahl, 40–41.

43. O. Malanchuk and J. S. Eccles, "Self-Esteem," in *Handbook of Girls' and Women's Psychological Health,* ed. J. Worell and C. D. Goodheart (Oxford: Oxford University Press, 2006), 149–156; J. S. Eccles, B. L. Barber, D. Jozefowicz, O. Malanchuk, and M. Vida, "Self-Evaluations of Competence, Task Values, and Self-Esteem," in *Beyond Appearances: A New Look at Adolescent Girls,* ed. N. Johnson, M. Roberts, and J. Worell (Washington, DC: American Psychological Association, 1999), 53–83.

44. M. Altabe, "Ethnicity and Body Image: Quantitative and Qualitative Analysis," *International Journal of Eating Disorders* 23 (1998), 153–159; Eccles et al., 53–83; S. M. Harris, "Racial Differences in Predictors of Women's Body Image Attitudes," *Women and Health* 2 (1994), 129–145.

45. Hunter, *Race, Gender,* 103–109; Neal and Wilson, 332–333.

46. V. M. Keith and M. S. Thompson, "Color Matters: The Importance of Skin Tone for African American Women's Self-Concept in Black and White America," in *In and Out of Our Right Minds: The Mental Health of African American Women,* ed. D. R. Brown and V. M. Keith (New York: Columbia University Press, 2003), 116–135; M. S. Thompson and V. M. Keith, "The Blacker the Berry: Gender, Skin Tone, Self-Esteem, and Self-Efficacy," *Gender and Society* 15 (2001), 336–357.

47. The correlation between skin tone and attractiveness was .20 and was significant at the .01 level.

48. Y. St. Jean and J. R. Feagin, *Double Burden: Black Women and Everyday Racism* (New York: Sharpe, 1998), 91–92.

49. Rosenberg, 99–127.

50. Harvey et al., 237–253.

51. M. L. Craig, *Ain't I a Beauty Queen: Black Women, Beauty, and the Politics of Race* (New York: Oxford University Press, 2002), 30–37.

52. M. E. Hill, "Race of the Interviewer and Perception of Skin Color: Evidence from the Multi-City Study of Urban Inequality," *American Sociological Review* 67 (2002), 99–108.

53. I. V. Blair, C. M. Judd, M. S. Sadler, and C. Jenkins, "The Role of Afrocentric Features in Person Perception: Judging by Features and Categories," *Journal of Personality and Social Psychology* 83, 1 (2002), 5–25; Maddox and Chase, 533–546.

54. K. Dion, "Physical Attractiveness and Evaluation of Children's Transgressions," *Journal of Personality and Social Psychology* 24, 2 (1972), 207–213.

55. J. Kirscheman and K. M. Neckerman, "Hiring Strategies, Racial Bias, and Inner-City Workers," *Social Problems* 38, 4 (1991), 433–447.

Chapter 3

Acknowledgments. For a complete version of this article, see Eduardo Bonilla-Silva and Amanda E. Lewis, "The New Racism: Toward an Analysis of the U.S. Racial Structure, 1960s–1990s," in *Race, Nation, and Citizenship,* ed. Paul Wong (Boulder, CO: Westview Press, 1999); and Eduardo Bonilla-Silva and Gianpaolo Baiocchi, "Anything But Racism: How Sociologists Limit the Significance of Racism," *Race and Society* 4 (2001), 117–131.

1. Silvio Rodríguez, "Resumen de Noticias." *A Final de este Viaje* (Spartacus Discos, 1995).

2. Edward E. Telles, "Ethnic Boundaries and Political Mobilization Among African Brazilians: Comparisons with the U.S. Case," in *Racial Politics in Contemporary Brazil,* ed. Michael Hanchard (Durham: Duke University Press, 1999), 82–97.

3. We are adapting Antonio Negri's idea of the "collective worker" to the situation of all those at the bottom of the racial stratification system. See Jim Fleming, ed., *Marx Beyond Marx: Lessons on the Grundrisse* (South Hadley, MA: Bergin and Garvey, 1984).

4. Victor M. Rodriguez, "Boricuas, African Americans, and Chicanos in the 'Far West': Notes on the Puerto Rican Pro-Independence Movement in California, 1960s–1980s," in *Latino Social Movements: Historical and Theoretical Perspectives,* ed. Rodolfo D. Torres and George Katsiaficas (New York: Routledge, 1999), 79–110.

5. Kerry Ann Rockquemore and Patricia Arend, "Opting for White: Choice, Fluidity, and Black Identity Construction in Post-Civil Rights America," *Race and Society* 5 (2002), 49–64.

6. Vilna Bashi, "Globalized Anti-Blackness: Transnationalizing Western Immigration Law, Policy, and Practice," *Racial and Ethnic Studies* 27 (2004), 584–606.

7. Margaret L. Hunter, *Race, Gender, and the Politics of Skin Tone* (New York: Routledge, 2005), 1–16.

8. Lourdes Martínez-Echazabal, "Mestizaje and the Discourse of National/Cultural Identity in Latin America, 1845–1959," *Latin American Perspectives* 25 (1998), 21–42.

9. Eduardo Bonilla-Silva, "'This Is a White Country': The Racial Ideology of the Western Nations of the World-System," *Sociological Inquiry* 70 (2000), 188–214.

10. Gilberto Freyre, *New World in the Tropics: The Culture of Modern Brazil* (New York: Knopf, 1959), 7.

11. Verena Martínez-Alier, *Marriage, Class and Colour in Nineteenth-Century Cuba: A Study of Racial Attitudes and Sexual Values in a Slave Society* (London: Cambridge University Press, 1974).

12. Jay Kinsbrunner, *Not of Pure Blood: The Free People of Color and Racial Prejudice in Nineteenth-Century Puerto Rico* (Durham, NC: Duke University Press, 1996), 1–18.

13. Peter Wade, *Blackness and Race Mixture: The Dynamics of Racial Identity in Colombia* (Baltimore: Johns Hopkins University Press, 1995), 341.

14. Kinsbrunner, 19–52.

15. Wade, 342.

16. Michel-Rolph Trouillot, *Haiti, State Against Nation: Origins and Legacy of Duvalierism* (New York: Monthly Review Press, 1990).

17. Richard Siddle, "Ainu: Japan's Indigenous People," in *Japan's Minorities: The Illusion of Homogeneity,* ed. Michael Weiner (New York: Routledge, 1997), 17–49.

18. Alejandro de la Fuente, "Race, National Discourse, and Politics in Cuba: An Overview," *Latin American Perspectives* 25 (1998), 43–69.

19. Martínez-Echazabal, 21–42.

20. Eduardo Bonilla-Silva, "Rethinking Racism: Toward a Structural Interpretation," *American Sociological Review* 62 (1997), 465–480.

21. Silvi Torres-Saillant, "The Tribulations of Blackness: Stages in Dominican Racial Identity," *Latin American Perspectives* 25 (1998), 126–146.

22. David T. Goldberg, *The Racial State* (Malden, MA: Blackwell Press, 2002), 74–97.

23. U.S. Bureau of the Census, *Population Projections of the United States by Age, Sex, Race, and Hispanic Origin: 1995 to 2050* (Washington, DC: U.S. Government Printing Office, 1996), 12.

24. Elizabeth M. Grieco and Rachel C. Cassidy, *Overview of Race and Hispanic Origin 2000* (Washington, DC: U.S. Government Printing Office, 2001), 3.

25. Aline Helg, "Race in Argentina and Cuba, 1880–1930: Theory, Policies, and Popular Reaction," in *The Idea of Race in Latin America, 1870–1940,* ed. Richard Graham (Austin: University of Texas Press, 1990), 37–70.

26. Jonathan W. Warren and France Winddance Twine, "White Americans, the New Minority?: Non-Blacks and the Ever-Expanding Boundaries of Whiteness," *Journal of Black Studies* 28 (1997), 200–218.

27. Eduardo Bonilla-Silva and Amanda E. Lewis, "The New Racism: Toward an Analysis of the U.S. Racial Structure, 1960s–1990s," in *Race, Nation, and Citizenship,* ed. Paul Wong (Boulder, CO: Westview Press, 1999), 55–101.

28. Roy L. Brooks, *Rethinking the American Race Problem* (Berkeley: University of California Press, 1990), 25–33.

29. For a detailed analysis of color-blind racism, see Eduardo Bonilla-Silva, *White Supremacy and Racism in the Post-Civil Rights Era* (Boulder, CO: Lynne Rienner, 2001), 137–166.

30. Clarence Lusane, *Race in the Global Era: African Americans at the Millennium* (Boston: South End Press, 1997), 1–20.

31. Robert Miles, *Racism After Race Relations* (London: Routledge, 1993), 80–106.

32. Robin Cohen, *Global Diasporas: An Introduction* (Seattle: University of Washington Press, 1997), 177–196.

33. Bonilla-Silva, "Rethinking Racism," 465–480.

34. For more on this topic, see Bonilla-Silva, "This Is a White Country," 188–214.

35. Rockquemore and Arend, 49–64.

36. Stephen Steinberg, *Turning Back: The Retreat from Racial Justice in American Thought and Policy* (Boston: Beacon Press, 1995), 107–136.

37. The 2003 U.S. Supreme Court decision in *Grutter v. Bollinger,* hailed by some observers as a victory, is at best a weak victory, because it allows for a "narrowly tailored" use of race in college admissions, imposes an artificial 25-year deadline for the program, and encourages a monumental case-by-case analysis for admitting students that is likely to create chaos and push institutions into making admissions decisions based on test scores.

38. *Parents Involved in Community Schools v. Seattle School District No. 1 et al.,* argued December 4, 2006; decided June 28, 2007; no. 05-908, 40–41.

39. We acknowledge that the United States has never had a monolithic racial order. Historically, areas that had "Latin American-like" racial situations, such as South Carolina and Los Angeles, have had more pluralistic racial orders. Nevertheless, it is possible to articulate the claim that, at the macro level during the slavery era, the time of Jim Crow, and during the post-Civil Rights era, there have been national trends that support the discussion. Varieties of racial orders and local exceptions to the national trend do not negate the national macrolevel trend.

40. Although the Bolivian census of 2001 reports that 71 percent of Bolivians self-identify as Indian, less than 20 percent have more than a high school diploma, and 58.6 percent live below the poverty line; 66 percent of Bolivians in the United States self-identify as white, and 64 percent have 12 or more years of education and a per-capita income comparable with that of whites (Censo Nacional de Población y Vivienda, *Bolivia: Caraterísticas de la Población, Serie Resultados,* vol. 4. [La Paz: Ministerio de Hacienda, 2002]). Thus, this seems like a case of self-selection—that is, Bolivians in the United States do not represent Bolivians in Bolivia.

41. The concentration of Puerto Ricans in the lower occupational categories is slightly less than 50 percent. However, when one subdivides the category "Sales and Office," where 20.46 percent of Puerto Ricans are located, one finds that Puerto Ricans are more likely to be represented in the low-paying jobs in that broad category.

42. Cecilia L. Ridgeway, "The Social Construction of Status Value: Gender and Other Nominal Characteristics," *Social Forces* 70 (1991), 367–386.

43. Michael Hanchard, *Orpheus and Power: The Movimento Negro of Rio de Janeiro and Sâo Paulo, Brazil, 1945–1988* (Princeton, NJ: Princeton University Press, 1994), 43–76.

44. Rodolfo de la Garza, Louis DeSipio, F. Chris Garcia, John Garcia, and Angelo Falcon, *Latino Voices: Mexican, Puerto Rican, & Cuban Perspectives on American Politics* (Boulder, CO: Westview Press, 1992), 21–46.

45. Leland T. Saito, *Race and Politics: Asian Americans, Latinos, and Whites in a Los Angeles Suburb* (Urbana: University of Illinois Press, 1998), 59.

46. Yolanda Niemann, Leilani Jennings, Richard Rozelle, James Baxter, and Elroy Sullivan, "Use of Free Response and Cluster Analysis to Determine Stereotypes of Eight Groups," *Personality and Social Psychology Bulletin* 20 (1994), 379–390.

47. Tacho Mindiola, Nestor Rodríguez, and Yolanda Niemann Flores, *Intergroup Relations Between Hispanics and Blacks in Harris County* (Houston, TX: University of Houston, Center for Mexican American Studies, 1996).

48. Nilda Flores-Gonzales, "The Racialization of Latinos: The Meaning of Latino Identity for the Second Generation," *Latino Studies Journal* 10 (1999), 3–31.

49. Suzanne Oboler, "'It Must Be a Fake!' Racial Ideologies, Identities, and the Question of Rights in Hispanics/Latinos," in *Hispanics/Latinos in the United States: Ethnicity, Race, and Rights,* ed. Jorge J. E. Gracia and Pablo De Greiff (New York: Routledge, 2000), 125–146.

50. David Howard, *Coloring the Nation: Race and Ethnicity in the Dominican Republic* (Boulder, CO: Lynne Rienner, 2001), 50–72.

51. Clara E. Rodriguez, *Changing Race: Latinos, the Census, and the History of Ethnicity in the United States* (New York: New York University Press, 1989), 87–105.

52. Lawrence Bobo, Camille Zubrinksy, James Johnson, Jr., and Melvin Oliver, "Work Orientation, Job Discrimination, and Ethnicity," *Research in the Sociology of Work* 5 (1995), 45–85.

53. Ibid., 78.

54. Ronald Weitzer, "Racial Prejudice Among Korean Merchants in African American Neighborhoods," *The Sociological Quarterly* 38 (1997), 587–606.

55. Michael Dawson, "Slowly Coming to Grips with the Effects of the American Racial Order on American Policy Preferences," in *Racialized Politics: The Debate About Racism in America,* ed. David O. Sears, Jim Sidanius, and Lawrence Bobo (Chicago: University of Chicago Press, 2000), 344–358.

56. Lawrence Bobo and Devon Johnson, "Racial Attitudes in a Prismatic Metropolis: Mapping Identity, Stereotypes, Competition, and Views on Affirmative Action," in *Prismatic Metropolis,* ed. Lawrence Bobo, Melvin Oliver, James Johnson, and Abel Valenzuela (New York: Russell Sage Foundation, 2000), 81–166.

57. Bobo and Johnson also show that Latinos tend to rate blacks negatively and that blacks tend to do the same regarding Latinos. They also found that Latinos, irrespective of national ancestry, self-rate lower than whites and Asians (blacks, however, self-rate at the same level with whites and as better than Asians). This pattern seems to confirm Latin Americanization as those at the bottom in Latin America tend to

have a diffused racial consciousness. Our contention seems further bolstered by their findings that "blacks give themselves ratings that tilt in an unfavorable dimension on the traits of welfare dependency and involvement with gangs" and that "for Latinos three of the dimensions tilt in the direction of negative in-group ratings" (Bobo and Johnson, 103).

58. Rachel F. Moran, *Interracial Intimacy: The Regulation of Race and Romance* (Chicago: University of Chicago Press, 2001), 103.

59. Greta A. Gilbertson, Joseph P. Fitzpatrick, and Lijun Yang, "Hispanic Inter-marriage in New York City: New Evidence from 1991," *International Immigration Review* 30 (1996), 445–459.

60. Harry H.L. Kitano and Roger Daniels, *Asian Americans: Emerging Minorities* (Englewood Cliffs, NJ: Prentice Hall, 2001), 187.

61. Mary C. Waters, *Black Identities: West Indian Immigrant Dreams and American Reality* (Cambridge, MA: Harvard University Press, 1999), 192–242.

62. Gilbertson et al., 445–459.

63. Moran, 42–60.

64. For some of the limitations of this index, see Eduardo Bonilla-Silva and Gianpaolo Baiocchi, "Anything But Racism: How Sociologists Limit the Significance of Racism," *Race and Society* 4 (2001), 117–131.

65. Douglas S. Massey and Nancy A. Denton, "Trends in the Residential Segregation of Blacks, Hispanics, and Asians: 1970–1980," *American Sociological Review* 52 (1987), 802–825.

66. John R. Logan, *From Many Shores: Asians in Census 2000.* Report by the Lewis Mumford Center for Comparative Urban and Regional Research (Albany, NY: University of Albany, 2001).

67. The dissimilarity index expresses the percentage of a minority population that would have to move to result in a perfectly even distribution of the population across census tracts. This index runs from 0 (no segregation) to 100 (total segregation) and is symmetrical (not affected by population size).

68. The exposure index measures the degree of potential contact between two populations (majority and minority) and expresses the probability of a member of a minority group meeting a member of the majority group. Like the dissimilarity index, it runs from 0 to 100, but unlike the dissimilarity index, it is asymmetrical (it is affected by population size).

69. Logan, 9.

70. William H. Frey and Reynolds Farley, "Latino, Asian, and Black Segregation in U.S. Metropolitan Areas: Are Multi-Ethnic Metros Different?" *Demography* 33 (1996), 35–50.

71. Camille Zubrinsky Charles, "The Dynamics of Racial Residential Segregation," *Annual Review of Sociology* 29 (2003), 167–207.

72. Frey and Farley, 35–50.

73. Logan, 9.

74. In the current study, we are using census data to make collective claims. Although there are variations among Cubans and other Latino groups in the United States, the lack of national data on phenotype precludes more detailed, systematic analysis. There is a small segment of African Cubans (black Cubans) in the U.S. Cuban population that is projected to become part of the collective American black. See Mirta Ojito, "Best of Friends, Worlds Apart," in *How Race Is Lived in America* by Correspondents of the *New York Times* (New York: Times Books, 2001), 23–40.

75. Bonilla-Silva, *White Supremacy,* 137–166.

76. Dawson, 344–358.

77. Milton Vickerman, *Crosscurrents: West Indian Immigrants and Race* (New York: Oxford University Press, 1997), 91–136.

78. Bonilla-Silva, *White Supremacy,* 167–192.

79. Kerry Ann Rockquemore and David L. Brunsma, *Beyond Black: Biracial Identity in America* (Thousand Oaks, CA: Sage Publications, 2002), 53–74.

80. Verna M. Keith and Cedric Herring, "Skin Tone and Stratification in the Black Community," *American Journal of Sociology* 97 (1991), 760–778.

81. Charles W. Mills, *The Racial Contract* (Ithaca, NY: Cornell University Press, 1997), 91–134.

Chapter 4

Acknowledgments. This chapter was originally written for *Is Lighter Better? Skin Tone Discrimination Among Asian Americans* by Joanne L. Rondilla and Paul Spickard (Rowman & Littlefield, 2007).

I thank the wonderful people at the Center for Race and Gender for organizing the Hierarchies of Color conference on December 2005. The conversations from that conference were immeasurable. I also thank Catherine Ceniza Choy, Paul Spickard, Margaret Hunter, Laura Perez, and Marcial Gonzalez for their continued support. Finally, thank you to Evelyn Nakano Glenn and Amy Fujiwara Shen for their work on this extremely important anthology.

1. "White Skin," Synovate, www.marketfacts.com/en/news/press_details.php?id=53 (accessed on December 15, 2004).

2. Margie Quimpo-Espino, "Can Her Face Launch P1B Worth of Sales?" *Philippine Daily Inquirer* (July 27, 2003); Linda Collard, *Asian Women in Pursuit of White Skin,* press release (June 16, 2004), www.marketfacts.com/en/news/press_details.php?id=53 (accessed December 15, 2004); Joanne L. Rondilla and Paul Spickard, *Is Lighter Better? Skin Tone Discrimination Among Asian Americans* (New York: Rowman & Littlefield, 2007), 27.

3. Stuart Hall, "Culture, Community and Nation," in *Representing the Nation: A*

Reader in Heritage and Museums, ed. David Boswell and Jessica Evans (New York: Routledge, 1999), 33–44, quote from 36.

4. Stuart Hall, "New Cultures for Old," in *A Place in the World? Places, Cultures and Globalization,* ed. Doreen Massey and Pat Jess (Oxford: Oxford University Press, 1996), 190.

5. Wendy Chapkis, *Beauty Secrets: Women and the Politics of Appearance* (Boston: South End Press, 1986), 37.

6. Patricia Hill-Collins, *Black Feminist Thought: Knowledge, Consciousness and the Politics of Empowerment* (New York: Routledge, 2000), 69.

7. Shiseido and Shu Uemura are available in free-standing boutiques or in fine department stores. Esolis, DHC, Pola are all Japan-based direct-sales companies with products that are available online, via mail-order catalogs, or through independent sales representatives.

8. Esolis catalog, March 2003, 2.

9. Rondilla and Spickard, 59.

10. Ibid., 50–59.

11. For a more thorough discussion, please see Rondilla and Spickard, especially Chapters 3 and 5.

12. Kathy Peiss, *Hope in a Jar: The Making of America's Beauty Culture* (New York: Metropolitan Books, 1998), 188.

13. Similar observations can be made about other parts of Asia. Additionally, tan skin (especially skin that looks like it has been enhanced through sun exposure or tanning processes) is a marker of leisure and is temporary. If someone is naturally dark skinned, the racial meanings are different. Naturally dark skin points toward a more permanent social difference presumed to be linked to one's genes.

14. Deborah Root, *Cannibal Culture: Art, Appropriation, and the Commodification of Difference* (Boulder, CO: Westview Press, 1998), 130.

15. Lilynda Agvateesiri, *Untitled.* Student paper (Santa Barbara: University of California, 2003).

16. Koichi Iwabuchi, *Recentering Globalization: Popular Culture and Japanese Transnationalism* (Durham: Duke University Press, 2002), 16.

17. Hannah Beech, "Eurasian Invasion," *Time Magazine* (April 16, 2001), www.time .com/time/printout/0,8816,106427,00.html (accessed February 25, 2007).

18. Ibid.

19. Margaret L. Hunter, *Race, Gender, and the Politics of Skin Color* (New York: Routledge, 2005), 57.

20. Hunter, 70–71.

21. Similar dynamics work in Cambodia, where a relatively dark-skinned local population has mixed to some degree with lighter skinned Chinese, Vietnamese, or French, with a hierarchy of light over dark also being formed.

22. Judith Williamson, "Woman Is an Island: Femininity and Colonization," in *Studies in Entertainment: Critical Approaches of Mass Culture,* ed. Tania Modleski (Bloomington: Indiana University Press, 1986), 101.

23. Collard.

24. Rondilla and Spickard, 60.

25. Esolis catalog, 2.

26. *Morena* refers to some one who is darker skinned, whereas *mestiza* refers to someone who is lighter skinned and of mixed race.

27. Lora Gahol, "Whiteners Won't Transform 'Morena' into 'Mestiza,'" *Philippine Daily Inquirer* (April 30, 2003).

28. Catherine Lutz and Jane L. Collins, *Reading National Geographic* (Chicago: University of Chicago Press, 1993), 56.

29. Miriam Jordan, "Creams for a Lighter Skin Capture the Asian Market; Especially in India Fair Color as a Cultural Virtue," *International Herald Tribune* (April 24, 1998).

30. Root, 9.

31. Williamson, 116.

32. Peiss, 146.

33. Ibid., 223.

34. Amina Mire, "Skin-Bleaching: Poison, Beauty, Power and the Politics of the Colour Line," *New Feminist Research* 28 (Winter/Spring 2001), 27.

35. Peiss, 223.

36. Kimberly DaCosta, *Making Multiracials: State, Family, and Market in the Redrawing of the Color Line* (Stanford: Stanford University Press, 2007), 166.

37. Rebecca King-O'Riain, *Pure Beauty: Judging Race in Japanese American Beauty Pageants* (Minneapolis: University of Minnesota Press, 2006) 22.

Chapter 5

Acknowledgments. I thank pageant coproducer Belva Davis and the Miss Bronze contestants who generously granted me interviews, helped me to locate others who were in the contest, and lent me Miss Bronze programs. I am also grateful to Jessica Fields, Stephanie Sears, and Evelyn Nakano Glenn for their helpful critical comments on drafts of this chapter.

1. For a more detailed discussion of the contests sponsored by the *New York Age,* the *Western American,* and the Miss Fine Brown Frame contest, see Maxine Leeds Craig, *Ain't I a Beauty Queen?: Black Women, Beauty and the Politics of Race* (New York: Oxford University Press, 2002), 45–64.

2. The articles and images were mainly published in two black newspapers: *The California Voice* and *The Sun-Reporter.* Additional articles were from the *Oakland Post, The Oakland Tribune,* and the *San Francisco Chronicle.*

3. The *Western American*'s 1927 contest, which similarly recruited black contestants of a variety of skin tones, occurred not long after the peak years of Marcus Garvey's black nationalist movement. Garvey's movement stimulated popular critiques of the privileged positions of blacks with light skin.

4. In this chapter I look critically at color discourse yet cannot avoid using it. My descriptions of contestant's colors are based on my own observations as well as on the way contestants described themselves and others throughout my interviews. During the course of an interview, a woman might shift her self-description from brown to dark. These self-descriptions and my attempts to categorize individuals in terms of color are relational. A black woman is dark in relation to another black woman who is lighter. In this chapter I use the categories of dark, brown, and light to locate women, as best I can, as they would have been categorized by their contemporaries.

5. Sander Gilman, *Making the Body Beautiful* (Princeton: Princeton University Press, 1999), 220.

6. Kathy Peiss, "Making Faces: The Cosmetics Industry and the Cultural Construction of Gender, 1890–1930," *Genders* Spring, 7 (1990), 164.

7. W. E. B. Du Bois, *The Souls of Black Folk* (New York: Signet Classic, 1995), 45.

8. In an earlier study I found similarly contradictory sentiments regarding skin color and beauty among twelve- to fifteen-year-old girls. See Maxine Leeds Craig, "Young African American Beauty and the Language of Beauty," in *Ideals of Feminine Beauty: Philosophical, Social, and Cultural Dimensions,* ed. Karen A. Callaghan (Westport, CT: Greenwood Press, 1994), 150.

9. See Sarah Banet-Weiser, *The Most Beautiful Girl in the World: Beauty Pageants and National Identity* (Berkeley: University of California Press, 1999), 6–10; Colleen Cohen Ballerino, Richard Wilk, and Beverly Stoeltje, eds., *Beauty Queens on the Global Stage: Gender, Contests, and Power* (New York: Routledge, 1996), 2; Rebecca Chiyoko King-O'Riain, *Pure Beauty: Judging Race in Japanese American Beauty Pageants* (Minneapolis: University of Minnesota Press, 2006), 76; Judy Tzu-Chun Wu, "'Loveliest Daughter of Our Ancient Cathay!' Representations of Ethnic and Gender Identity in the Miss Chinatown U.S.A. Beauty Pageant," *Journal of Social History* 31, 1 (Fall 1997), 6; Christine R. Yano, *Crowning the Nice Girl: Gender, Ethnicity, and Culture in Hawai'i's Cherry Blossom Festival* (Honolulu: University of Hawai'i Press, 2006), 5.

10. "There She Goes . . . ," [Home Edition], *Los Angeles Times,* October 24, 2004, M4. By way of comparison, 9.8 million viewers watched the 2006 Miss America pageant.

11. Unless otherwise indicated, all quotations are from interviews conducted by the author.

12. Kay Wahl, "She Also Cooks . . . " *The Oakland Tribune,* May 12, 1963, S7. I am grateful to Jessica Weiss for calling my attention to this published interview.

13. Korie Edwards, Katrina M. Carter-Tellison, and Cedric Herring, "For Richer, For Poorer, Whether Dark or Light: Skin Tone, Marital Status, and Spouse's Earnings," in *Skin Deep: How Race and Complexion Matter in the "Color-Blind" Era,* ed. Cedric Herring, Verna Keith, and Hayward D. Horton (Urbana: University of Illinois Press, 2004), 73.

14. St. Clair Drake and Horace R. Cayton, *Black Metropolis: A Study of Negro Life in a Northern City* (New York: Harper & Row, 1945), 503.

15. Margaret Hunter, "Light, Bright, and Almost White: The Advantages and Disadvantages of Light Skin," in *Skin Deep: How Race and Complexion Matter in the "Color-Blind" Era,* ed. Cedric Herring, Verna Keith, and Hayward D. Horton (Urbana: University of Illinois Press, 2004), 38.

16. Bart Landry, *The New Black Middle Class* (Berkeley: University of California Press, 1987), 24–25.

17. This name, and the names of all contestants who were not crowned Miss Bronze, are pseudonyms.

18. Laila Haidarali, "Polishing Brown Diamonds: African American Women, Popular Magazines, and the Advent of Modeling in Early Postwar America," *Journal of Women's History* 17, 1 (Spring 2005), 31.

19. Julie Bettie, *Women Without Class: Girls, Race, and Identity* (Berkeley: University of California Press, 2003), 50.

20. Craig, 139–140.

21. For a discussion of skin color and wealth, see Elizabeth I. Mullins and Paul Sites, "The Origins of Contemporary Eminent Black Americans: A Three-Generation Analysis of Social Origin," *American Sociological Review* 49 (October 1984), 681. For a discussion of hair texture and status, see Ingrid Banks, *Hair Matters: Beauty, Power, and Black Women's Consciousness* (New York: New York University Press, 2000), 28–30.

Chapter 6

Acknowledgments. I am grateful to the faculty and staff of the Center for Race and Gender at the University of California, Berkeley, for organizing the conference Hierarchies of Color, for which this paper was originally prepared. Inviting me to participate in this conference pushed me to probe further the problem of color and colorism in South Asian diasporas. I thank volume editor Evelyn Nakano Glenn and my anonymous reviewers for their helpful comments and suggestions. I also express my deep gratitude to my colleague Don Kulick for his close and patient scrutiny of my initial draft. Parts of this chapter appear in Khan, Aisha, *Callaloo Nation: Metaphors of Race and Religious Identity among South Asians in Trinidad* (Durham: Duke University Press, 2004).

1. Daniel Segal, "'Race' and 'Colour' in Pre-Independence Trinidad and Tobago," in *Trinidad Ethnicity,* ed. Kevin Yelvington (Knoxville: University of Tennessee Press, 1993), 81–115.

2. Aisha Khan, "What Is 'a Spanish'?: Ambiguity and 'Mixed' Ethnicity in Trinidad," in *Trinidad Ethnicity*, ed. Kevin Yelvington (Knoxville: University of Tennessee Press, 1993), 180–207.

3. Kelvin Singh, "Indians in the Larger Society," in *Calcutta to Caroni: The East Indians of Trinidad*, ed. John LaGuerre (St. Augustine: University of the West Indies, 1985), 33–60.

4. Sidney Mintz, "Review of *A Framework for Caribbean Studies*" by M. G. Smith, *Boletin Bibliografico de Antropologia Americana* 8, 1 (1957), 189–194.

5. Donald Brenneis, "Talk and Transformation," *Man* (NS) 22 (1987), 499–510; Robin Sheriff, *Dreaming Equality: Color, Race, and Racism in Urban Brazil* (New Brunswick: Rutgers University Press, 2001).

6. Susan Bayly, "Caste and 'Race' in the Colonial Ethnography of India," in *The Concept of Race in South Asia*, ed. Peter Robb (Delhi: Oxford University Press, 1997), 165–218.

7. Ashis Nandy, *The Intimate Enemy: Loss and Recovery of Self Under Colonialism* (Delhi: Oxford University Press, 1983); John D. Rogers, "Racial Identities and Politics in Early Modern Sri Lanka," in *The Concept of Race in South Asia*, ed. Peter Robb (Delhi: Oxford University Press, 1997), 146–164; Bayly, 165–218; Tony Ballantyne, *Orientalism and Race: Aryanism in the British Empire* (London: Palgrave, 2002).

8. Rogers, 163–164.

9. Peter Robb, "Introduction: South Asia and the Concept of Race," in *The Concept of Race in South Asia*, ed. Peter Robb (Delhi: Oxford University Press, 1997), 1–76.

10. Romila Thapar, "The Image of the Barbarian in Early India," *Comparative Studies in Society and History* 13, 4 (1971), 408–436.

11. Ibid., 410.

12. Ibid., 411.

13. Damodar Dharman Kosambi, *Ancient India: A History of Its Culture and Civilization* (New York: Pantheon, 1965), 81.

14. Arthur Llewellyn Basham, *The Wonder That Was India* (London: Sidgwick and Jackson, 1961), 24.

15. Kosambi, 72.

16. Bayly, 169.

17. Kenneth A. R. Kennedy, "Have Aryans Been Identified in the Prehistoric Skeletal Record from South Asia? Biological Anthropology and the Concepts of Ancient Races," in *The Indo-Aryans of Ancient South Asia: Language, Material Culture and Ethnicity*, ed. George Erdosy (Berlin: Walter de Gruyter, 1995), 32–66.

18. Ballantyne, 19, 31.

19. Ibid., 44; Zaheer Baber, "'Race,' Religion and Riots: The 'Racialization' of Communal Identity and Conflict in India," *Sociology* 38, 4 (2004), 701–718; Deepa Reddy, "The Ethnicity of Caste," *Anthropological Quarterly* 78, 3 (2005), 543–584.

20. Ballantyne, 48.

21. Ibid., 54.

22. Padma Rangaswamy, *Namaste America: Indian Immigrants in an American Metropolis* (University Park: Pennsylvania State University Press, 2000), 44, quoted in Sunil Bhatia, *American Karma: Race, Culture, and Identity in the Indian Diaspora* (New York: New York University Press, 2007), 86.

23. Monisha Das Gupta, *Unruly Immigrants: Rights, Activism, and Transnational South Asian Politics in the United States* (Durham: Duke University Press, 2006).

24. Ibid., 37, 46.

25. Gary Taylor, *Buying Whiteness: Race, Culture, and Identity from Columbus to Hip Hop* (London: Palgrave Macmillan, 2005), 56, 63, 59–60.

26. E. F. L. Wood, *West Indies Report: Visit to the West Indies and British Guiana, December 1921–February 1922* (London: His Majesty's Stationery Office, 1922), 23

27. A. Hyatt Verrill, *West Indies of Today* (New York: Dodd, Mead, 1931), 186.

28. William Agnew Paton, *Down the Islands: A Voyage to the Caribbees* (New York: Charles Scribner's Sons, 1887), 198.

29. Alfred Radford, *Jottings on the West Indies and Panama* (London: William Whiteley, 1886), 35

30. Vidia Surujprasad Naipaul, *The Enigma of Arrival* (New York: Knopf, 1987).

31. Thapur, 435.

Chapter 7

1. Oracy Nogueira, *Tanto Preto Quanto Branco: Estudos de Relações Raciais* (São Paulo: T.A. Queiroz, 1985).

2. As we know, *race,* and therefore the idea of *race mixture,* is a social construction. However, I have tried to avoid placing these and other race-related terms or categories (e.g., *black*) in quotations to facilitate smoother reading.

3. I use the term *race blindness* to refer to that aspect of Mexico's national ideology that asserts the irrelevance and nonexistence of race and racism in society. I use this term as opposed to *color blindness,* because, in Mexico, there is a clear distinction between race and color, with the national ideology most strongly referencing the former. Furthermore, there is a societal taboo surrounding the term "race" that does not exist with the term "color."

4. Patrick J. Carroll, *Blacks in Colonial Veracruz* (Austin: University of Texas Press, 2001), 3.

5. An estimated 200,000 slaves were brought from Africa in colonial times, according to Bobby Vaughn, "Race and Nation: A Study of Blackness in Mexico" (PhD dissertation, Stanford University, 2001), 18. The "great wave" of Cuban migration brought 2,716 Cubans to Veracruz. See Bernardo García Díaz, "La Migración Cubana a Veracruz 1870–1910," in *La Habana/Veracruz, Veracruz/La Habana: Las Dos Orillas,* ed. Bernardo García Díaz and Sergio Guerra Vilaboy (Xalapa: Univer-

sidad Veracuzana, 2002), 297–320. In addition, a very small Indigenous population composed mostly of migrants from neighboring towns or states resides in the urban centers. The lack of a strong local indigenous "group" makes the Indian question less salient in Veracruz compared with some other regions in Mexico, although it is part of the local discourse on *mestizaje*. See Judith Friedlander, *Being Indian in Hueyapan: A Study of Forced Identity in Contemporary Mexico* (New York: St. Martin's Press, 1975), 71–79; Vaughn, 99–104.

6. All the names used in this chapter are pseudonyms.

7. Although the significance depends on context, the addition of "-ito/-ita" to the end of a word in Spanish represents the diminutive form.

8. Matthijs Kalmijn, "Trends in Black/White Intermarriage," *Social Forces* 72 (1993), 137–138; Zhenchao Qian, "Breaking the Racial Barriers: Variations in Interracial Marriage Between 1980 and 1990," *Demography* 34 (1997), 273; John Burdick, *Blessed Anastacia: Women, Race, and Popular Christianity in Brazil* (New York: Routledge, 1998), 26–42; Edward E. Telles, *Race in Another America: The Significance of Skin Color in Brazil* (Princeton: Princeton University Press, 2004), 189–191.

9. The last race question was asked in 1921. For a more detailed discussion, see Mara Loveman, "Nation-State Building, 'Race,' and the Production of Official Statistics: Brazil in a Comparative Perspective" (PhD dissertation, University of California, Los Angeles, 2001), 327.

10. Colin Palmer, *Slaves of a White God: Blacks in Mexico, 1570–1650* (Cambridge: Harvard University Press, 1976), 1; Patrick J. Carroll, *Blacks in Colonial Veracruz* (Austin: University of Texas Press, 2001), 80; R. Douglas Cope, *The Limits of Racial Domination: Plebeian Society in Colonial Mexico City, 1660–1720* (Madison: University of Wisconsin Press, 1994), 83; Gonzalo Aguirre Beltrán, "The Integration of the Negro into the National Society of Mexico," in *Race and Class in Latin America,* ed. Magnus Mörner (New York: Columbia University Press, 1970), 11–27; Gonzalo Aguirre Beltrán, *La Población Negra de México: Estudio Ethnohistórico* (Veracruz: Fondo de Cultura Económica, 1989); Gonzalo Aguirre Beltrán, *Cuijla: Esbozo Ethnográfico de un Pueblo Negro* (Mexico D.F.: Fondo de Cultura Económica, 1958).

11. People prefer to speculate that individuals are from Cuban origin as opposed to slave origin, because the latter holds a greater social stigma. However, because the number of slaves brought from Africa far exceeds the number of Cubans of African descent who immigrated to Veracruz, the majority of the African-origin population in Veracruz is likely to be of slave origin.

Chapter 8

1. Charis Thompson, "Race Science," *Theory, Culture & Society* 23 (2006), 2–3.2.

2. Compare, for example, regional variations in race categories used for data collection in assisted reproductive technologies presented at the 2002 annual meeting

of the American Society for Reproductive Medicine. Dr. Cristy James and colleagues from the University of Alabama in the southern United States reported on a study that compared African American women and Caucasian women. Dr. Bevilacqua and colleagues in Boston divided their patients into four groups of Caucasian, African American, Asian, and Hispanic women patients. In addition, Asian categories tend to be more finely differentiated on the West Coast and in Hawaii, and Caribbean categories are more differentiated in east and southeast clinics.

3. This visual logic is important. The fact that one chooses an adult woman when choosing an egg donor—as it were, a reproductive/sexual partner/substitute—but one chooses a baby who will look something like the donor did as a baby when buying sperm underlies deep gender differences in reproduction and sexuality that are beyond the scope of this chapter.

4. Donor Concierge, www.donorconcierge.com/id70.html (accessed 7/23/2008).

5. http://eggdonationindia.com/becoming_a_donor.htm (accessed 7/23/2008).

6. See Charis Thompson, "Why We Should, in Fact, Pay for Egg Donation," *Regenerative Medicine* 2, 2 (2007), 203–209, for an elaboration of some of these arguments.

7. *De-kinned* is my word to link a history of the denial of kinship to the families of slaves with the continued disproportionate separation by the state of African American children from their biological parents. See, for example, Dorothy Roberts, *Shattered Bonds: The Color of Child Welfare* (New York: Basic Books: 2002).

8. For a locus classicus, see Nella Larsen, *Passing* (Harmondsworth: Penguin, [1929] 2003). For a wonderful recent novel on multiple forms of passing, one of which concerns a woman's phenotypically invisible African ancestry, which is revealed in the birth of her darker skinned children, see Patricia Powell, *The Pagoda* (Orlando: Harvest Books, 1998).

9. The history of this country is tied in numerous ways to racialized restrictions on citizenship and kinship. See Evelyn Nakano Glenn, *Unequal Freedom: How Race and Gender Shaped American Citizenship and Labor* (Cambridge: Harvard University Press, 2002). Visible blackness, in which skin tone has always been important, played a role in a person's status as free or slave, in applying the one-drop rule, and in deciding with whom an individual might (be forced to) procreate, and the subsequent identity and belonging of children. The history of antimiscegenation laws is one strand illustrative of this state of affairs. The first antimiscegenation law, prohibiting marriage between whites and free blacks was passed during the colonial era in 1691, in the British colony of Virginia. Of the thirteen founding colonies in 1776, seven enacted laws prohibiting interracial marriage. In *Pace v. Alabama,* 1883, the U.S. Supreme Court declared antimiscegenation laws to be constitutional. States' antimiscegenation laws were not repealed nationwide until they were finally declared unconstitutional in a unanimous 1967 decision by the U.S. Supreme Court in *Virginia v. Loving.* South Carolina and Alabama did not remove their invalidated antimiscegenation laws from

state law until 1998 and 2000, respectively. Literature on racial passing often makes reference to the unpredictable phenotype of children.

10. Within the United States, this kind of gradient also exists between states. The legality of different procedures as well as the availability and terms of insurance coverage varies among states. Internationally, exchange rates and costs of procedures as well as the availability of donors and surrogates also create reproductive tourism gradients.

Chapter 9

Acknowledgments. This research extends earlier work on Indian matrimonials conducted in collaboration with Ramdas Menon of the Texas Department of Health. I thank Hsin Chin Chen for assistance with the preparation of graphs, and Amanda Grunden, Katie Wood, Cara Karline, and Rika Muhl for coding the ads.

1. Nirad Choudhuri, *The Autobiography of an Unknown Indian* (New Delhi: Jaico, 1951), 121.

2. Amali Philips, "Gendering Colour: Identity, Femininity and Marriage in Kerala," *Anthropologica* 46 (2004), 261.

3. Sucheta Mazumdar, "Racist Responses to Racism: The Aryan Myth and South Asians in the United States," *South Asia Bulletin* 9, 1 (1989), 47–55.

4. Roksana Rahman, "Color as a Status: The Role of Skin Color Among Hindu Indian Women" (master's thesis, Rutgers University, 2002).

5. Vijay Prashad, *The Karma of Brown Folk* (Minneapolis: University of Minnesota Press, 2000).

6. Rosemary George, "'From Expatriate Aristocrat to Immigrant Nobody': South Asian Racial Strategies in the Southern Californian Context," *Diaspora* 6, 1 (2004), 31–60.

7. Mazumdar, 50.

8. George, 31–60.

9. Zareena Grewal, "Marriage in Color: Race, Religious Authority and Spouse Selection in Four Muslim Communities in Michigan" (paper presented at the AMSS 32nd annual conference, Indiana University, 2003).

10. Dhoolekha Raj, *Where Are You From? Middle-Class Migrants in the Modern World* (Berkeley: University of California Press, 2003), 136.

11. Sarita Sahay and Niva Piran, "Skin Color Preferences and Body Satisfaction among South Asian-Canadian and European-Canadian Female University Students," *The Journal of Social Psychology* 137, 2 (1997), 161–171.

12. Tara Jethwani, "Revisioning Boundaries: A Study of Interracial Marriage among Second Generation Asian Indian Women in the U.S." (PhD dissertation, Rutgers University, 2002).

13. Abdallah M. Badahdah and Kathleen Tiemann, "Mate Selection Among Muslims Living in America," *Evolution and Human Behavior* 26 (2005), 432–440.

14. F. de Singly, "The Maneuvers of Seduction: An Analysis of Matrimonial Advertisements," *Revue Francaise de Sociologie* 25, 4 (1984), 523–559; H. Ahluwalia, "Matrimonial Advertisements in Punjab," *The Indian Journal of Social Work* 30, 1 (1969), 55–64; K. Anand, "An Analysis of Matrimonial Advertisements," *Sociological Bulletin* 14, 1 (1965), 59–71; K. R. Murthy and A. B. Ranga Rao, "A Sociological Analysis of the Content in Matrimonial Advertisements in South India," *Indian Journal of Social Work* 44, 4 (1984), 377–386.

15. Harjinder Singh, "A Content Analysis of Matrimonial Advertisements of Indians Abroad," *Man in India* 57, 1 (1977), 69–74; Ramdas Menon and Jyotsna Vaid, "The Ideal Mate: An Analysis of Matrimonial Advertisements in the Indian Immigrant Press" (paper presented at the conference on South Asia, University of Wisconsin at Madison, 1987).

16. Gura Bhargava, "Seeking Immigration Through Matrimonial Alliance: A Study of Advertisements in an Ethnic Weekly," *Journal of Comparative Family Studies* 19, 2 (1988), 245–259; Ramdas Menon, "Arranged Marriages Among South Asian Immigrants," *Sociology and Social Research* 73, 4 (1989), 180–181.

17. Jyotsna Vaid and Ramdas Menon, "From Sham Marriages to Innocent Divorces: A Study of Matrimonial Ads in the Immigrant Press" (paper presented at the Association for Asian American Studies, Ithaca, NY, 1993); Jyotsna Vaid, "Stigmatized or Self-Actualized? Gendered Portrayals of Divorce in Indian matrimonials" (paper presented at national South Asian Women's Conference, "Forging New Identities in Cross-Cultural America," Los Angeles, CA, 1994); Jyotsna Vaid, "Indian Matrimonial Advertisements: Discourses of the Commodified Self" (invited address, University of Colorado at Boulder, 1998); Jyotsna Vaid and Rashmi Luthra, "The ABC(D)s of Matrimonial Advertisements: Reading Between the Lines" (paper presented at the annual conference on multiethnic literature of the United States, "Contentious Intersections, Still: Race, Gender, Class, Ethnicity," Texas A&M University, 1994).

18. Chitra Divakaruni, *Wheat Complexions and Pink Cheeks,* www.rediff.com/news/2001/apr/02usspec.htm (accessed August 30, 2005).

19. Noel Gist, "Mate Selection and Mass Communication in India," *Public Opinion Quarterly* 17, 4 (1953–54), 481–495.

20. Arthur Niehoff, "A Study of Matrimonial Advertisements in North India," *The Eastern Anthropologist* 12, 2 (1959), 73–86.

21. Musab U. Siddiqi and Earl Y. Reeves, "A Comparison of Marital Preference of Asian Indians in Two Different Cultures," *International Journal of Sociology of the Family* 19, 1 (1989), 21–36.

22. Vaid, "Indian Matrimonial Advertisements," 1998 (unpublished).

23. Raj, 136.

24. Sayantani Dasgupta and Shamita Das Dasgupta, "Bringing up Baby: Raising a 'Third World' Daughter in the 'First World,'" in *Dragon Ladies, Asian American*

Feminists Breathe Fire, ed. Sonia Shah (Boston: South End Press, 1997), 182–199; Amita Handa, *Of Silk Saris and Mini-skirts: South Asian Girls Walk the Tightrope of Culture* (Toronto: Women's Press, 2003); Keith Maddox and Stephanie Gray, "Cognitive Representations of Black Americans: Reexploring the Role of Skin Tone," *Personality and Social Psychology Bulletin* 28, 2 (2002), 250–259.

Chapter 10

1. See Cedric Herring, Verna M. Keith, and Hayward Derrick Horton, eds. *Skin Deep: How Race and Complexion Matter in the "Color Blind" Era* (Chicago: Institute for Research on Race and Public Policy, 2003); Margaret Hunter, *Race, Gender, and the Politics of Skin Tone* (New York: Routledge, 2005); and Keith B. Maddox, "Perspectives on Racial Phenotypicality Bias," *Personality and Social Psychology Review* 8 (2004), 383–401.

2. Jean Michel Massing, "From Greek Proverb to Soap Advert: Washing the Ethiopian," *Journal of the Warburg and Courtauld Institutes* 58 (1995), 180.

3. Timothy Burke, *Lifebuoy Men, Lux Women: Commodification, Consumption, and Cleanliness in Modern Zimbabwe* (Durham: Duke University Press, 1996), 189; Nakedi Ribane, *Beauty: A Black Perspective* (Durban: University of KwaZulu-Natal Press, 2006), 12.

4. James Muzondidya, *Walking a Tightrope: Towards a Social History of the Coloured Community of Zimbabwe* (Trenton, NJ: Africa World Press, 2005), 23–24.

5. Antoine Mahe, Fatimata Ly, and Jean-Marie Dangou, "Skin Diseases Associated with the Cosmetic Use of Bleaching Products in Women from Dakar, Senegal," *British Journal of Dermatology* 148, 3 (2003), 493–500.

6. Malangu Ntambwe, "Mirror Mirror on the Wall, Who is the FAIREST of Them All?" *Science in Africa, Africa's First On-Line Science Magazine* (March 2004), www .scienceinafrica.co.za/2004/march/skinlightening.htm (accessed May 1, 2007); Paul Margulies, "Cushing's Syndrome: The Facts You Need to Know," www.medhelp.org/ www/nadf4.htm (accessed May 1, 2007).

7. *Telling It Like It Is: 10 Years of Unsustainable Development in Ireland* (Dublin: Earth Summit, Ireland, Ltd., 2002), 13–14; Julia Chadwick, "Arklow's Toxic Soap Factory," *Wicklow Today.com*, June, 2001, www.wicklowtoday.com/features/mercurysoap .htm (accessed April 18, 2007).

8. Dara De Faoite, "Investigation into the Sale of Dangerous Mercury Soap in Ethnic Shops," *The Observer*, May 27, 2001, http://observer.guardian.co.uk/uk_news/story/ 0,6903,497227,00.html (accessed May 1, 2007); Michael O'Farrell, "Pressure Mounts to Have Soap Plant Shut Down," *Irish Examiner*, August 26, 2002, http://archives.tcm.ie/ irishexaminer/2002/08/26/story510455503.asp (accessed May 1, 2007).

9. Antoine Mahe et al., "An Epidemiologic Survey on the Cosmetic Use of Bleaching Agency by the Women of Bamako, Mali," *Annals of Dermatology and [Venereology]*

120 (1993), 870–873; N. Malangu and G. A. Ogunbanjo, "Predictors of Topical Steroid Misuse Among Patrons of Pharmacies in Pretoria, *South African Family Practice* 48, 1 (2006), 14; P. Del Guidice and P. Yves, "The Widespread Use of Skin Lightening Creams in Senegal: A Persistent Public Health Problem in West Africa," *The International Journal of Dermatology* 41 (2002), 69–72; S. B. Adebajo, "An Epidemiological Survey of the Use of Cosmetic Skin Lightening Cosmetics Among Traders in Lagos, Nigeria," *West African Journal of Medicine* 21, 1 (2002), 51–55.

10. Erin Dooley, "Sickening Soap Trade," *Environmental Health Perspectives* October (2001), available at www.ehponline.org/docs/2001/109-10/forum.html; Iyamide Thomas, "'Yellow Fever': The Disease That Is Skin Bleaching," *Mano Vision*, 33 (2004), 34. Also available from www.manovision.com/ISSUES/ISSUE33/33skin.pdf (accessed May 7, 2007).

11. Futhi Ntshingila, "Female Buppies Using Harmful Skin Lighteners," *Sunday Times,* South Africa, November 27, 2005, www.sundaytimes.co.za (accessed January 25, 2006).

12. Ibid.

13. Kathy Russell, Midge Wilson, and Ronald Hall, *The Color Complex: The Politics of Skin Color Among African Americans* (New York: Harcourt Brace Jovanovich, 1992), 24–40.

14. Audrey Elisa Kerr, "The Paper Bag Principle: The Myth and the Motion of Colorism," *Journal of American Folklore* 118 (2005), 271–289.

15. Kathy Peiss, *Hope in a Jar: The Making of America's Beauty Culture* (New York: Metropolitan Books, 1998), 41, 42.

16. Ibid., 210, 212. Under pressure from African American critics, Nadolina reduced the concentration to 6 percent in 1937 and 1.5 percent in 1941.

17. Peiss, 67–70. See also A'Lelia Bundles, *On Her Own Ground: The Life and Times of Madam C. J. Walker* (New York: Scribner, 2001).

18. Peiss, 205, 213, 212; J. H. Harmon, "The Negro as a Local Business Man," *The Journal of Negro History,* 14, 2 (1929), 138; Robert Mark Silverman, "The Effects of Racism and Racial Discrimination on Minority Business Development: The Case of Black Manufacturers in Chicago's Ethnic Beauty Aids Industry," *Journal of Social History* 31, 3 (1998), 579–580.

19. Products offered at online stores, including ebonyline.com (www.ebonyline .com/skin-fade-cream-skin-tone-cream.html), TexasBeautySupply (www.TexasBeauty Supplies.com), Allure Beauty Supply (www.allurebeautysupply.com/Face-Skincare_ c_113-1-3.html), and Avre products (www.avreskincare.com/skin_menu.html). One online store offers an alternative approach that advocates products that purport to nourish melanin pigments (www.africanamericanskincare.com/).

20. Discussions on Bright Skin Forum, Skin Lightening Board, http://excoboard. com/exco/forum.php?forumid=65288 (accessed May 11, 2005); Pallid Skin Lighten-

ing System, www.avreskincare.com/skin/pallid/index.html; advertisement for Swiss Whitening Pills, www.skinbleaching.net (accessed July 5, 2005).

21. See Aisha Kahn's and Jyotsna Vaid's chapters in this volume.

22. David Arnold, "Race, Place and Bodily Difference in Early Nineteenth Century India," *Historical Research* 77 (2004), 263, 162.

23. Based on examining entries on Internet forums found on Herbal Salon.com and IndiaParenting.com, www.indiaparenting.com/beauty/beauty041book.shtml (accessed November 2005).

24. Based on examining a list of Indian skincare manufacturers and suppliers, and descriptions of their products, www.indianindustry.com/herbalcosmetics/10275. htm (accessed November 2005), and also linked websites of Indian manufacturers and suppliers.

25. Susan Runkle, "Making 'Miss India': Constructing Gender, Power and Nation," *South Asian Popular Culture* 2, 2 (2004), 145–159.

26. Susan Runkle, "The Beauty Obsession," *Manushi* 145 (2005), www.indiatogether .org/manushi/issue145/lovely.htm (accessed September 18, 2006).

27. Reyna Mae L. Tabbada, "Trouble in Paradise," Press release, September 20, 2006, www.bulatlat.com/news/6-33/6-33-trouble.htm (accessed May 5, 2007).

28. In 2004, overseas workers remitted an estimated $10.7 billion according to the Bangko Sentral ng Pilipinas, the central bank of the Republic of the Philippines. Table on remittances found at www.bsp.gov.ph/statistics/spei/tab11.htm (accessed May 5, 2007).

29. Rhacel Parrenas, *Servants of Globalization: Women, Migration, and Domestic Work* (Stanford: Stanford University Press, 2001).

30. www.synovate.com/knowledge/infact/issues/200406 (accessed March 21, 2007).

31. Skin whitening forums found at www.candymag.com/teentalk/index.php/ topic,131753.0.html and www.rexinteractive.com/forum/topic.asp?TOPIC_ID=41 (accessed June 10, 2007).

32. http://yumeimise.com/store/index.php (accessed May 5, 2007).

33. Makiko Ashikari, "Urban Middle-Class Japanese Women and Their White Faces: Gender, Ideology, and Representation," *Ethos* 31, 1 (2003), 9–11, 3–4, 3.

34. "Intelligence on the Cosmetic Market in Japan," Intage, 2001, www.intage .co.jp/express/01_08/market/index1.html (accessed June 14, 2006). Based on scanning products in a Japanese market in Little Tokyo in Los Angeles, September 2005.

35. "Prairie Plants Take Root in Cosmetics Industry, *Saskatchewan Business Unlimited* 10, 1 (2005), 1–2.

36. Exhibitor information for Beautyworld, Japan, May 8–10, 2006, www .beautyworldjapan.com/en/efirst.html (accessed June 14, 2007).

37. "Prairie Plants Take Root"; Health, Beauty & Personal Grooming: A Global Nielsen Consumer Report (Haarlem, the Netherlands: The Nielsen Company, March

2007). Also available from www.acnielsen.co.in/news/20070402.shtml (accessed May 3, 2007).

38. Nancy Ley Stepan, *The Hour of Eugenics: Race, Gender, and Nation in Latin America* (Ithaca: Cornell University Press, 1991), 135.

39. Matthew C. Guttman, *The Meanings of Macho: Being a Man in Mexico City* (Berkeley: University of California Press, 1996), 40; Ruben Martinez, *Crossing Over: A Mexican Family on the Migrant Trail* (New York: Henry Holt, 2001); Marcia Farr, *Rancheros in Chicagocan: Language and Identity in a Transnational Community* (Austin: University of Texas Press, 2006), Chapter 5.

40. Jamie Winders, John Paul Jones III, and Michael James Higgins, "Making *Gueras*: Selling White Identities on Late-Night Mexican Television," *Gender, Place and Culture* 12, 1 (2005), 77–78.

41. Allen Knight, "Racism, Revolution, and *Indigenismo*: Mexico, 1910–1940," in *The Idea of Race in Latin America, 1870–1940,* ed. Richard Graham (Austin: University of Texas Press, 1990), 71–114, 100.

42. New York Department of Health and Mental Hygiene, "NYC Health Dept. Warns Against Use of 'Skin Lightening' Creams Containing Mercury or Similar Products Which Do Not List Ingredients," press release, January 27, 2005, www.nyc.gov/html/doh/html/pr/pr008-05.shtml (accessed May 7, 2007).

43. Centers for Disease Control and Prevention, "Update: Mercury Poisoning Associated with Beauty Cream—Arizona, California, New Mexico, and Texas," *Morbidity and Mortality Weekly Report* 45, No. 29 (July 26, 1996, 33-3; [Atlanta, GA: Centers for Disease Control and Prevention, July 26, 1996] U.S. Food and Drug Administration, "FDA Warns Consumers Not to Use Crema De Belleza." FDA statement, issued July, 23, 1996, available at www.cfsan.fda.gov/~lrd/belleza.html (accessed August 17, 2008).

44. Discussion of the ingredients in White Secret, www.vsantivirus.com/hoax-white-secret.htm (accessed August 16, 2008).

45. Winders et al., 80–84.

46. I say that Stiefel targets Latin America because it markets other dermatology products, but not skin lighteners, in the competitive Asian, Middle Eastern, African, and European countries. Information about Stiefel products obtained at its corporate website, www.stiefel.com/why/about.aspx (accessed May 1, 2007).

47. Peiss, 85, 149, 224.

48. Ibid., 150–151, 148–149.

49. Many of the products used by older white and Asian women to deal with age spots are physician-prescribed pharmaceuticals, including prescription-strength hydroquinone formulas. See information on one widely used system, Obagi, www.obagi.com/article/homepage.html (accessed December 13, 2006).

50. Stephanie Wong, "Whitening Cream Sales Soar as Asia's Skin-Deep Beau-

ties Shun Western Suntans," *The Manila Bulletin Online,* www.mb.com.ph/issues/ 2004/08/24/SCTY2004082416969.html# (accessed March 24, 2007).

51. L'Oreal product lines, www.loreal.com/_en/_ww/index.aspx?FROM=WW-Dispatch-LOREAL-CORPORATE; worldwide sales of L'Oreal, www.loreal.com/_en/_ ww/index.aspx?direct1=00001&direct2=00001/00002&direct3=00001/00002/00003; information on three products, www.vichy.com/gb/biwhite/, www.2.lancome.com/_ int/_en/catalog/product1.aspx?prdcode=110222&CategoryCode=AXESkincare%5E F1_Correction_taches_Protection%5EF2_Correction_taches&, www2.lancome.com/_ int/_en/search/results.aspx?; international, www.laroche-posay.com/_int/_en/index .aspx; Mexico, www.laroche-posay.com.mx/_es/_zal/; Brazil, www.laroche-posay.com .br/_pt/_br/index.aspx (all accessed May 1, 2007).

52. Shiseido, Annual report (2006), 34. Also available at www.shiseido.co.jp/e/ annual/html/index.htm. Data on European, American, and Japanese markets, www .shiseido.co.jp/e/story/html/sto40200.htm. World employment figures, www.shiseido .co.jp/e/story/html/sto40200.htm. White Lucent, www.shiseido.co.jp/e/whitelucent_ us/products/product5.htm. White Lucency, www.shiseido.co.jp/e/whitelucency/ (all accessed May 6, 2007).

53. Unilever, Annual report (2006), www.unilever.com/ourcompany/investorcen-tre/annual_reports/archives.asp (accessed May 6, 2007).

54. Unilever, Report on Earnings, www.unilever.com/ourcompany/investorcentre/ understanding_unilever/default.asp (accessed May 6, 2007); fact sheet, www.unilever .com/ourcompany/investorcentre/understanding_unilever/factsheet.asp; information on Ponds, www.unilever.com/ourbrands/personalcare/Ponds.asp; information on brands; Unilever, Annual Report and Accounts (2006), 6, www.unilever.com/ourcompany/ investorcentre/annual_reports/annual_report_Form.asp (accessed May 6, 2007).

55. Runkle, "The Beauty Obsession."

56. In February 2007, the HLL board of directors approved a name change to Hindustan Unilever Unlimited (HUL), press release, www.hll.com/mediacentre/ mediacentre_2007.asp (accessed May 6, 2007). Ayurvedic Fair & Lovely, www.hll .com/brands/fairnlovely.asp (accessed May 6, 2007); Susan Runkle, "The Beauty Obsession."

57. HLL, "Fair & Lovely Launches Oil-Control Fairness Gel," press release (April 27, 2004), www.hll.com/mediacentre/release.asp?fl=2004/PR_HLL_042704.htm (ac-cessed May 6, 2007); HLL, "Fair & Lovely Unveils Premium Range," press release (May 25, 2004), www.hll.com/mediacentre/release.asp?fl=2004/PR_HLL_052104_2 .htm (accessed May 6, 2007).

58. Pond's Femina Miss World site, http://feminamissindia.indiatimes.com/ articleshow/1375041.cms; All India Democratic Women's Association object to skin lightening ad, www.aidwa.org/content/issues_of_concern/women_and_media.php; reference to Fair & Lovely campaign, www.aidwa.org/content/issues_of_concern/

women_and_media.php; HLL, "Fair & Lovely Launches Foundation to Promote Economic Empowerment of Women," press release (March 11, 2003), www.hll.com/mediacentre/release.asp?fl=2003/PR_HLL_031103.htm (all accessed December 2, 2006).

59. "India debates 'racist' skin cream ads," *BBC News World Edition* (July 24, 2003), http://news.bbc.co.uk/1/hi/world/south_asia/3089495.stm (accessed May 8, 2007).

Chapter 11

Acknowledgments. This chapter has benefited from comments that I received on earlier drafts from participants at a history of technology in Africa workshop organized by Keith Breckenridge and Gabrielle Hecht, as well as from Jordanna Bailkin, Tani E. Barlow, Stephanie M.H. Camp, Evelyn Nakano Glenn, Kenda Mutongi, Uta G. Poiger, Sarah Abreveya Stein, and Andrew Zimmermann. I am also grateful to Hilary Carmen, Lindsay Clowes, and Dan Magaziner for sharing research materials with me, and to my undergraduate and graduate research assistants at the University of Washington who collected some of the other sources. A Charles A. Ryskamp Fellowship from the American Council of Learned Societies, a National Endowment for the Humanities Fellowship, and the Graduate School and History Department at the University of Washington generously provided funding for research and writing.

1. "Battle Against Skin Lighteners Ends," *Sowetan* (August 30, 1990).

2. For example, see Maxine Leeds Craig, *Ain't I a Beauty Queen?: Black Women, Beauty, and the Politics of Race* (Oxford: Oxford University Press, 2002), 26; Susannah Walker, *Style & Status: Selling Beauty to African American Women, 1920–1975* (Lexington: The University Press of Kentucky, 2007), 68. This scholarship has paid greater attention to hair straighteners than skin lighteners. Notable exceptions include Kathy Peiss, *Hope in a Jar: The Making of America's Beauty Culture* (New York: Metropolitan Books, 1998); Modern Girl Around the World Research Group [Tani E. Barlow, Madeleine Yue Dong, Uta G. Poiger, Priti Ramamurthy, Lynn M. Thomas, and Alys Eve Weinbaum], "The Modern Girl Around the World: A Research Agenda and Preliminary Findings," *Gender & History* 17, 2 (2005), 245–294.

3. Michel Foucault, "Technologies of the Self" in *Technologies of the Self: A Seminar with Michel Foucault,* ed. Luther H. Martin, Huck Gutman, and Patrick Hutton (Amherst: University of Massachusetts Press, 1988), 16–49; Modern Girl Around the World Research Group, 249.

4. Thomas McCarthy, "The Critique of Impure Reason: Foucault and the Frankfurt School," *Political Theory* 18, 3 (1990), 437–469.

5. Peiss, 26–32, 40–43, 226; Cleveland R. Denton, Aaron Bunsen Lerner, and Thomas B. Fitzpatrick, "Inhibition of Melanin Formation by Chemical Agents," *Journal of Investigative Dermatology* 18, 2 (1952), 119–135; Modern Girl Around the World Research Group, 270.

6. A. J. Christopher, "'To Define the Indefinable': Population Classification and the Census in South Africa," *Area* 34, 4 (2002), 401–408.

7. Peiss, 108–109.

8. Shane White and Graham White, *Stylin': African American Expressive Culture from Its Beginnings to the Zoot Suit* (Ithaca: Cornell University Press, 1998), 189–190.

9. Peiss, 207–213.

10. "The Opening of Vast Unexplored Market," *Bantu World* (May 26, 1934), 1.

11. James Campbell, "The Americanization of South Africa" in *'Here, There and Everywhere': The Foreign Politics of American Popular Culture*, ed. Reinhold W. Wagnleitner and Elaine T. May (Hanover, NH: University Press of New England, 2000), 34–63.

12. "Remarkable Business Acumen of Negro Woman Shown in Her Work," *Bantu World* (November 11, 1933), 10.

13. Lynn M. Thomas, "The Modern Girl and Racial Respectability in 1930s South Africa," *The Journal of African History* 47 (2006), 461–490.

14. D. F. Nealon, "Ammoniated Mercury and the Skin," *Drug and Cosmetic Industry* 52, 2 (1943), 159–162; Denton et al.

15. Peiss, 149–150.

16. Lynn M. Thomas, "Technocultural Narratives of Race Reversal and the Transnational Trade in Skin Lighteners" (paper presented at the Workshop on the History of Technology in Africa, Ithala, South Africa, July 13–17, 2006).

17. James R. Korombi, "Hair Straightening," *Bantu World* (March 4, 1939), 5.

18. James Campbell, "T.D. Mweli Skota and the Making and Unmaking of a Black Elite," (paper presented at the University of the Witwatersrand History Workshop, February 9–14, 1987); J. D. Mweli Skota, Correspondence, historical papers, University of Witwatersrand AD2781, letter from Zilpah T. D. Skota to J. D. Mweli Skota, April 17, 1941.

19. Belinda Bozzoli with the assistance of Mmantho Nkotsoe, *Women of Phokeng: Consciousness, Life Strategy and Migrancy in South Africa, 1900–1983* (Portsmouth, NH: Heinemann, 1991), 102.

20. Nakedi Ribane, *Beauty: A Black Perspective* (Durban: University of KwaZulu-Natal Press, 2006), 105, 12.

21. Issac Schapera, *Married Life in an African Tribe* (New York: Sheridan House, 1941), 46–48; Monica Hunter, *Reaction to Conquest: Effects of Contact with Europeans on the Pondo of South Africa* (London: Oxford University Press, 1936), 222–226.

22. Timothy Burke, *Lifebuoy Men, Lux Women: Commodification, Consumption, and Cleanliness in Modern Zimbabwe* (Durham: Duke University Press, 1996), 168–169, 189, 192.

23. Ibid., 119, 158–159, 168–169.

24. Irwin Stanley Manoim, "The Black Press 1945–1963: The Growth of the Black Mass Media and Their Role as Ideological Disseminators" (master's thesis, University of Witwatersrand, 1983), 9–18.

25. Manoim, 62–79; Sonja Laden, "'Making the Paper Speak Well,' or, the Pace of Change in Consumer Magazines for Black South Africans," *Poetics Today* 22, 2 (2001), 515–548.

26. Superskin Bleach ad, *Zonk!* 3 (January 1951), 39.

27. This claim is based on a survey at five-year intervals of the newspaper the *Afro-American* (Baltimore) from 1920 through 1965.

28. Sweet Sue ad, *Zonk!* 3 (April 1951), 10.

29. Herman Negro Molla, "Beauty Competition," *Zonk!* 3 (April 1951), 4.

30. "Aunt Thandi Replies to Correspondents," *Zonk!* 4 (April 1952), 33.

31. "Album of Advertisements Which Appeared in African Newspapers," 1953–1957, historical papers, University of Witwatersrand, 2A427.

32. Lindsay Clowes, "A Modernised Man? Changing Constructions of Masculinity in *Drum* Magazine, 1951–1984" (PhD dissertation, University of Cape Town, 2002), 4.

33. Bu-Tone Products ad, *Drum,* East African ed. (January 1958), 46–47.

34. Artra Skin Tone Cream ad, *Drum,* East African ed. (October 1959), 72.

35. Thomas, "Technocultural Narratives of Race Reversal," 18–24.

36. Manoim, 26–32.

37. Market Research Africa (Rhodesia), *Profile of Rhodesia: African* (Salisbury, 1972) reproduced and discussed in Burke, 168–169.

38. L. M. Guthrie, African Market Sterling Drug (S.A.) (Pty) Ltd., Durban, "Successes and Failures in Bantu Marketing," in *The Urban Bantu Market: Understanding Its Complexities and Developing Its Potential—2 Day Seminar, February 1969, Durban* (Durban: The National Development and Management Foundation, 1969), 63–69.

39. Super Rose ad, *Drum* (January 1957).

40. Guthrie, 69; Burke, 180 and 263, note 38 explains that the Ambi license was obtained in 1963.

41. Phyllis Ntantala, *A Life's Mosaic: The Autobiography of Phyllis Ntantala* (Berkeley: University of California Press, 1993), 129–130.

42. Emma Mashinini, *Strikes Have Followed Me All My Life: A South African Autobiography* (London: Women's Press, 1989), 9.

43. R. K. Deppe, *Bureau of Market Research Report No. 39* (Pretoria: University of South Africa, 1974), 25–33, 73; R. K. Deppe, *Bureau of Market Research Report No. 48* (Pretoria: University of South Africa, 1975), 45–47, 79.

44. Ribane, 51, 54.

45. Andrew M. Ivaska, "'Anti-Mini Militants Meet Modern Misses': Urban Style, Gender and the Politics of 'National Culture' in 1960s Dar es Salaam, Tanzania," *Gender & History* 14, 3 (2002), 584–607.

46. Mahmood Mamdani, *Imperialism and Fascism in Uganda* (Trenton: Africa World Press, 1984), 54.

47. Kenya, *National Assembly Debates,* April 4, 1968, 1589–1590; November 28, 1968, 3660–3661; and March 30, 1971, 1376–1379.

48. Ali Mazrui, "A Discourse on Mixed Reactions to—Miniskirts," *Sauti ya Mabibi* 1, 8 (1969), 2–5, 8, 17, 21.

49. Lindsay Clowes, "Are You Going to be MISS (or MR) Africa?" *Gender & History* 13, 1 (2001), 14–15; Kenya, *National Assembly Debates,* March 30, 1971, 1376–1379.

50. Audrey Wipper, "African Women, Fashion, and Scapegoating," *Canadian Journal of African Studies* 6, 2 (1972), 329–349.

51. James Matthews and Gladys Thomas, *Cry Rage!* (Johannesburg: Spro-cas Publications, 1972), 48.

52. Karis and Gerhart Collection, historical papers, University of Witwatersrand: Interviews with Malusi Mpumlwana, Thoko Mbanjwa, and Mamphela Ramphele, Cape Town; and Malusi Mpumlwana, August 7, 1989, Uitenhage.

53. Mashinini, 9.

54. Deppe, *Bureau of Market Research Report No. 48,* 46–47.

55. Thomas, "Technocultural Narratives of Race Reversal," 22–23.

56. B. Bentley-Phillips and Margaret A. H. Bayles, "Cutaneous Reactions to Topical Application of Hydroquinone: Results of a 6-Year Investigation," *South African Medical Journal* 49 (1975), 1391; D. Saffer, H. Tayob, and P. L. A. Bill, "Correspondence: Continued Marketing of Skin-Lightening Preparations Containing Mercury," *South African Medical Journal* 50, 39 (1976), 1499.

57. M. Dogliotti, I. Caro, R. G. Hartdegen, and D. A. Whiting, "Leucomelanoderma in Blacks: A Recent Epidemic," *South African Medical Journal* 48 (1974), 1555–1558; G. H. Findlay, J. G. L. Morrison, and I. W. Simson, "Exogenous Ochronosis and Pigmented Colloid Milium from Hydroquinone Bleaching Creams," *British Journal of Dermatology* 93 (1975), 614.

58. Interview by author with Dr. Hilary Carmen, August 15, 2004, Johannesburg.

59. National Archives and Record Administration, College Park, MD, Records of FDA, RG 88, General Subject Files, 1974, 581.1: Dr. Leonard J. Trilling, Assistant Director for Medical Review, Division of Cosmetics Technology, Department of Health, Education, and Welfare to H. Wulffhart Wins Products (PTY) Limited, Johannesburg, South Africa, March 6, 1974.

60. Thomas, "Technocultural Narratives of Race Reversal," 20–24.

61. Findlay et al., 613–622.

62. G. H. Findlay and H. A. De Beer, "Chronic Hydroquinone Poisoning of the Skin from Skin-Lightening Cosmetics: A South African Epidemic of Ochronosis of the Face in Dark-Skinned Individuals," *South African Medical Journal* 57, 187 (1980), 187–190.

63. B. Bentley-Phillips and Margaret A. H. Bayles, "Acquired Hypomelanosis: Hyperpigmentation Following Reactions to Hydroquinones," *British Journal of Dermatology* 90, 232 (1974), 233.

64. Bentley-Phillips and Bayles, "Cutaneous Reactions," 1394.

65. Findlay et al., 614; G. H. Findlay, "Ochronosis Following Skin Bleaching with Hydroquinone," *American Academy of Dermatology Journal* 6, 6 (1982), 1093.

66. Findlay and De Beer, 188.

67. Interview with Dr. Carmen.

68. "If the Health Department Keeps It's Promise. . . . Say Goodbye to Skin Lightening Cream," *Learn and Teach* 2, 3 (1982), 2–4; interview with Dr. Carmen.

69. "You and Your Body . . . Your Skin," *Upbeat* 1, 5 (1981), 23; "If the Health Department Keeps Its Promise"; "Skin Lightening Creams: A Big New Problem," *Learn and Teach* 2, 5 (1982), 1–3; "The Learn and Teach Challenge," *Learn and Teach* 2, 5 (1982), 4; interview with Dr. Carmen.

70. Via Palestrant, Consumer Affairs Manager, Checkers South African Limited to Ellen Kuzwayo, President, The National Black Consumers Association, Johannesburg, March 30, 1987; Press conference with Ellen Kuzwayo and Dr. Hilary Carmen, "Discussion: Ban of Hydroquinone and Other Harmful Ingredients in Skin Lighteners," March 9, 1988; J. Tatham, Vice President, The Housewives' League of South Africa, Johannesburg to Director General, Foodstuffs, Cosmetics & Disinfectants Act, Department of Health and Population Development, Pretoria, March 16, 1988. Photocopies of these documents and those cited in the next two notes are in my possession.

71. Dr. Mary Ann Sher, Chairman, Dermatological Society of South Africa to Dr. C. E. M. Viljoen, Secretary General, Medical Association of South Africa, November 29, 1988; interview with Dr. Carmen.

72. "Press Announcement: The Skin Lightening Industry," June 24, 1988; Dr. Mary Ann Sher, Chairman, Dermatological Society of South Africa to Professor Tager, Chairman, Business Practice Committee, Parklands, July 6, 1988; interview with Dr. Carmen. In recent years, Kenya, Uganda, and the Gambia passed similar bans grounded in medical arguments.

73. Interview with Dr. Carmen; interview with Dr. Jameela Aboobaker, July 19, 2007, Durban; Ribane, 53.

74. McCarthy, 458.

Chapter 12

1. Cheryl Harris, "Whiteness as Property," *Harvard Law Review* 106 (1993), 1709–1791.

2. Taunya Lovell Banks, "Colorism: A Darker Shade of Pale," *U.C.L.A. Law Review* 47 (2000), 1714–1715.

3. Tanya Katerí Hernández, "Multiracial Discourse: Racial Classification in an Era of Color-Blind Jurisprudence," *Maryland Law Review* 57 (1998), 128, note 160.

4. Michael Omi, "Out of the Melting Pot and into the Fire: Race Relations Policy," in *The State of Asian Pacific America: Policy Issues to the Year 2020* (Los Angeles: LEAP, 1993), 199214.

5. Gunnar Myrdal, *An American Dilemma: The Negro Problem and Modern Democracy* (New York: Harper & Brothers, 1944), 697.

6. E. Franklin Frazier, *Black Bourgeoisie* (Glencoe, IL: Free Press, 1957), 135.

7. Michael Hughes and Bradely R. Hertel, "The Significance of Color Remains: A Study of Life Chances, Mate Selection, and Ethnic Consciousness Among Black Americans," *Social Forces* 68 (1990), 1105–1120; Verna M. Keith and Cedric Herring, "Skin Tone and Stratification in the Black Community," *American Journal of Sociology* 97 (1991), 760–778; Richard Seltzer and Robert C. Smith, "Color Differences in the Afro-American Community and the Differences They Make," *Journal of Black Studies* 21 (1991), 279–286.

8. Aaron Gullickson, "The Significance of Color Declines: A Re-Analysis of Skin Tone in Post-Civil Rights America," *Social Forces* 84 (2005), 157–180.

9. Arthur H. Goldsmith, Darrick Hamilton, and William Darity, Jr., "Shades of Discrimination: Skin Tone and Wages," *The American Economic Review* 96 (2006), 242–245.

10. Walter Allen, Edward Telles, and Margaret Hunter, "Skin Color, Income and Education: A Comparison of African Americans and Mexican Americans," *National Journal of Sociology* 12 (2000), 129–180; Carlos H. Arce, Edward Murguia, and W. Parker Frisbie, "Phenotype and Life Chances Among Chicanos," *Hispanic Journal of Behavioral Sciences* 9 (1987), 19–32; Jeremiah Cotton, "More on the Cost of Being a Black or Mexican American Male Worker," *Social Science Quarterly* 66 (1985), 867–885; Edward E. Telles and Edward Murguia, "Phenotypic Discrimination and Income Differences Among Mexican Americans," *Social Science Quarterly* 71 (1990), 682–696; Edward Murguia and Edward E. Telles, "Phenotype and Schooling Among Mexican Americans," *Sociology of Education* 69 (1996), 276–289.

11. Joni Hersch, "Profiling the New Immigrant Worker: The Effects of Skin Color and Height," *Journal of Labor Economics* 26(2) (2008), 345–386.

12. Ibid., 12.

13. Dwayne Christian Butler Proctor, "Shades of Guilt: A Mass Media Effects Experiment Answering Why Dark Skin Implies Guilt for Jurors" (PhD dissertation, University of Connecticut, 1999), 80, 81.

14. Jennifer L. Hochschild and Vesla Weaver, "The Skin Color Paradox and the American Racial Order," *Social Forces* 86 (2007) 643–670.

15. Naya Terkildsen, "When White Voters Evaluate Black Candidates: The Processing Implications of Candidates Skin Color, Prejudice, and Self-Monitoring," *American Journal of Political Science* 37 (1993), 1032–1053.

16. Jerry Kang, "Cyber-race," *Harvard Law Review* 113 (2000), 1131–1208.

17. Jerry Kang, "Trojan Horses of Race," *Harvard Law Review* 118 (2005), 1489–1593.

18. Irene V. Blair, Charles M. Judd, and Kristine M. Chapleau, "The Influence of Afrocentric Facial Features in Criminal Sentencing," *Psychological Science* 15 (2004), 674–679.

19. Irene V. Blair, "The Malleability of Automatic Stereotypes and Prejudice," *Personality and Social Psychology Review* 6 (2002), 242–261; Irene V. Blair, Charles M. Judd, and Jennifer L. Fallman, "The Automaticity of Race and Afrocentric Facial Features in Social Judgments," *Journal of Personality and Social Psychology* 87 (2004), 763–778.

20. Blair et al., "The Influence of Afrocentric Facial Features," 677, 678.

21. Ibid., 677, 678.

22. Banks, 1710.

23. 42 United States Code Service § 1981 (2006).

24. 42 United States Code Service § 2000e-2(a) (1) (2006).

25. *Walker v. Secretary of the Treasury, I.R.S., 742* Federal Supplement 670 N.D. Georgia 1990.

26. *Franceschi v. Hyatt Corp., 782* Federal Supplement 712, D. P.R. 1992 (722).

27. *Johnson v. Wegman's,* 1998 U.S. Dist. LEXIS 356 W.D. N.Y. 1998.

28. *Maingi v. IBP, Inc.,* 1993 United States Appeals LEXIS 27352 10th C.A. 1993.

29. *Vester v. Henderson,* 178 Federal Supplement 2d 594, M.D. North Carolina 2001.

30. *Santiago v. Stryker Corp.,* 170 Federal Supplement 2d 93, D.P.R. 1998 (96).

31. *Felix v. Marquez,* 24 Employment Practices Decisions (CCH) P31, 279, D.D.C. 1980.

32. Banks, 1740–1741.

33. *Rodriguez v. Gattuso,* 795 Federal Supplement 860, N.D. Ill. 1992.

34. Ibid., 865.

35. Trina Jones, "Shades of Brown: The Law of Skin Color," *Duke Law Journal* 49 (2000), 1487–1557.

36. Ibid., 1497–1498, 1544.

37. Charles R. Lawrence, III, "The Id, the Ego and Equal Protection: Reckoning with Unconscious Racism," *Stanford Law Review* 39 (1987), 317–388; Jody Armour, *Negrophobia and Reasonable Racism: The Hidden Costs of Being Black in America* (New York: New York University Press, 1997); Kang, "Trojan Horse of Race."

38. Blair, "The Malleability of Automatic Stereotypes," 242–261.

39. Irene V. Blair, "The Efficient Use of Race and Afrocentric Features in Inverted Faces," *Social Cognition* 24 (2006), 563–579; Blair et al., "The Automaticity of Race and Afrocentric Facial Features," 763–778.

40. Armour.

41. Blair et al., "The Automaticity of Race."

42. *United States v. White,* No. 1:00-CR-81-01, W.D. Michigan 2000.

43. John Terrence A. Rosenthal, "Batson Revisited in America's 'New Era' of Multiracial Persons," *Seton Hall Law Review* 33 (2002), 67–108.

44. Ibid., 100.

45. Ibid., 101.

46. *Batson v. Kentucky*, 476 United States Reports 79 (1986).

47. Wolf Blitzer, "The Situation Room," Transcript in the CNN Library, September 6, 2005, http://transcripts.cnn.com/TRANSCRIPTS/0509/01/sitroom.02.html (accessed July 22, 2008).

Chapter 13

1. EEOC Press Release, "EEOC Settles Color Harassment Lawsuit with Applebee's Neighborhood Bar and Grill," August 7, 2003, www.eeoc.gov/press/8-07-03.html [hereinafter, "EEOC Press Release"]. The manager reportedly referred to Mr. Burch with terms like "tar baby," "black monkey," "porch monkey," "jig-a-boo," and "blackie." He also told Mr. Burch to bleach his skin. Dana Hedgpeth, "Settlement Reached in Color-Bias Suit: Black Worker at Applebee's Said Lighter-Skinned Black Supervisor Harassed Him," *Washington Post*, August 8, 2003, E4; Marjorie Valbrun, "EEOC Sees Rise in Intrarace Complaints of Color Bias," *Wall Street Journal*, August 8, 2003, B1.

2. Color discrimination filings with the EEOC have increased by at least 125 percent since the mid 1990s, from 413 in fiscal year (FY) 1994 to 932 in FY 2004. U.S. Equal Employment Opportunity Commission, "Race/Color Discrimination: Statistics," www.eeoc.gov/types/race.html.

3. Hedgpeth, E4.

4. From 1994 to 2002, about twenty complaints led to lawsuits. The remainder were settled out of court. The majority of EEOC charges in 2002 were in the Northeast (44%), followed by the West (21%), South (15%), Midwest (12.5 %), and Southwest (7.5%). EEOC Press Release.

5. This chapter draws from my earlier, more detailed treatment of this topic. See Trina Jones, "Shades of Brown: The Law of Skin Color," *Duke Law Journal* 49 (2000), 1487.

6. *Plessy v. Ferguson*, 163 U.S. 537, 540 (1896).

7. *Brown v. Board of Educ.*, 347 U.S. 483 (1954) (invalidating state-sponsored segregation in education).

8. *Loving v. Virginia*, 388 U.S. 1 (1967) (holding Virginia's antimiscegenation statutes unconstitutional).

9. See, for example, *Loving v. Virginia*, 388 U.S. 1, 4 (citing Va. Code Ann. § 20-59, 20-58 which prohibited marriage between "any white person" and "a colored person"); see also Tex. Const., art. VII, § 7 ("Separate schools shall be provided for the white and colored races") (repealed August 5, 1969); Act of March 13, 1901, ch. 7, 1901 Tenn. Pub. Acts 9 (prohibiting "white and colored persons" from attending the same educational institutions).

10. Civil Rights Act of 1964, Pub. L. No. 88-352, 78 Stat. 241 (codified as amended in scattered sections of 42 U.S.C.).

11. See *Rodriguez v. Gattuso*, 795 F. Supp. 860, 865 (N.D. Ill. 1992); *Felix v. Marquez*, 24 Empl. Prac. Dec. (CCH) para. 31,279 (D.D.C. 1980). For cases dealing directly with allegations of colorism, see, for example, *Arrocha v. City Univ. of New York*, 2004 U.S. Dist. LEXIS 4486 (E.D.N.Y. 2004); *Brack v. Shoney's, Inc.*, 249 F. Supp. 2d 938 (W.D. Tenn. 2003); *Rios v. Aramark Corp.*, 139 F. Supp. 2d 210 (D.P.R. 2001). See also cases listed in Jones, 1532–1535, footnotes 186–203.

12. See Ian F. Haney Lopez, "The Social Construction of Race: Some Observations on Illusion, Fabrication, and Choice," *Harvard Civil Rights and Civil Liberties Law Review* 29 (1994), 7, 11–16.

13. 42 U.S.C. § 3601 et seq.

14. 42 U.S.C. § 2000e.

15. 42 U.S.C. § 1981.

16. 42 U.S.C. § 1983.

17. The Court subjects race claims to strict scrutiny, the most demanding review level. *Adarand Constructors, Inc. v. Pena*, 515 U.S. 200, 227, 235–240 (1995); *Grutter v. Bollinger*, 539 U.S. 306, 321, 334 (2003). In contrast, sex-based classifications are subject to intermediate scrutiny, or midlevel review. See *Craig v. Boren*, 429 U.S. 190, 197 (1976); *J.E.B. v. Alabama*, 511 U.S. 127, 135–137 (1994). Age- and class-based distinctions are subject only to rational basis review, or minimal scrutiny. See *Massachusetts Bd. of. Ret. v. Murgia*, 427 U.S. 307, 313–314 (1976); *San Antonio Independent School District v. Rodriquez*, 411 U.S. 1 (1973).

18. Under Title VII, plaintiffs can bring disparate treatment claims, which require a showing of intentional discrimination, or disparate impact claims, which do not require evidence of intent, but require proof of a disparate impact on a protected classification from use of neutral criteria (e.g., a high school diploma requirement that disparately affects African Americans or Latinos). In disparate treatment cases, a defendant may offer a legitimate, nondiscriminatory reason for its action (if the case is based on circumstantial evidence), such as *McDonnell Douglas v. Green*, 411 U.S. 792 (1973), or establish that the requirement being imposed was a bona fide occupational qualification (in cases of facial distinctions), 42 U.S.C. § 2000e-2(e). In contrast, a defendant responding to a disparate impact claim must show that the neutral criteria were job related for the position in question and were justified by business necessity, 42 U.S.C. § 2000e-2(k).

19. See, for example, *Rios v. Aramark Corp.*, 139 F. Supp. 2d 210 (D.P.R. 2001); *Walker v. Internal Revenue Service*, 742 F. Supp. 670 (N.D. Ga. 1990); *Felix v. Marquez*, 27 Empl. Prac. Dec. (CCH) par. 32, 241 (D.D.C. 1981).

20. 42 U.S.C. § 2000e-2.

21. 42 U.S.C. § 1981.

22. See *Johnson v. Railway Express Agency*, 421 U.S. 454, 459–460 (1975).

23. See, for example, *Walker v. Internal Revenue Service,* 713 F. Supp. 403, 406 (N.D. Ga. 1989); *Felix v. Marquez,* 24 Empl. Prac. Dec. (CCH) par. 31, 279 (D.D.C. 1980).

24. *Walker v. Internal Revenue Service,* 713 F. Supp. 403, 406 (N.D. Ga. 1989).

25. See 110 Cong. Rec. H-2552-55 (daily ed. February 8, 1964), reprinted in U.S. EEOC, Legislative History of Titles VII and XI of Civil Rights Act of 1964, 3193–3194 (recounting exchange between representatives regarding the legality of an employer's refusal to hire a person because the applicant was too dark).

26. EEOC Press Release, EEOC Race/Color Discrimination (describing color as a race-related characteristic).

27. See *Asgrow Seed Co. v. Winterboer,* 513 U.S. 179, 187 (1995).

28. For additional arguments for coverage under Section 1981, see Jones, 1535 (referencing the legislative history of Section 1981).

29. *Saint Francis College v. Al-Khazraji,* 481 U.S. 604 (1987).

30. Ibid., 613.

31. See *Hansborough v. City of Elkhart Parks and Recreation,* 802 F. Supp. 199, 207 (N.D. Indiana 1992) (requiring "a substantial preliminary showing when one person alleges discrimination by another black person").

32. See Devon Carbado and G. Mitu Gulati, "The Fifth Black Woman," *Journal of Contemporary Legal Issues* 11 (2001), 701–729.

33. See *Sere v. Board of Trustees,* 628 F. Supp. 1543, 1546 (N.D. Ill. 1986), aff'd, 852 F.2d 285 (7th Cir. 1988) (refusing "to create a cause of action that would place [the court] in the unsavory business of measuring skin color and determining whether the skin pigmentation of the parties is sufficiently different to form the basis of a lawsuit").

34. See Ian F. Haney Lopez, *White by Law: The Legal Construction of Race* (New York: New York University Press, 1996).

35. See, for example, *Rios v. Aramark Corp.,* 139 F. Supp. 2d 210 (D.P.R. 2001).

Chapter 14

1. Color discrimination has also come to be recognized as a claim under the Civil Rights Act of 1866, 42 U.S.C. § 1981, which grants to all persons the same right to "make and enforce contracts . . . as is enjoyed by white citizens." Trina Jones, "Shades of Brown: The Law of Skin Color," *Duke Law Journal* 49 (2000), 1487–1557 (detailing the development of color discrimination as a legal cause of action).

2. Patrick Mirza, "A Bias That's Skin Deep," *Human Resources Magazine* December (2003), 62–67.

3. Marjorie Valbrun, "EEOC Sees Rise in Intrarace Complaints of Color Bias," *Wall Street Journal* (August 7, 2003), 7; U.S. Equal Employment Opportunity Commission, *EEOC Press Release, Takes New Approach to Fighting Racism and Colorism in*

the 21st Century Workplace: E-Race Initiative to Highlight New and Emerging Discrimination Issues Nationwide (2007).

4. Taunya Lovell Banks, "Colorism: A Darker Shade of Pale," *University of California Los Angeles Law Review* 47 (2000), 1705–1746.

5. *Cubas v. Rapid American Corp.*, 420 F. Supp. 663 (E.D. Pennsylvania 1976). Although the court solely discusses Cubas' case as a racial discrimination case, I incorporate it here as a color discrimination case because of the way in which the plaintiff focuses upon her nonwhite status as salient to the case in a manner that implicated color discrimination.

6. *Manzanares v. Safeway*, 593 F.2d 968 (10th Cir. 1979). Although the plaintiff did not assert a color claim separately from his racial discrimination claim, much of his assessment of being racially discriminated against as a Mexican American was rooted in his experience of being nonwhite in physical appearance in ways that could characterize the case as a color discrimination case as well.

7. It has been empirically documented that the vast majority of civil rights claims never reach trial because judges dismiss the lawsuits upon defense motions for summary judgment. Theresa Beiner, "The Misuse of Summary Judgment in Hostile Environment Cases," *Wake Forest Law Review* 34 (1999), 71–134.

8. *Galdamez v. Potter*, 415 F.3d 1015 (9th Cir. 2005).

9. *Torres v. White*, 46 Fed. Appx. 738, 741 (6th Cir. 2002).

10. *Metzger v. Martinez*, 48 Fed. Appx. 660, 664 (9th Cir. 2002).

11. This helps to explain why even in cases in which a supervisor testifies that no racial discrimination against an Afro-Latino employee can exist when no other African Americans have complained of racial discrimination in the workplace, that a court can still recognize that a prima facie case of employment discrimination has been set out by an Afro-Latino employee terminated and then replaced by a white Anglo employee. The white versus nonwhite paradigm assists the court in identifying a cognizable claim for discrimination. See *O'Loughlin, Sr. v. Procon*, 627 F. Supp. 675, 678 (E.D. Texas 1986) (recognizing an African Cuban plaintiff's prima facie claim for racial discrimination but noting that it was rebutted by the employer's articulation of legitimate justification for termination in the plaintiff's unwillingness to cooperate with coworkers or to perform his duties in a workmanlike manner). Indeed, the power of the white versus nonwhite paradigm for judicial recognition of discrimination even extends to the related context of discrimination in housing. See *Rodriguez v. Gattuso*, 795 F. Supp. 860 (N.D. Illinois 1992) (recognizing the color-based housing discrimination claim of an Afro-Latino plaintiff who was denied available housing by a white Anglo prospective landlord).

12. *Felix v. Marquez*, 27 Empl. Prac. Dec. P 32,241, 22,2768 n. 6 (D.D.C. 1981).

13. Banks.

14. Nancy A. Denton and Douglas S. Massey, "Racial Identity Among Caribbean Hispanics: The Effect of Double Minority Status on Residential Segregation," *Ameri-*

can Sociological Review 54 (1989), 790–808; Laura Padilla, "Internalized Oppression and Latinos," *Texas Hispanic Journal of Law and Policy* 7 (2001), 61–113; Eric Uhlmann, Nilanjana Dasgupta, Angelica Elgueta, Anthony G. Greenwald, and Jane Swanson, "Subgroup Prejudice Based on Skin Color Among Hispanics in the United States and Latin America," *Social Cognition* 20 (2002), 198–225.

15. Sonya M. Tafoya, "Shades of Belonging: Latinos and Racial Identity," *Harvard Journal of Hispanic Policy* 17 (2004/2005), 58–78.

16. Carmen Luz Valcarel, "Growing up Black in Puerto Rico," in *Challenging Racism and Sexism: Alternatives to Genetic Explanations,* ed. Ethel Tobach and Betty Rosoff (New York: The Feminist Press, 1994), 284–294.

17. Marta I. Cruz-Janzen, "Y Tu Abuela A'onde Esta?," *SAGE Race Relations Abstracts* 26 (2001), 7–24.

18. Ariel E. Dulitzky, "A Region in Denial: Racial Discrimination and Racism in Latin American," in *Neither Enemies Nor Friends: Latinos, Blacks, Afro-Latinos,* ed. Anani Dzidzienyo and Suzanne Obeler (New York: Palgrave Macmillan, 2005), 39–59.

19. *Falero v. Santiago,* 10 F. Supp. 2d 93 (D. Puerto Rico 1998).

20. John Valery White, "The Irrational Turn in Employment Discrimination Law: Slouching Toward a Unified Approach to Civil Rights Law," *Mercer Law Review* 53 (2002), 709–810.

21. *Ash v. Tyson Foods, Inc.,* 126 S. Ct. 1195 (2006).

22. *Falero v. Santiago.*

23. U.S. Equal Employment Opportunity Commission, *Compliance Manual* (District of Columbia EEOC, 2006).

24. Banks.

25. U.S. Census Bureau, *The Hispanic Population in the United States* (District of Columbia: U.S. Census Bureau, 2002).

26. Rakesh Kochhar, *Pew Hispanic Center Latino Labor Report 2006: Strong Gains in Employment* (2006); Bureau of National Affairs, "Second-Generation Latinos to Exert Major Workforce Influence, Pew Report Says," *Daily Labor Report* 15 (Arlington: BNA,2003), A7.

27. Office of Advocacy, U.S. Small Business Administration, *Minorities in Business* (District of Columbia: U.S. Small Business Administration, 1999).

28. Tanya Katerí Hernández, "Latino Inter-Ethnic Employment Discrimination and the 'Diversity' Defense," *Harvard Civil Rights Civil Liberties Law Review* 42 (2007), 259–316.

29. Tanya Katerí Hernández, "Multiracial Matrix: The Role of Race Ideology in the Enforcement of Antidiscrimination Laws: A United States–Latin America Comparison," *Cornell Law Review* 87 (2002), 1093–1176.

30. Eduardo Bonilla-Silva and David Dietrich, "The Latin Americanization of U.S. Race Relations: A New Pigmentocracy," Chapter 3; Tanya Katerí Hernández,

"'Multiracial' Discourse: Racial Classifications in an Era of Color-Blind Jurisprudence," *Maryland Law Review* 57 (1998), 97–173.

31. Eduardo Bonilla-Silva, *Racism Without Racists: Color-Blind Racism and the Persistence of Racial Inequality in the United States* (Lanham, MD: Rowman & Littlefield, 2003), 53–73.

Index